YEATS AND ARTISTIC POWER

Yeats and Artistic Power

Phillip L. Marcus
Professor of English
Cornell University, Ithaca, New York

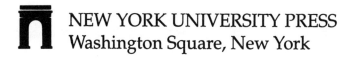
NEW YORK UNIVERSITY PRESS
Washington Square, New York

© Phillip L. Marcus 1992

First published in the U.S.A. in 1992 by
NEW YORK UNIVERSITY PRESS
Washington Square
New York, N.Y. 10003

Library of Congress Cataloging-in-Publication Data
Marcus, Phillip L., 1941–
Yeats and artistic power / Phillip L. Marcus.
p.   cm.
Includes bibliographical references and index.
ISBN 0–8147–5471–6
1. Yeats, W. B. (William Butler), 1865–1939—Aesthetics.
2. Poetics.   II. Title.   II. Series.
PR5908.A35M37   1992
821'.8—dc20

Printed in Hong Kong

In memory of my mother
Virginia Brenna Marcus
1914–1991

Contents

Preface

In the late 1960s, while doing research for *Yeats and the Beginning of the Irish Renaissance* (1970), I became interested in Yeats's aesthetic of artistic power. Although that interest manifested itself in only the briefest way in that book, it continued to develop throughout the next two decades, stimulated first by my work on *The Death of Cuchulain* and then by a growing sense of its crucial place in Yeats's entire oeuvre. In 1979 I devoted an essay to the subject, and it found its way into many of my other publications as well. Writing a preface to a new edition of the *Irish Renaissance* book in 1987 offered me the opportunity to give the aesthetic the importance it seemed to deserve in relation to the concerns of that volume, but also made me realise that really to do justice to it would require much more space than was there available. The present study was the result of that realisation.

Although Yeats's concern with the power of art to shape life has been given *some* consideration in many studies of his work, most frequently in connection with 'The Statues' or *The King's Threshold*, it has never to my knowledge been the focal point of any other extended examination, or taken seriously as a concept. My own researches, in any case, have been conducted independently. On the other hand, I owe an immense debt of a more general kind to the outstanding body of scholarship devoted to Yeats in recent decades by such figures as Douglas Archibald, George Bornstein, Curtis Bradford, David R. Clark, Richard Ellmann, Edward Engelberg, Warwick Gould, George M. Harper, Daniel Harris, John Kelly, William M. Murphy, William H. O'Donnell, James Olney, Stephen Parrish, Michael J. Sidnell, Ronald Schuchard, Jon Stallworthy, Donald T. Torchiana, Thomas Whitaker and F.A.C. Wilson. More specific debts are acknowledged in the notes following the text.

It is particularly pleasant to acknowledge the contribution of the many students with whom I have explored the work of Yeats over the years, especially Kent Gilges, Nicholas Halmi, Lahney Preston, Keith Dunlop and Alexis Wilson. My own teachers Frederick R. McLeod and John V. Kelleher have been shaping my understanding of life as well as art for as long as I can remember, and I hope they will recognise some of that influence here. Margaret

Cannon of Macmillan has been an enthusiastic and supportive editor, and Anne Rafique copyedited the manuscript admirably. Barbara Panetta, Nell Gutman, Sheila Metzner and Marie Sophie Wilson all patiently responded to queries concerning a potential jacket illustration that could not in the end be used. Others to whom I am indebted in various ways include Michael Colacurcio, Wayne Furman, A. Walton Litz, Richie Moran, Phillis Molock, Marian Reiner, Edgar Rosenberg, Daniel R. Schwarz, Linda Shaughnessy and Lydia Zelaya. The understanding and support of Brenda Marcus, Patrick Marcus, Leonard Marcus and Mary Marcus Ferguson have sustained me through many vicissitudes. To my mother, who was always there for me, I owe a special debt of gratitude; this book is dedicated to her memory.

An earlier version of some of the material in Chapter 2 appeared as the 'Preface to the New Edition' in the second edition of *Yeats and the Beginning of the Irish Renaissance* and is drawn upon here with the permission of Syracuse University Press. Earlier versions of some of the material in Chapter 3 appeared as 'Artificers of the Great Moment: An Essay on Yeats and National Literature' in the *Colby Library Quarterly* and 'Incarnation in "Middle Yeats"' in *Yeats Annual* No. 1 and are drawn upon here with the permission of the respective editors, Douglas Archibald and Richard J. Finneran. An earlier version of some of the material in Chapter 4 appeared as 'The Authors Were in Eternity – or Oxford: George Yeats, George Harper, and the Making of *A Vision*' in Richard J. Finneran (ed.), *Yeats: An Annual of Critical and Textual Studies*, Vol. VI (1988), © by the University of Michigan 1989, and is drawn upon here with the permission of the University of Michigan Press.

For permission to quote from copyright materials, acknowledgement is gratefully made to the following:

To Peters, Fraser and Dunlop and the Joan Daves Agency for quotations from Frank O'Connor, *The Wild Bird's Nest: Poems from the Irish* (Dublin: Cuala Press, 1932).

To Oxford University Press for quotations from Kathleen Raine (ed.), *Letters on Poetry from W. B. Yeats to Dorothy Wellesley* (London and New York: Oxford University Press, 1964).

To Michael Butler Yeats, Anne Butler Yeats, the Macmillan Press Ltd, Macmillan Publishing Company and A. P. Watt Ltd for quotations from Allan Wade (ed.), *The Letters of W. B. Yeats*, Copyright 1953, 1954 by Anne Butler Yeats, copyright renewed 1982 by Anne Butler Yeats; from Denis Donoghue (ed.), *Memoirs*, copyright ©

1972 by M. B. Yeats and Anne Yeats, copyright © 1972 by Denis Donoghue; and from 'The Choice', copyright 1933 by Macmillan Publishing Company, renewed 1961 by Bertha Georgie Yeats, in Peter Allt and Russell K. Alspach (eds), *The Variorum Edition of the Poems of W. B. Yeats*. Also to Michael Butler Yeats, Anne Butler Yeats and A.P. Watt Ltd for quotations from John P. Frayne (ed.), *Uncollected Prose by W. B. Yeats*, Vol. 1, copyright © 1970 by John P. Frayne and Michael Yeats.

Permission to quote from unpublished materials by W. B. Yeats was generously granted by Michael Butler Yeats, Anne Butler Yeats, A. P. Watt Ltd, Oxford University Press, John Kelly, Ronald Schuchard, and the Foster-Murphy Collection, Department of Rare Books and Manuscripts, the New York Public Library, Astor, Lenox and Tilden Foundations.

The painting by AE reproduced as a jacket illustration is in the collection of Phillip L. Marcus and is used by kind permission of Colin Smythe.

Key West, Florida   PHILLIP L. MARCUS
June 1991

List of Abbreviations

The works listed below are cited in the text by abbreviation and page number.

Au   *Autobiographies* (London: Macmillan, 1955).

AVA   *A Critical Edition of Yeats's 'A Vision'* (1925), eds George Mills Harper and Walter Kelly Hood (London: Macmillan, 1978).

AV B   *A Vision* (London: Macmillan, 1962).

CL1   *The Collected Letters of W. B. Yeats*, Vol. 1: *1865–95*, eds John Kelly and Eric Domville (Oxford: Clarendon Press, 1986).

E&I   *Essays and Introductions* (London and New York: Macmillan, 1961).

Ex   *Explorations*, sel., Mrs W. B. Yeats (London: Macmillan, 1962; New York: Macmillan, 1963).

L   *The Letters of W.B. Yeats*, ed. Allan Wade (London: Rupert Hart-Davis, 1954; New York: Macmillan, 1955).

LDW   *Letters on Poetry from W. B. Yeats to Dorothy Wellesley*, intro. Kathleen Raine (London and New York: Oxford University Press, 1964).

LNI   *Letters to the New Island*, eds George Bornstein and Hugh Witemeyer, *The Collected Works of W.B. Yeats*, Vol. VII (London and New York: Macmillan, 1989).

LTSM   *W. B. Yeats and T. Sturge Moore: Their Correspondence, 1901–1937*, ed. Ursula Bridge (London: Routledge and Kegan Paul; New York: Oxford University Press, 1953).

LTWBY   *Letters to W. B. Yeats*, eds Richard J. Finneran, George Mills Harper and William M. Murphy (London: Macmillan; New York: Columbia University Press, 1977).

Mem   *Memoirs*, ed. Denis Donoghue (London: Macmillan, 1972; New York: Macmillan, 1973).

Myth   *Mythologies* (London and New York: Macmillan, 1959).

OBMV   *The Oxford Book of Modern Verse, 1892–1935*, chosen by W. B. Yeats (Oxford: Clarendon Press, 1936).

SB   *The Speckled Bird, With Variant Versions*, ed. William H. O'Donnell (Toronto: McClelland and Stewart, 1976).

SS   *The Senate Speeches of W. B. Yeats,* ed. Donald R. Pearce
         (Bloomington: Indiana University Press, 1960; London:
         Faber and Faber, 1961).

UP1   *Uncollected Prose by W. B. Yeats,* Vol. 1, ed. John P. Frayne
         (London: Macmillan; New York: Columbia University
         Press, 1970).

UP2   *Uncollected Prose by W. B. Yeats,* Vol. 2, eds John
         P. Frayne and Colton Johnson (London: Macmillan,
         1975; New York: Columbia University Press, 1976).

VP   *The Variorum Edition of the Poems of W. B. Yeats,* eds Peter
         Allt and Russell K. Alspach (1957; reprinted New York
         and London: Macmillan, 1973).

VPl   *The Variorum Edition of the Plays of W. B. Yeats,* ed. Russell
         K. Alspach, corrected second printing (London and New
         York: Macmillan, 1966).

VSR   *The Secret Rose: Stories by W. B. Yeats: A Variorum Edition,*
         eds Warwick Gould, Phillip L. Marcus, and Michael J.
         Sidnell, new edn, revised and enlarged (London:
         Macmillan, 1991).

Wade   *Allan Wade, A Bibliography of the Writings of W. B. Yeats,*
         3rd edn, rev. Russell K. Alspach (London: Rupert Hart-
         Davis, 1968).

YBIR   Phillip L. Marcus, *Yeats and the Beginning of the Irish
         Renaissance,* 2nd edn (Syracuse, NY: Syracuse University
         Press, 1987).

YL   Edward O'Shea, *A Descriptive Catalog of W. B. Yeats's
         Library* (New York and London: Garland, 1985).

1

Introduction: Cast Your Mind on Other Days

In Tom Stoppard's brilliant play *Travesties* (1975), the character Henry Carr reminisces about a dream in which in an effort to discomfit his old adversary James Joyce he had '*flung* at him – "And what did you do in the Great War?"' only to have Joyce reply 'I wrote *Ulysses*.'[1] The victory was Joyce's in the battle of wit; but Carr's evocation of the well-known slogan from World War I recruiting posters forces us to consider the foundation of that victory. Millions *had* fought. Many of those, as well as many who for one reason or another had not fought, had written poems, plays, fiction they hoped would influence the conduct or the outcome of the War.[2] But the serious implication of Joyce's witticism is that his withdrawal to neutral Switzerland, for peace in which to work on the novel, was justified not by any political effect or intent the (unfinished) book might have but by its intrinsic artistic merit, its greatness. Periods of war or intense political activity bring with them demands that art in some way contribute to the cause. Even some of the Dadaists, whose movement had begun in Zurich during Joyce's stay there, had seen their supposedly meaningless art as an effort of this kind: according to Hans Arp, 'revolted by the butchery of the 1914 World War, we in Zurich devoted ourselves to the arts. While the guns rumbled in the distance, we sang, painted, made collages and wrote poems with all our might. We were seeking an art based on fundamentals, to cure the madness of the age, and a new order of things that would restore the balance between heaven and hell. We had a dim premonition that power-mad gangsters would one day use art itself as a way of deadening men's minds.'[3] I can still remember during the conflict in Vietnam hearing a professor of mathematics at Cornell read with passion his own poem beginning 'Goddamn it, Lady Bird, you're not going to the hairdresser this afternoon if *I* can help it.' He *couldn't*, or at least so it seemed, and the poem was no *Ulysses* meritwise – but at least, the audience felt, he was trying to do something. At this same period violence was breaking out in

Northern Ireland and in 'Summer 1969' Joyce's countryman Seamus Heaney depicted himself in Spain, significantly sweating 'my way through [and thus in a sense re-enacting] the life of Joyce' when he heard the familiar call to give up his own detachment and create engaged art.[4] For Irish writers, in fact, the tumultuous history of their country has made such expectations the norm.

In 1892 W. B. Yeats first published 'Apologia addressed to Ireland in the coming days', a confident assertion that his occult interests were not inappropriate for a *national* writer. The deftness with which he made his case can be seen in his reiteration of the word *'druid'* (1.32) with its fusion of Irish and occult associations. His concomitant claim to be *'True brother of that company / Who sang to sweeten Ireland's wrong, / Ballad and story, rann and song'* reflects an equal subtlety (*VP* 137-9). *'Ireland's wrong'* recalls the formulaic militancy of Young Ireland, a movement Yeats had already come to associate with Nationalist propaganda in bad verse; and the name of one of its chief sinners in that regard, Thomas Davis, appears among the list of those with whom a few lines later Yeats hopes he will be *'counted one.'*[5] On the other hand, *'sweeten'* implies something less militant, but still positive, and in some undefined way beneficial to the nation. The paradox originated in potentially opposed desires on Yeats's part: to serve his country and to create great art. The ambiguity of the passage may have been intentional, protecting Yeats by allowing different audiences to interpret it in different ways. At this point in his career, after all, he could count among his readers everything from 'hillside men' scheming or dreaming of armed insurrection against England to *fin de siècle* companions of the Cheshire Cheese devoted to the religion of *l'art pour l'art*. But he had in fact already formulated an aesthetic that he believed would allow him not only to satisfy both desires but even to reconcile them, while negotiating the tricky passage between the Scylla of facile political rhetoric in the manner of the poetry of *The Nation* and the Charybdis of detachment or cosmopolitanism.[6] Some indication of the means he envisaged can be found in the address to *future* readers with which the poem ends, and more in the famous late poem to which those lines proleptically lead us:

> *I cast my heart into my rhymes,*
> *That you in the dim coming times*
> *May know how my heart went with them*
> *After the red rose bordered hem.* (*VP* 139; 1892 version)

The 'hem', as previous lines have suggested, is that of Divine Wisdom, linked with Ireland since the beginning of time. The phrases 'cast my heart' and 'coming times,' as well as the syntactic connection of future and past around a 'that [pronoun] may [verb]' construction, point towards Part V of 'Under Ben Bulben':

> Irish poets, learn your trade,
> Sing whatever is well made,
> Scorn the sort now growing up
> All out of shape from toe to top,
> Their unremembering hearts and heads
> Base-born products of base beds.
> Sing the peasantry, and then
> Hard-riding country gentlemen,
> The holiness of monks, and after
> Porter-drinkers' randy laughter;
> Sing the lords and ladies gay
> That were beaten into the clay
> Through seven heroic centuries;
> Cast your mind on other days
> That we in coming days may be
> Still the indomitable Irishry.[7]

Here the relationship between art and nationalism is defined openly, and allows us to see more clearly what the 'Apologia' had only implied. The 'indomitable Irishry' – again the spirit of the phrase is that of *The Nation* – will derive their strength from the poets, whose work embodies ideal images from the past to inspire them.

In the eighties and nineties Yeats had found in a variety of Irish and foreign sources the simple but empowering concept (most memorably expressed by Oscar Wilde in the dazzling paradoxes of 'The Decay of Lying') that 'life imitates art'. Early on Yeats realised that the process need not, and in fact generally should not, involve efforts like those of the Young Irelanders to exert an *immediate* influence, or to influence *directly* a large audience. 'An unkind Providence', he wrote, 'has granted to us Irish folk a terrible love of immediate results, wholly fatal to great work' (*LNI* 48).[8] Haste could threaten formal and technical perfection, but that was not all. Form was the essential fabric of vision, and the artists had to be true to that vision, never, for example, sacrificing a necessary complexity of expression in the interest of easy intelligibility. Such faithfulness was essential because the true artist was in fact a seer: 'When a man writes any work of genius, or invents some creative action, is it not because some knowledge or power has come into his mind from beyond his mind?' (*Au* 272). Wisdom came 'from among the spirits' (*UP2* 232; also *E&I* 184) or from the collective unconscious, the realm of the archetypes (*E&I* 102, 50); and as Yeats wrote Robert Bridges in 1896, 'I do most firmly believe that all art is dedicated to wisdom and not because it teaches anything but because it reveals divine substances' (*L* 268; also *E&I* 193). In the Edenic past, the 'Golden Age', those 'substances' had had concrete form and were readily accessible, but since 'the fall into division' the arts had become 'the only means of conversing with eternity left to man on earth' (*Mem* 189; *UP2* 131). 'Visions of these eternal principles or characters of human life appear to poets in all ages'; so for the visionary artist the past and the imagination led to the same reality, and if he or she could give vision an adequate embodiment, it would eventually influence at least a few individuals, and through them others, until society as a whole had been changed by imitating the incarnated ideal images (*E&I* 158–9). Thus in 'To a Shade', the targets of Yeats's satire are condemned for having rejected the Lane pictures, which 'had they only known, / Had given their children's children loftier thought, / Sweeter emotion, working in their veins / Like gentle blood' (*VP* 292). Then Parnell, to whom the poem was addressed, might have found in this sweetening of Ireland's wrong a hope that would have quieted his restless shade. Shortly after Yeats wrote this poem, the Easter Rising, led by a man who had looked for inspiration to the ancient Irish epic figure of Cuchulain, had provided him with what he would come to see as a quintessential example of art's transforming power. The accompanying violence and tragedy suggested a troubling aspect of that power, but did not deter him from continuing repeatedly to cast his own mind on other days; and even in his last play, *The Death of Cuchulain*, he looked to the past for an image to inspire an Ireland he knew he would never live to see. The central importance in his life and work of the shaping power of art constitutes the argument of this study.

The lines in 'Under Ben Bulben' V about the 'lords and ladies gay / That were beaten into the clay', a by-product of Yeats's work with Frank O'Connor on translations of Irish poetry, echo not only the folk lyric 'Kilcash':

> Your courtyard's filled with water
> And the great earls where are they?
> The earls, the lady, the people
> Beaten into the clay.[9]

but also the great bardic poet Aogán O'Rathaille's 'Cabhair Ní Ghairfead' ('Last Lines'):

> I shall go after the heroes, ay, into the clay! (*WBN* 23)

Both poems date from the dark era of the Penal Laws, and O'Raithaille's articulates a particularly bleak sense of an ending. It was in fact written during his last illness and thus also corresponds in his career to 'Under Ben Bulben' with its inclusion of the poet's self-composed epitaph.[10] But significantly, although the present moment is a dark one in Yeats's poem, too, his tone is far more positive, precisely because *he* did not feel impotent, condemned to a fruitless nostalgia for an irretrievable past. As the allusion to O'Rathaille suggests, in 'Under Ben Bulben' Yeats adopted the bardic role and spoke in the bardic voice himself. The proud tradition of the Gaelic professional poets had come to an end in the eighteenth century, but Yeats anticipated Daniel Corkery in arguing that the essence of the tradition survived among the downtrodden peasantry; and (here he and Corkery would part company) that *he* was a legitimate present incarnation of it. The bardic inheritance entitled him to the bards' aristocratic position in society, to their obsessive concern with formal perfection, to their subject-matter, and to their fierce allegiance to the native tradition in the face of the development of the English drive to domination.[11] All these elements are suggested in Part V. The bards were associated with the mysteries of the Druids, and their inheritance also incorporated esoteric wisdom, a concern only implicit in this section of the poem but central in Parts I and II: 'ancient Ireland knew it all.'

There seem in fact to have been several classes or categories of literary men in early Ireland, our information about which becomes less and less certain as we push back further in time. According to medieval metrical tracts, 'the *bard* was simply a poet and versifier; the *fili* a poet, but also a scholar and guardian of traditional knowledge; he is especially a prophet and a seer and can wield supernatural powers.'[12] As one modern scholar describes the distinction, 'although the bard with his praise-poetry for the kings and nobles was an important person in society, the *fili* was even more eminent. The word came to mean 'poet', but in origin it had more of the meaning of "seer"; and at one time the *fili* may have had some of the attributes of the Druid. The *fili* could practise divination by means of various rites. He was also accredited with the supernatural powers of blemishing, or causing death, by satire.'[13] The poetry composed by the *fili* (later *file*) was 'a statement of the way things were, are, and will be', incarnated in literary form (Nagy 24). His function as revealer of hidden truth had a 'shamanic' quality – that is, he 'knows, "sees", and can communicate because he is regularly transported into the otherworld, or because he becomes possessed by otherworldly inspirational forces' (*Nagy* 25). The link with Druidism has been interpreted variously. The poets may have been a distinct but related group; in early Christian times they were perhaps a 'protective metamorphosis' of the ancient Druidic order, or at least the inheritors of its functions (Nagy 26–7, 237). James Carney has called the *ollamh* (the highest rank of poet) 'the shadow of a high-ranking pagan priest or druid.'[14] Keating, writing in the seventeenth century, referred to one individual as *file* and *draoi* interchangeably.[15] (In 'The Madness of King Goll' Yeats, with pardonable uncertainty, called one minor character in successive revisions 'Druid', 'old man', and 'Ollave' [*VP* 82].) Robert Graves argued in *The White Goddess* that the poetic 'colleges' preserved the ancient beliefs and ceremonies of the Goddess religion and related fertility cults, often concealing their lore by means of allegories, symbolism, and language codes.[16] Although there was an esoteric aspect to their wisdom, their verses and tales were designed to serve as 'mythical models' intended to be 'imitated' (perhaps not literally) by the people of early Celtic society.[17] The literary men were also involved with the laws of the country, which eventually became the special province of a distinct group, the brehons or *breithemain* (Carney 109, *RPES* 48).

The relationship among poet, king or patron, their land and people, fertility rites and the occult, encomia and satiric verse, and literary and political power was extremely complex:

> This [bardic] organisation preserved and propagated ideas on the nature of kingship and in these ideas we find our best relics of pre-Christian religion. A king married his territory: if he was effective and behaved as a king should, according to the ethical system of the poets, his land was fertile and bore fruit. If the king

was bad, according to this ethical system, the land was barren. . . .
[I]n certain families it was an ollav who presided at an inauguration
and who handed the prince the rod or wand which symbolised
his mystic union with the land, with growth and fertility. Here
the ollav is acting a part which is elsewhere played by a bishop:
he is the intermediary between the prince and the mysterious
powers of nature.

The satiric verse of the poets was regarded with such awe because

satire in origin is a religious sanction and represents the means
which the pagan 'church' used in order to exercise power over
the state. If an ollav satirises a prince he is in effect telling him
that the forces of nature, with which he, the ollav, is in
communion, are not satisfied: the result of the satire is an injury
to the king's honour (which may show physically as blisters on
his face) and possibly a blight on the land. The converse of this
necessarily holds: when a poet praises a king he is assuring him
that the powers of nature find him pleasing and that the marriage
is going well. Hence the poem of praise, as well as the satire, is in
origin a religious act. There is a close and mystic bond between
the prince and his ollav, and this may have something to do with
the fact that the ollav or druid was the prince's only possible
approach to the earth goddess whose husband he was. This may
explain the idea, basic to Irish thinking, that prince and ollav are
in a symbolic sense husband and wife.[18]

Obviously the 'legislative' role of the literary class was public and
highly visible. Members of that class were trained for their duties in
special schools, with the course lasting from seven to twelve years
and including the mastery of extremely complex metrical systems
as well as historical and occult lore. In the law tracts, the rank of the
ollamh was equivalent to that of a petty king, and he was legally
entitled to rewards for praise poems and to hospitality for a retinue
of up to twenty-four men.[19] A verse from a fifteenth-century manuscript combines the fertility element with the importance of
obedience to the monarch:

> If you have a feeble king
> Or him offend in anything,
> On the rich earth it bodes ill
> And works confusion in your will.[20]

In practice the relationship of bard to patron was subject to abuse, and there were many instances of insincere praise for gain, exorbitant demands, and offering one's services to the highest bidder.[21] Periodic efforts were made to curb or suppress the order, but it continued to exist.[22] The advent of Christianity also affected the literary tradition, but it persisted and even flourished for centuries, until the destruction of the indigenous Irish social patterns upon which its existence depended.[23] Even then vestiges of it survived, in such forms as peasant poets and storytellers and the inclusion of tale-telling as a feature of seasonal festivals, christenings, weddings and wakes (Rees 210–2).

Yeats, who typically chose to blur whatever distinctions of class and function might have existed and referred to the entire early Irish literary tradition as 'bardic' (a practice I have consequently adopted in this study), had become aware of that tradition quite early in his career, undoubtedly aided in recognising certain aspects of it by his own occult studies and pursuits, and saw in it a paradigm of the visionary Irish artist that offered coherence for his own complex poetic identity.[24] Through it he was able to 'hammer into unity' what had seemed disparate interests in 'a form of literature, in a form of philosophy, and a belief in nationality', so that all three became discrete expressions 'of a single conviction' (*Ex* 263).

As seers, the bards had had direct access to ideal images. Viewed historically, those images were to be found in the past, closer in time to the Edenic or pre-lapsarian state, and in sacred texts where they had been embodied by bardic predecessors and preserved through a tenaciously conservative tradition. That tradition also incorporated stories of the deeds of earlier heroes and kings, which might themselves serve as vehicles for esoteric wisdom (*RPES* 131). In the Middle Ages Irish and Christian history were reconciled in such syncretisms as the *Lebor Gabála* or *Book of Invasions*. At a more mundane level, legends provided support for dynastic claims. Thus the past was a crucial part of the bardic model. In a recent study of 'Historical Need and Literary Narrative', Donnchadh O' Corráin has observed that 'ownership of the past was, in a sense, control of the future'; and K. Theodore Hoppen, focussing upon more recent times, generalises similarly: 'Since at least the seventeenth century almost every group with an axe to grind has thought it imperative to control the past in order to provide support for contemporary arguments and ideologies.'[25] The early Irish obsession with the past was given added force by the English conquest and Ascendancy dilemmas of identity.[26] If a figure such as Daniel O'Connell had seen such an obsession as a barrier to national development, Douglas Hyde had urged his audience 'to never forget' the past in the speech that led to the founding of the Gaelic League.[27] Yeats, always impatient with the merely historical or antiquarian, recognised early in his career that such control of the past viewed as a vital force in his own time was crucial to the realisation of his own ambitions as a national writer.

His bardic inheritance entitled Yeats also to claim for himself their *power*. With a political shrewdness too often denied him, he anticipated Michel Foucault in his concern with mechanisms by which power 'reaches into the very grain of individuals, touches their bodies, and inserts itself into their actions and attitudes, their discourses, learning processes and everyday lives.'[28] In 1900 Yeats had asserted that it is

> only those things which seem useless or very feeble that have any power, and all those things that seem useful or strong, armies, moving wheels, modes of architecture, modes of government, speculations of the reason, would have been a little different if some mind long ago had not given itself to some emotion … and shaped sounds or colours or forms, or all of these, into a musical relation, that their emotion might live in other minds. A little lyric evokes an emotion, and this emotion gathers others about it … and at last … as it grows more powerful, it flows out, with all it has gathered, among the blind instincts of daily life, where it moves a power within powers.'[29]

Bardic power, though it appears comically in the bards' supposed ability to rhyme rats to death, was usually no laughing matter. In the *Táin Bó Cúalnge*, fear of their satire drove Ferdiad to fight his blood brother Cuchulain; and a sixteenth-century treaty weighed satire by the poets and excommunication by the Church as equivalent sanctions. Yeats himself termed the bards 'the most powerful influence in the land. … No gift they demanded might be refused them. One king being asked for his eye by a bard in quest of an excuse for rousing the people against him plucked it out and gave it. Their rule was one of fear as much as love. A poem and an incantation were almost the same. A satire could fill a whole countryside with famine.' As he noted in the same context, that fear survived in his own day among the country people.[30] *The King's Threshold* makes it clear that he saw such beliefs positively, as images of the power of bardic art to shape life. As seers in possession of esoteric knowledge, as inheritors of tradition and celebrators of an ideal heroic order, the bards combined the national and the occult and could bring the past to bear upon the present. Their patrons had often been chieftains, nobles, men at arms who both appreciated complex art and could put ideals into action. Similarly, the image of a heroic figure such as Cuchulain could move modern Irishmen to emulation, and thus mould the future along heroic lines – as well as bringing the soul of man to God.

When Yeats began his career as an *Irish* writer, Parnell's star was at its zenith and political excitement was running high; even more compelling to him was the Fenian tradition, represented by his mentor John O'Leary, who had himself been inspired by Davis and his school but was well aware of their literary weaknesses (*Au* 209). The young poet felt himself unsuited by temper, talent, and commitment to conflicting values to produce writing that would be obviously and immediately relevant to the national cause, though occasionally he made such efforts. Meanwhile, his developing aesthetic provided the compensatory thought that the real forces behind the great political events of the day might not in fact be the obvious ones. Such was his point in the survey of Irish literature he made in August 1894 as an introduction to his influential anthology *A Book of Irish Verse*. He began with a vignette featuring the peasant poets on whom the mantle of the bards had fallen: 'The great bardic order, with its perfect artifice and imperfect art, had gone down in the wars of the seventeenth century, and poetry had found shelter amid the turf-smoke of the cabins.'[31] Yeats was obviously well aware that bardic passion for the 'well made' had too often degenerated into an obsession with form at the expense of vision, and perhaps felt that the transition into a less exalted milieu had had a positive effect in this regard.[32] In any event, the songs of poets like O'Sullivan the Red (Eoghan Ruadh O'Súilleabháin) 'had made the people, crushed by the disasters of the Boyne and Aughrim, remember their ancient greatness' (xii). Precisely this process was the subject of 'Under Ben Bulben' V, and putting it into practice would be his goal throughout his career. Compared to the battles, the songs of the poets might seem insignificant, but 'the powers that history commemorates are but the coarse effects of influences delicate and vague as the beginning of twilight, and in those days these influences were woven like a web about the hearts of men by farm-labourers, peddlers, potato-diggers, hedge-schoolmasters, and grinders at the quern' (xii).

After discussing the limitations of the Young Ireland movement, which he saw as essentially a new start rather than a continuation of the native line, Yeats ended with some consideration of his own time. In his view, Trinity College, the antithesis of Young Ireland politically, had had a similarly deleterious effect upon the literature of Ireland. But there, too, he saw at work the bardic tradition, even in its debased form: Trinity's 'few poëts have been awakened by the influence of the farm-labourers, potato-diggers, peddlers, and hedge-schoolmasters of the eighteenth century, and their imitators in this' (xxv). (A further manifestation was Yeats's own fascination with O'Sullivan, whom he was already using as a persona in what were to become the *Stories of Red Hanrahan*, and the interest he was to develop in the still later peasant poet Raftery, who a few years after he wrote this introduction would be brought to his attention by Lady Gregory and Douglas Hyde.) That Ireland in the nineties, cut off from the support of the educated classes, was the home of a renascent national literature showed clearly 'how strong a wind blows from the ancient legends of Ireland, how vigorous an impulse to create is in her heart to-day.' Perhaps the new literature would become 'great enough to lead a world sick with theories to those sweet well-waters of primæval poetry, upon whose edge still linger the brotherhoods of wisdom, the immortal moods' (xxv–xxvi). As 'primæval' suggests, the new 'bardic' writers would be drawing upon the past in order to shape the future, using those 'ancient legends' to put Irish readers in the present in touch with archetypal images that were their national heritage. Art, then, might influence life in ways that were more profound than *any* merely political event.

Ironically, Yeats's awareness of the central importance of bardic influence upon the national consciousness had come partly from the work of a TCD man, Standish James O'Grady, which he was to claim 'started us all.'[33] In an 1895 article, Yeats praised O'Grady as the best of modern Irish prose writers but went on to detect elements of Nationalist feeling at a period in Irish history when the Unionist O'Grady had seen only the clash of an old order with a new, the Irish petty chieftains of the sixteenth century warring with each other rather than presenting a united front to the Elizabethan invaders (*UP1* 369). When O'Grady charged Yeats with anachronism,

Yeats wrote a letter in which he defended his view with an argument O'Grady's own early work had helped inspire:

> Then too, one cannot forget a lot of gaelic poems life 'the battle song for the clans of Wicklow' (translated by Ferguson). Is it not possible that while the racial unity of England expressed itself in a method of government, the racial unity of Ireland expressed it self in things like the bardic order & in popular instincts & prejudices. That while the English nobles therefore expressed English racial purpose at its best, the Irish nobles, warped by their little princedoms & their precarious dynasties were more for themselves & less for Ireland, than the bards, & harpers & the masses of the people? You of course know & I do not. You speak from particular knowledge, I from general principles merely.
>
> (CL1 472)

Yeats could in fact have found support for his theory in English Tudor chronicles unsympathetic to the Irish cause. In one such account, the bards are said to be 'very hurtfull to the comonwhealle, for they chifflie manyntayne the rebells.... Their furst practisse is, if they se anye younge man discended of the septs of *Ose* or *Max*, ... then will they make him a Rime, wherein they will commend his father and his aunchetours, ... and in the ende they will compare them to Aniball, or Scipio, or Hercules, or some other famous person; wherewithall the pore foole runs madde, and thinkes indede it is so.'[34] Could those 'other famous persons' have included 'that famous man Cuchulain'? One can imagine an English chronicler writing in 1916 of the Easter Rising. Again, Spenser had told of how the bards, held 'in so high regard and estymacion amongst them, that none dare displease them', were wont to choose notorious rebels as their models: 'him they sett upp and glorifie in theire rymes, him they prayse to the people, and to young men make an example to followe.'[35] Indeed, an exhortation similar to the one in Ferguson's poem can be found in a poem by the bard Giolla Brighde Mac Con Midhe written less than a century after the first Normans had landed on the Irish shore.[36]

But for Yeats the importance of his theory went beyond historical controversy. By this point in his career he had encountered enough opposition to his ideals for a modern national literature so that he found increasingly attractive the view that the bardic order had itself been a key force behind the emergence of Irish national or 'racial' feeling and therefore that he more than the Young Irelanders spoke with the true voice of the Irish nation and could shape its future. In succeeding years, as the attacks on him grew increasingly vitriolic, he was able to articulate his own position with increasing confidence and defiance. The letter to O'Grady could almost be said to constitute an embryonic scenario for *The King's Threshold*, written in 1903 at the period when the work of Synge was about to become the target of similarly intense hostility; in it the poets assert their rightful predominance over the nobles because their songs, filled with Edenic images, are responsible for the greatness of their society itself, and for ushering in 'the great race that is to come' (*VPl* 311). That ringing phrase echoes the title of the 'Apologia' and anticipates 'Under Ben Bulben'.

Reverberations of the same letter can be felt even to the very end of Yeats's career, for after the passage about the bards he went on to encourage O'Grady regarding the publication of new versions of the later portions of his retellings of the Cuchulain saga: 'For the story from the laying on of the spell till the death, as you tell it in the 'history', is not less than any epic tale in the world' (*CL1* 472). Yeats had already learned from O'Grady to see the Irish epics as bardic constructs of ideal images upon which a great nation might be based, and from his studies of folklore and the occult that such legends were archetypal, partook of the divine reality behind or within the fallen world, and thus might be used to evoke that reality (see also *Au* 372–4). As he wrote of 'The Valley of the Black Pig', 'All these battles [implied in the poem] ... are one. Once a symbolism has possessed the imagination of large numbers of men, it becomes ... an embodiment of disembodied powers, and repeats itself in dreams and visions, age after age' (*VP* 810). Thus he would declare in the essay 'Magic' that 'I cannot now think symbols less than the greatest of all powers' (*E&I* 49). It was for such reasons that Irish writers would have to make the legends the subject of their art: 'From that great candle of the past we must all light our little tapers' (*LNI* 66). It seems particularly fitting, therefore, that *The Death of Cuchulain*, Yeats's own final attempt to carry on the bardic tradition and shape the future of his nation, should have taken as its subject the same event whose incarnation in O'Grady's work he had praised so long before.

The present study is designed to complement and extend my *Yeats and the Beginning of the Irish Renaissance* (1970; second edition, 1987), a general survey of Yeats's conception of national literature and of his efforts to develop a literary movement along its lines. The argument of that book still seems to me to be sound, and I have taken it for granted here. With it as background, I have focused in this new study upon the relationship between art and life and the importance of the concept of art's shaping power to his aesthetic of national literature. In chapter 2 I examine the emergence of Yeats's concern with the concept in his work of the eighties and nineties, including a consideration of possible sources. The theatre movement subjected him to intensified pressure to defend his ideals. Consequently, chapter 3 is devoted to the period from the turn of the century to the Rising and its aftermath; *The King's Threshold* and other plays, as well as several lyrics, essays, and polemic writings all receive attention. Against his discouragement over what he saw as the increasingly philistine middle class Ireland of the new century he reaffirmed the power of art to change its values. The establishment of the Free State seemed to provide a dramatic opportunity for the realisation of Yeats's dreams for his country: all existing institutions would be questioned, and an independent Ireland would at last be free to develop without the hindering force of foreign ideologies. Chapter 4 analyses a number of major texts from the 1920s and 1930s that together chronicle the vicissitudes of his efforts to wield artistic power in a nation he had thought, over-optimistically, would be as pliable as warm wax. *Last Poems and Two Plays*, the contents and order of which he decided shortly before his death, was designed to give his aesthetic a determining place. The Conclusion briefly considers some implications of 'the example of Yeats' for more recent literature and for contemporary critical theory and practice. It attempts to make the end of the study the point of departure for a new beginning.

2

The Early Work

I

The key features of Yeats's concern with the power of art emerge simultaneously with his interest in the literature of his own country.[1] They already pervade an essay on Sir Samuel Ferguson that he published in 1886:

> Sir Samuel Ferguson's special claim to our attention is that he went back to the Irish cycle [of legends], finding it, in truth, a fountain that, in the passage of centuries, was overgrown with weeds and grass, so that the very way to it was forgotten of the poets; but now that his feet have worn the pathway, many others will follow, and bring thence living waters for the healing of our nation, helping us to live the larger life of the Spirit, and lifting our souls away from their selfish joys and sorrows to be the companions of those who lived greatly among the woods and hills when the world was young.... Well then, perhaps, some one will say, if [Deirdre's lament] has come from so far off, what good can it do us moderns, with our complex life? Assuredly it will not help you to make a fortune, or even live respectably that little life of yours. Great poetry does not teach us anything – it changes us. Man is like a musical instrument of many strings, of which only a few are sounded by the narrow interests of his daily life; and the others, for want of use, are continually becoming tuneless and forgotten. Heroic poetry is a phantom finger swept over all the strings, arousing from man's whole nature a song of answering harmony. It is the poetry of action, for such alone can arouse the whole nature of man. It touches all the strings – those of wonder and pity, of fear and joy. It ignores morals, for its business is not in any way to make us rules for life, but to make character. It is not, as a great English writer has said, 'a criticism of life', but rather a fire in the spirit, burning away what is mean and deepening what is shallow. (*UP1* 82–4)

15

Ferguson had cast his mind on other days (as Yeats under O'Leary's influence was doing even as he wrote the essay) and found in the early legends and literature of Ireland the inspiration for much of his own poetry, including *Conary* and *Deirdre* (which Yeats particularly admired), the epic *Congal*, and numerous shorter poems. In stressing that 'many others will follow' in Ferguson's pioneering footsteps, Yeats was not only suggesting that *he* had chosen to follow them but also anticipating what became the address to 'Irish poets' in 'Under Ben Bulben'. The essay is as emphatic as the poem would be about the effect of the process.

A modern literature grounded in 'the Irish cycle' will 'bring thence living waters for the healing of our nation.' Ferguson was to be enumerated in the 'Apologia addressed to Ireland in the coming days' as one of those who 'sang to sweeten Ireland's wrong . . .', and we can see Yeats here describing the effects of such work in terms general enough to apply to someone who, except for a brief moment of Nationalist enthusiasm, had been a staunch supporter of the Union. Ferguson himself had declared that 'the poets will save the people', but few of his or Yeats's readers would have assumed that this meant propaganda verse.[2] The fountain of healing waters has symbolic associations with fertility rites and their esoteric spiritual equivalents. Interfused with the political implications are overtones of the occult preoccupations in which Yeats – quite unlike Ferguson in this regard – was deeply immersed. Obviously he was already suggesting that the Irish tradition led back to the Divine Wisdom and that the modern poet's task was to bring the ideal world to bear upon his own time and nation. A passage Yeats wrote near the turn of the century, in an 1898 defence of the use of the legendary materials in modern literature, glosses the reference to Arnold:

> I believe that all men will more and more reject the opinion that poetry is 'a criticism of life,' and be more and more convinced that it is a revelation of a hidden life, and that they may even come to think 'painting, poetry, and music' 'the only means of conversing with eternity left to man on earth'.[3]

The Ferguson piece implies the pre-lapsarian and explicitly evokes the heroic (Congal and his men are referred to as 'indomitable pagans'), again pointing ahead towards 'Under Ben Bulben' (*UP1* 85). The lines there about contemporary Irishmen 'all out of shape from toe to top' have their antecedents here, too. One of the effects of 'heroic poetry' is to 'arouse the whole nature of man' – what Yeats was later to call Unity of Being, a state comparable to a 'perfectly proportioned human body'.[4] This (rather than Young Ireland verse) is the true 'poetry of action'; it *changes* rather than teaches, serving the national cause by *making character*. From Unity of Being multiplied would come, presumably, Unity of Culture – an indomitable Irishry.[5]

II

The human propensity to imitate literary models was part of Yeats's own experience from early childhood, when the stable-boy's volume of 'Orange rhymes' led him to fantasise about becoming 'as brave and handsome as the young men in the story-books' (*Au* 14). Not long afterwards *The Lay of the Last Minstrel* made him wish to become a magician, and Hamlet became 'an image of heroic self-possession for the poses of youth and childhood to copy' (*Au* 46–7). John Butler Yeats, seeking always in literature 'the lineaments of some desirable, familiar life' may also have played a role, for Yeats, while still in art school, would say that unless he could be sure the arts would 'make us happier' he would never write again (*Au* 65, 86). His earliest literary sources for an aesthetic of artistic power would most likely have been Shelley and Standish O'Grady, but all *certain* evidence of his familiarity with the relevant texts post-dates 1886. Tracing the history of the concept up to Yeats's own time offers a context within which to explore his indebtedness.

In considering the origins of the concept we find that, as with the history of so many questions, our starting point must be Plato. Plato's famously negative attitude towards the artist was based on the assumption of a fundamental ontological separation between the realm of the Ideas and the products of art; the latter, as copies of a Nature itself only an imperfect copy, were twice removed from reality and moving in the wrong direction.

A more positive view of the poet's role could be found in Aristotle's *Poetics*. In a famous passage in Chapter IX he argued that poets were superior to historians: 'poetry is both more philosophical and more serious than history, since poetry speaks more of universals, history of particulars'.[6] But Aristotle's rationalising, 'secular' principles have the counterbalancing effect of robbing the universals of the divine lustre associated with them by Plato, and the reader in search of a position in which the artist's elevation was not bought at such a cost would have to look elsewhere (Halliwell 12). Cicero and especially Plotinus offered precisely what was wanted.

According to Cicero, 'nor did [Pheidias], when he formed Jupiter or Minerva, have before his eyes a model which he followed strictly, but in his own mind did he have an extraordinary idea of beauty, this he contemplated, on this he fixed his attention, and to rendering this he directed his art and his hand.... These forms of things Plato calls *ideas*....'[7] The fifth *Ennead* of Plotinus addressed the question even more directly:

> Still the arts are not to be slighted on the ground that they create by imitation of natural objects; for, to begin with, these natural objects are themselves imitations; then, we must recognise that they give no bare reproduction of the thing seen but go back to the Ideas from which Nature itself derives, and, furthermore, that much of their [that is, the artists'] work is all their own; they are holders of beauty and add where nature is lacking. Thus Pheidias wrought the Zeus upon no model among things of sense but by apprehending what form Zeus must take if he chose to become manifest to sight.[8]

Yeats may or may not have known the passage from Cicero; Plotinus was to become one of his great favorites, but precisely what if anything he had read this early in his life remains uncertain. He was to link Pheidian sculpture with the general problem in two of his most famous poems on the subject, 'The Statues' and 'Under Ben Bulben'. We begin to see in any case that he was working, as he liked to do, within a tradition.

From Plotinus that tradition leads to Renaissance Neoplatonism and Sir Philip Sidney's *An Apology for Poetry*. Sidney drew upon Aristotle (giving him a distortedly idealistic emphasis) as well as the Neoplatonic tradition in order to buttress his claims for the poets (Halliwell 18–9). In one passage he wrote of how 'any understanding knoweth the skill of the artificer standeth in that *Idea* or fore-conceit of the work, and not in the work itself. And that the poet hath that *Idea* is manifest by delivering them forth in such excellency as he hath imagined them. Which delivering forth also is not wholly imaginative, as we are wont to say by them that build castles in the air, but so far substantially it worketh, not only to make a Cyrus, which had been but a particular excellency, as nature might have done, but to bestow a Cyrus upon the world to make many

Cyruses. . . .'[9] Here there is a clear anticipation of Yeats's idea of the artist offering an embodiment of a divine type, or archetype, that will be imitated in the fallen world. Moving from the Classical to the Christian in his next argument, Sidney drew an analogy between Maker and maker: the former, 'having made man to His own likeness, set him beyond and over all the works of that second nature, which in nothing he showeth so much as in poetry, when with the force of a divine breath he bringeth things forth far surpassing her doings, with no small argument to the incredulous of that first accursed fall of Adam: sith our erected wit maketh us know what perfection is, and yet our infected will keepeth us from reaching unto it' (17). The poets in *The King's Threshold*, placing images of the life that was in Eden about the childbed of the world, and the 'globe-trotting Madam' of 'Under Ben Bulben' IV whose bowels are enflamed by the 'half-awakened Adam' of the Sistine Chapel as part of the process of 'profane perfection', may come to our minds.

Sidney's moralistic stress throughout on art's positive effects on its audience constitutes an important contribution to the tradition. Elsewhere in the *Apology* he anticipates Shelley and O'Grady (as we shall see) by observing that 'Homer, a Greek, flourished before Greece flourished', and 'as by him their learned men took almost their first light of knowledge, so their active men received their first motions of courage' (62). So an Irish Homer might develop indomitability in his countrymen. Sidney himself provided the basis for such a geographical transposition. He knew that 'in our neighbor country Ireland, where truly learning goeth very bare, yet are their poets held in a devout reverence'; and his concluding satiric dismissal of those still unsympathetic to poetry refers to being 'rhymed to death, as it is said to be done in Ireland' (9, 89).

Perhaps because of its transcendentalist element, the concept seems to have found no powerful advocates during the Neoclassic era, but it reappeared dramatically in the age of Romanticism, especially in Shelley, one of Yeats's earliest literary enthusiasms, and in Blake, who became a dominant influence by the late 1880s.

III

In 1893, Yeats praised Shelley's *A Defence of Poetry* as one of the most 'fundamental' and 'philosophic' tracts 'in modern English criticism', but although his deep immersion in Shelley even predates his com-

mitment to *Irish* literary identity, we lack specific evidence that he
had read the *Defence* by the time he wrote his pieces on Ferguson in
1886.[10] If so, he certainly found there an argument passionate and
memorable enough to have exerted a powerful formative influence
upon the position he himself was developing; if he only encountered
it later, it supplemented and nuanced his own arguments as well as
offering the sanction of a significant precursor.

Shelley's essay had been a response to Peacock's 'Four Ages of
Poetry'. Peacock had attacked literature on utilitarian grounds and
even depicted bards as 'always ready to celebrate the strength of
[the king's] arm, being first duly inspired by that of his liquor'.[11]
During the period when Yeats was writing the Ferguson essays he
had almost certainly encountered the native Irish satire of the bards
and challenge to their civic power that he would remember and
later make the foundation of *The King's Threshold*, so Shelley's point
of departure would have been significant to him; Yeats later quoted
the most salient passage from the *Defence* in his essay 'The Philosophy
of Shelley's Poetry', written after his own idea of art had come
under fire from fellow Nationalists (*IGE* 93–5). The foundation of
Shelley's Neoplatonically inspired 'defence' was the argument that
poets were in direct touch with ultimate reality, the realm of the
Ideas. 'A poet participates in the eternal, the infinite, and the one; as
far as relates to his conceptions, time and place and number are
not'; and a poem 'is the creation of actions according to the unchangeable forms of human nature, as existing in the mind of the
creator, which is itself the image of all other minds'.[12] Shelley
noted, in another passage Yeats cited, that 'in the earlier epochs of
the world' poets had been known as 'legislators or prophets: a poet
essentially comprises and unites both these characters. For he not
only beholds intensely the present as it is, and discovers those laws
according to which present things ought to be ordered, but he
beholds the future in the present, and his thoughts are the germs of
the flower and the fruit of latest time' (104). The concern here with
the artist's impact upon the future runs throughout the essay.

Shelley stressed, as Yeats was to do, that the influence of art might
be so subtle as to pass unapprehended. He compared the poet to a
nightingale, 'who sits in darkness and sings to cheer its own solitude with sweet sounds; his auditors are as men entranced by the
melody of an unseen musician, who feel that they are moved and
softened, yet know not whence or why' (109). The nightingale
image itself suggests that audience impact and social change need

not be the poet's *motivations* at all. The impact would be no less
great. Echoing Sidney and anticipating O'Grady (as well as 'The
Statues'), Shelley claimed that 'the poems of Homer and his
contemporaries were the delight of infant Greece; they were the
elements of that social system which is the column upon which all
succeeding civilization has reposed' (109). Homer 'embodied the
ideal perfection of his age in human character'; he wrote of heroes,
and those who read him 'were awakened to an ambition of
becoming like to Achilles, Hector, and Ulysses: the truth and beauty
of friendship, patriotism, and persevering devotion to an object,
were unveiled to their depths in these immortal creations' (109–10).
The process sounds very much like that Yeats was to delineate, the
sentiments of the audience being 'refined and enlarged by a
sympathy with such great and lovely impersonations, until from
admiring they imitated, and from imitation they identified themselves
with the objects of their admiration' (110). Yeats, it will be recalled,
had rejected the Arnoldian concern with art as a pedagogic moral
force. Here, too, he had been anticipated by Shelley, who had
similarly substituted a far more profound influence exerted by art,
which 'awakens and enlarges the mind itself by rendering it the
receptacle of a thousand unapprehended combinations of thought'
(111). Again we may observe the equivalent of Yeats's concept of
Unity of Being.

Shelley devoted several pages of his essay to charting the relationship of art to the rise and fall of civilizations, pages suggestive of
Yeats's own vision of history. Thus, for example, he asserted that at
the end of the Classical era,

> the ancient system of religion and manners had fulfilled the circle
> of its evolutions. And the world would have fallen into utter
> anarchy and darkness, but that there were found poets among
> the authors of the Christian and chivalric systems of manners
> and religion, who created forms of opinion and action never before
> conceived; which, copied into the imaginations of men, became
> as generals to the bewildered armies of their thoughts. (122)

Arnold's ignorant armies clashing by night and Yeats's 'Confusion
fell upon our thought' from 'Under Ben Bulben' and the 'mere anarchy'
of 'The Second Coming' share aspects of Shelley's vision here. Shelley
noted only in passing 'the evil produced by these systems' and only
to deny that any 'portion of it can be attributed to the poetry they

contain' (122). Art's potentially baneful effects were a problem that Yeats would dwell upon at length and more darkly. Shelley saw links in the chain of the 'tradition' running from Pythagoras through Plato to Christianity, and even discerned a Celtic contribution. The 'sacred and eternal truths' contained in the 'perennial philosophy' were divulged by Christ, so that Christianity became 'the exoteric expression of the esoteric doctrines of the poetry and wisdom of antiquity' and '[t]he incorporation of the Celtic nations with the exhausted population of the south, impressed upon it the figure of the poetry existing in their mythology and institutions' (124). Another portion of the historical survey described the appearance of 'the poetry of sexual love' during the Middle Ages: 'It was as if the statues of Apollo and the Muses had been endowed with life and motion, and had walked forth among their worshippers; so that earth became peopled by the inhabitants of a diviner world. The familiar appearances and proceedings of life became wonderful and heavenly, and a paradise was created as out of the wrecks of Eden' (125). Apollo (reincarnate as Cuchulain) was later to stalk through the Post Office, artists from Seanchan to Calvert and Wilson, Blake and Claude would offer the soul Edenic images.

Through all the vicissitudes of history, poetry itself survived, and Shelley described its survival as Yeats would increasingly come to describe its influence:

> The sacred links of that chain have never been entirely disjoined, which descending through the minds of many men, is attached to those great minds, whence as from a magnet the invisible effluence is sent forth; which at once connects, animates and sustains the life of all. It is the faculty which contains within itself the seeds at once of its own and of social renovation. (120)

In the optimistic 1880s Yeats may not have found such a passage particularly germane, but a similar thought would sustain him in less happy times ahead.

Near the end of the essay Shelley, whose perhaps embarrassingly naive sympathy with the Irish national struggle George Bornstein has noted Yeats's silence about, referred to revolution in more general terms and asserted that poetry was 'the most unfailing herald, companion, and follower of the awakening of a great people' (143).[13] Here he stressed the *power* of art, repeating the word three times in as many consecutive sentences, and helped give emphasis to the famous final sentence. Such power would work even through poets of Shelley's own time who were scarcely in sympathy with his own visions. In a rhetorical flourish he caught even them up in his net, declaring that 'poets are the hierophants of an unapprehended inspiration; the mirrors of the gigantic shadows which futurity casts upon the present; the words which express what they understand not; the trumpets which sing to battle and feel not what they inspire; the influence which is moved not, but moves. Poets are the unacknowledged legislators of the world' (144). If the power seated on the throne of the souls of such poets produces an 'electric life which burns within their words', how much more efficacious would be the words of the *conscious* hierophants such as Yeats? The *Defence*, then, offered him a source for virtually every aspect of the concept that would figure significantly in his own thought.

Although Yeats was soon to help bind his national and occult concerns together by claiming that Irish blood flowed through the veins of William Blake and consequently an Irish spirit through his work, he made no such claims for Shelley. Standish O'Grady in a way provided a link, for he was himself an admirer of Shelley and had published a pamphlet entitled *Scintilla Shelleiana: Shelley's Attitude Towards Religion* in 1875. His 'Histories' may reflect the influence of the *Defence*; in any case, they adapt comparable arguments to a specifically Irish context.

'O'Grady was the first, and we had read him in our teens' – so Yeats was to recall in *The Trembling of the Veil* (*Au* 221). He wrote also that 'I think it was his "History of Ireland, Heroic Period", that started us all.'[14] The two volumes of O'Grady's *History* had been published in 1878 and 1880, and the first (and only) volume of the *History of Ireland: Critical and Philosophical* in 1881, so Yeats *could* have read them in his teens. But his interest in the Irish legendary materials presumably post-dated the fateful encounter with O'Leary; and Yeats's imprecision with dates has itself become almost legendary. In 'A General Introduction for my Work' he recalled that after reading the Young Irelanders at O'Leary's suggestion he had turned from 'the literature of the point of view' back to Homer and 'those that fed at his table'. O'Leary had sent him to O'Curry for information on the *Irish* heroic era, but 'his unarranged and uninterpreted history' had defeated Yeats's 'boyish indolence'. 'Then somebody, not O'Leary, told me of Standish O'Grady and his interpretation of Irish legends' (*E&I* 511). This might well have taken place by the time he wrote the Ferguson essays, for it seems likely that Yeats had been led to

Ferguson as part of the same quest for imaginative versions of the Irish tales; if not, the encounter came soon afterwards, for there seems to be an echo of the *History* in an essay Yeats published in 1887. Whether O'Grady had brought inspiration or only reinforcement, his impact upon Yeats's imagination must have been strengthened by the passion and enthusiasm with which he, like Shelley, made his case.

Although working in the infancy of Celtic and Irish historical scholarship, and without any knowledge of the Irish language, O'Grady was well aware that the surviving documents were at best untrustworthy guides to the real events of Ireland's early history. But unlike so many other scholars, he saw in such materials something at least as important:

> The legends represent the imagination of the country; they are the kind of history which a nation desires to possess. They betray the ambition and ideals of the people, and, in this respect, have a value far beyond the tale of actual events and duly recorded deeds, which are no more history than a skeleton is a man. Nay, too, they have their own reality. They fill the mind with an adequate and satisfying pleasure. They present a rhythmic completeness and a beauty not to be found in the fragmentary and ragged succession of events in time.[15]

O'Grady lacked the Neoplatonic strain found in Shelley, but the language in such a passage, in which completeness and beauty are set up against 'events in time', could easily be taken in such a sense by someone (such as Yeats) who did belong within that tradition. As John Kelly has suggested, Yeats seems to have been echoing this particular passage in his 1887 essay on the bardic hero Finn (Fionn Mac Cumhaill):

> Under all these old legends there is, without doubt, much fact, though, I confess, I care but little whether there be or not. A nation's history is not in what it does, this invader or that other; the elements or destiny decides all that; but what a nation imagines that is its history, there is its heart; than its legends, a nation owns nothing more precious.[16]

In O'Grady's view, 'early Irish history is the creation mainly of the bards' (1,19). Writing in 1890, Yeats would speculate in very similar terms that 'Cuchullin, Finn, Oisin, St. Patrick, the whole ancient world of Erin may well have been sung out of the void by the harps of the great bardic order' (*UP1* 164).

O'Grady's model for the influence of the bards upon the actual life of their country was ancient Greece:

> To the Greek bards who shaped the mythology of Hellas we must remotely attribute all the enormous influence which Greece has exercised on the world. But for them, the Greece that we know would not have been; without them the Iliad and Odyssey would never have arisen, nor the Athenian drama, nor Greek art, nor architecture. All of these, as we find them, are concerned with the gods and heroes who were the creations of pre-historic bards. It was they, namely, these pre-historic unremembered Greeks, who supplied the types, and the fire, ideality, and creative impulses. The great age of Hellas was not an accident, but an emergence into light, and a bursting as it were into flower of that which was generated and nursed in earlier obscurer centuries. Those rude elder forgotten bards were the root of all that floral magnificence of the Periclean and subsequent ages.[17]

O'Grady was very close here to Shelley. In the essay on Finn, Yeats had offered the suggestion that 'without her possible mythical siege of Troy, perhaps, Greece would never have had her real Themopylæ'.[18] Five decades later, still meditating on the relationship between art and life in *On the Boiler*, he was still focusing upon the experience of Greece:

> There are moments when I am certain that art must once again accept those Greek proportions which carry into plastic art the Pythagorian numbers, those faces which are divine because all there is empty and measured. Europe was not born when Greek galleys defeated the Persian hordes at Salamis, but when the Doric studios sent out those broad-backed marble statues against the multiform, vague, expressive Asiatic sea, they gave to the sexual instinct of Europe its goal, its fixed type.[19]

Yeats's use of 'type' glosses the same word in O'Grady and makes explicit what he might have seen in such a passage, the 'type' being comparable to the Jungian archetypes, to the Platonic Ideas, and to Shelley's 'unchangeable forms of human nature, as existing in the mind of the creator'.[20]

O'Grady frequently drew analogies between Irish and Greek culture, presumably in part to aggrandise the indigenous tradition, which had been studiedly ignored by the masters during his years in school and at TCD. He was a Unionist in politics, because he considered it in Ireland's best interest economically and politically to be part of the Empire, but his love of his country was as intense as any Young Irelander's and attracted Nationalist readers to his work. He argued that the bards had created the Heroic Age at an era when 'the national idea had laid hold upon the Irish mind' (I, 23–4). The bards had had a *national* motive, and the ideal worlds they created constituted a model 'for all succeeding ages' (I, 24). 'With their imagined gods and superhuman heroes, [they] breathed into the land and people the gallantry and chivalrousness, the prevailing ideality, the love of action and freedom, the audacity and elevation of thought, which, underneath all rudeness and grotesquerie, characterizes those remnants of their imaginings, and which we would believe no intervening centuries have been powerful wholly to annul' (*HCP* 61). O'Grady was clearly hoping to affect *current* attitudes, and it must have been exhilarating for a young Nationalist artist to find him speculating 'when I consider the extraordinary stimulus which the perusal of that literature gives to the imagination, even in centuries like these, and its wealth of elevated and intensely human characters, that, as I anticipate, with the revival of Irish literary energy and the return of Irish self-esteem, the artistic craftsmen of the future will find therein, and in unfailing abundance, the material of persons and sentiments fit for the highest purposes of epic and dramatic literature and of art, pictorial and sculptural' (*HCP* 61). O'Grady's words, strikingly prophetic in 1881, proved to be quite true, and Yeats would become a primary force in their realisation. The rediscovery of the early legends and literature did provide a crucial stimulus to the Irish Literary Revival, and Yeats himself was quick to feel their power and recognise their literary potential and their importance and utility in relation to the national cause (*YBIR* 223–75). After the Revolution, they seemed to many outmoded. In 1926, feeling some disappointment with a free Ireland that seemed to have forgotten its heroic inspiration, Yeats castigated Irish clerical narrowmindedness in an article entitled 'The Need for Audacity of Thought' (*UP2* 461–5). This echo of O'Grady, who had argued that the idealism nourished by the bards had made Ireland receptive to Christianity (I,vii), may have been coincidental; but in the late 1930s, with the entire literary movement apparently a spent force, Yeats's mind consciously turned back to O'Grady. The 'superhuman' heroes appear in the opening lines of 'Under Ben Bulben', later in which Yeats addressed the 'artistic craftsmen' of the day and urged them to use materials such as those O'Grady had recommended, for similar purposes; the catalogue of subjects and values there even corresponds to the (more abstract) one in O'Grady.

In *The Death of Cuchulain* Yeats offered a last example of how such advice might be put into practice. O'Grady himself had attempted to bring about the realisation of his prophecy. Despite its title, the famous two-volume *History* was made up primarily of literary renderings of the old texts, and even included an epic invocation of the 'Spirits of the ancient bards, my ancestors' (I, 48–9). Moreover, in 1882 the relevant portions were gathered into a single volume under the title *Cuculain: An Epic*. In his Introduction to *Fighting the Waves* (1934) Yeats would recall that 'in the eighties of the last century Standish O'Grady, his mind full of Homer, retold the story of Cuchulain that he might bring back an heroic ideal'; in the same passage Yeats went on to treat his own Cuchulain cycle as a continuation of O'Grady's endeavour.[21] At the time he wrote that Introduction the cycle remained incomplete, but in ensuing years he would come to feel that a change in European thought had made the time ripe at last, and *The Death of Cuchulain* was the result.

We have already seen Yeats in 1895 praising O'Grady's version of the story of Cuchulain's death and trying to help him find publishers for new versions of the saga; in *The Trembling of the Veil*, considering the failure of these efforts, Yeats speculated that if they 'had got all his histories and imaginative works into the hands of our young men, he might have brought the imagination of Ireland nearer the Image and the honeycomb' (*Au* 221). As it was, O'Grady directly or indirectly had had a major role in the shaping of modern Ireland not only through his impact upon literary figures such as Yeats, AE, and Lady Gregory, but, still more dramatically, upon figures such as Pearse. (My own copy of the *History: Critical and Philosophical*, bearing the signature of Ernie O'Malley, who was a generation younger than Pearse, offers a token of the continuing hold of O'Grady's work upon the revolutionary imagination.) So O'Grady provided Yeats with a model early in his career, and remained to the end of it a symbol of the power art might have.

IV

The concept of art Yeats was developing was strengthened and supplemented by an Irishman very different from O'Grady: Oscar

Wilde. The brilliant paradoxes and wit of 'The Decay of Lying', Wilde's first prose dialogue, make it almost unforgettable; and for Yeats the impact must have been intensified considerably by Wilde himself reading him the proofs of the periodical version of the essay in the elegant white rooms in Chelsea on Christmas Day, 1888 (*Au* 134–5). Wilde's essay was, as he admitted to a friend, '*au fond* . . . serious', and it left its mark on many of his contemporaries.[22] It became, in Richard Ellmann's words, 'the *locus classicus* for the expression of the converging aesthetic ideas of writers everywhere. Art was not to be put down by politics, economics, ethics, or religion. Its pride and power could no longer be challenged as frivolous or futile. Degeneration was regeneration. By cunning and eloquence Wilde restored art to the power that the romantic poets had once claimed for it, able once again to legislate for the world'.[23] The essay appeared in Wilde's *Intentions*, published in 1891; and at that time Yeats praised the volume as 'a wonderful book' and said it 'hides within its immense paradox some of the most subtle literary criticism we are likely to see for many a long day' (*CL1* 252; *UP1* 204).

Wilde had been piecing together his central paradox, life's imitation of art, as early as 1882;[24] and by the time he wrote 'The Decay of Lying' the argument was an elaborate one, enriched with a philosophical context that draws upon Plato in a way quite antithetical to Plato's own view:

> Art finds her own perfection within, and not outside of, herself. She is not to be judged by any external standard of resemblance. She is a veil, rather than a mirror. . . . She makes and unmakes many worlds. . . . Hers are the 'forms more real than living man', and hers the great archetypes of which things that have existence are but unfinished copies.[25]

Wilde was probably using Plato metaphorically rather than metaphysically, as his further statement that 'a great artist invents a type' suggests (307; see also 314). Nevertheless, he came out sounding like Cicero and Plotinus, who had identified the products of the artist's imagination with the Ideas; Plotinus had added that much of the artists' work was 'all their own; they are holders of beauty and add where nature is lacking.' Later in 'The Decay of Lying' Wilde referred (with some humour) to psychical research, and in regard to the Church claimed there was nothing 'better for the culture of a country than the presence in it of a body of men whose duty it is to believe in the supernatural, to perform daily miracles, and to keep alive that mythopœic faculty which is so essential for the imagination' (316–17). Such passages would have made it easier for Yeats to take Wilde's 'spiritual' language literally and thus to assimilate Wilde's position to his own idea of the *visionary* artist.

In describing the *process* by which art moulds life, Wilde used an image that stayed in Yeats's mind for decades:

> The Greeks ... understood this, and set in the bride's chamber the statue of Hermes or of Apollo, that she might bear children as lovely as the works of art that she looked at in her rapture or her pain. They knew that Life gains from Art not merely spirituality, depth of thought and feeling, soul-turmoil or soul-peace, but that she can form herself on the very lines and colours of art, and can reproduce the dignity of Pheidias as well as the grace of Praxiteles. (307–8)

The reference to Pheidias provides a link back to Cicero and Plotinus, but also to a source Wilde had found much closer to hand, Walter Pater's *Studies in the History of the Renaissance*. The essay on Winckelmann had quoted Winckelmann himself to the effect that 'the Spartan women set up in their bedchambers a Nireus, a Narcissus, or a Hyacinth, that they might bear beautiful children....'[26] But earlier in the volume Pater had already defined the 'law of the most excellent Greek sculptors, of Pheidias and his pupils, which prompted them constantly to seek the type in the individual, to abstract and express only what is structural and permanent ...', and Wilde was merging elements from his 'golden book' (*Renaissance* 51–2; *Au* 130). The idea that the artist could bring his world 'spirituality, depth of thought and feeling' might have seemed to Yeats like an echo of his own phrase from the Ferguson article – 'a fire in the spirit, burning away what is mean and deepening what is shallow.' The image of the artist affecting the child through the mother suggested a slow, *indirect* form of influence, but also a deep and organic one – appropriate for describing the distinction Yeats would come increasingly to emphasise between the influence of immediately intelligible but superficial and inferior 'popular' literature such as that of the Young Irelanders and difficult, esoteric work like so much of his own. Half a century later Yeats returned to the passage not only in 'The Statues' but also in the final lyric of *The Death of Cuchulain*. Like Wilde in the *fin de siècle*, Yeats in the late 1930s was seeking regeneration in a time of degeneration. Wilde had gone on to claim that the Greeks had opposed realism in art because

> they felt that it inevitably makes people ugly, and they were perfectly right. We try to improve the conditions of the race by means of good air, free sunlight, wholesome water, and hideous bare buildings for the better housing of the lower orders. But these things merely produce health, they do not produce beauty. For this, Art is required, and the true disciples of the great artist are not his studio-imitators, but those who become like his works of art, be they plastic as in the Greek days, or pictorial as in modern times; in a wold, Life is Art's best, Art's only pupil. (308)

Wilde's essay offered the hint of a remedy far more attractive than 'eugenics' for that decline of the race Yeats would so controversially lament in *On the Boiler*.[27] And Wilde's ensuing historical survey of the relationship between art and the age (proleptic, like that in Shelley's *Defence*, of 'Dove or Swan') suggested in its witty assertion that 'the Japanese people are the deliberate self-conscious creation of certain individual artists' just the sort of programme Yeats was to devote much of his life to an attempt to realise (314–6).[28]

It seems inevitable that William Blake, in whose work Yeats was becoming so deeply immersed during the period in which he had encountered 'The Decay of Lying', would also provide support for his thinking about the purpose and power of art. Blake had spoken as inspired bard in *Milton*;[29] and, however improbable from a scholarly point of view, Yeats's belief in Blake's 'Irishness' made it possible to see him as part of the *Irish* bardic tradition: 'His descent from a stock who had seldom lacked their attendant banshee . . . may well have had much to do with his visionary gift'; his poetry had 'an Irish flavour, a lofty extravagance of invention and epithet, recalling the *Tain Bo Cuilane* and other old Irish epics, and his mythology brings often to mind the tumultuous vastness of the ancient tales of god and demon that have come to us from the dawn of mystic tradition in what may fairly be called his fatherland' (I, 2–4; also *YBIR* 24). The link here between 'ancient Ireland' and 'the dawn of mystic tradition' situates Blake (whose place in the Neoplatonic tradition has been convincingly demonstrated by Kathleen Raine and George M. Harper) as squarely as Shelley behind the 'Apologia' and 'Under Ben Bulben'. It was Blake who had referred to 'Poetry,

Painting, and Music, – the three powers in man of conversing with Paradise which the flood did not sweep away.'[30] The art capable of doing this was not in the ordinary sense an imitation of life. 'Why are copies of nature incorrect, 'Blake had asked rhetorically, 'while copies of imagination are correct?' (II, 392). Yeats wrote 'true art is expressive and symbolic, and makes every form, every sound, every colour, every gesture, a signature of some unanalyzable imaginative essence. False art is not expressive but mimetic ...' (*IGE* 217). Imagination was the faculty by which the 'hidden life' sought by Yeats was revealed: 'The world of imagination is the world of eternity. ... There exist in that eternal world the eternal realities of everything which we see reflected in this vegetable glass of nature.' (II, 394) Yeats, in the essay on Blake's illustrations to Dante, observed that 'he had learned from Jacob Boehme and from old alchemist writers that imagination was the first emanation of divinity, "the body of God", "the Divine members", and he drew the deduction, which they did not draw, that the imaginative arts were therefore the greatest of Divine revelations' and discussed Blake's belief 'that the figures seen by the mind's eye, when exalted by inspiration, were "eternal existences", symbols of divine essences", and his corresponding hatred of any 'grace of style that might obscure their lineaments' (*IGE* 170, 182).[31] The natural world was the fallen world, the realm of Plato's incorrect copies, but the visionary artist could lead the soul of man back to God, could help regain Paradise through his art. Blake himself had claimed that 'the Nature of my work is Visionary or Imagination. It is an endeavour to restore what the Ancients called the golden age.'[32] The urgency that pervades Blake's statements clearly arises from his sense of the artist's responsibility to change and shape the life of his world.

Blake's *Descriptive Catalogue* threw light on the process as he envisioned it. His underlying assumptions were remarkably congruent with those Yeats himself had been formulating since his discovery of Theosophy. In 'The Celtic Element in Literature' Yeats wrote of the universal uniformity of 'the ancient religion of the world' (*IGE* 275). Under the influence of Jacob Bryant's *A New System, or, An Analysis of Ancient Mythology* (1774–6), Blake had argued that 'the Antiquities of every Nation under Heaven are no less sacred than those of the Jews. They are the same thing. ... All had originally one language, and one religion: this was the religion of Jesus, the Everlasting Gospel' (II, 374–5; *Ex* 43). Correlatively, he asserted of Chaucer's Canterbury pilgrims that they were 'the characters which

compose all ages and nations. As one age falls another rises different
to mortal sight, but to immortals only the same; for we see the same
characters repeated again and again. . . .' The pilgrims were 'lineaments
of universal human life . . .' (II, 365); 'Every one is an Antique Statue,
the image of a class, not of an imperfect individual' (II, 368). As Yeats
described Blake's view, which sounded like the relevant passage in
Pater, 'inspiration was to see the permanent and characteristic in all
forms' (*IGE* 183); it was an easy step to identify these universal images
with the Ideas or archetypes. The visionary artist saw experience in
precisely this way: 'Visions of these eternal principles or characters
of human life appear to poets in all ages' (II, 368). Blake himself had
had such visionary experiences, 'having been taken in vision into
the ancient republics, monarchies, and patriarchates of Asia' where
he saw the 'wonderful originals' of which the best Classical sculpture
had been copies. He had 'endeavoured to emulate the grandeur of
those seen in his vision, and to apply it to modern Heroes on a smaller
scale' (II, 364). The figures of Nelson and Pitt in his paintings were
new incarnations of ancient heroic types, in a way proleptic of Yeats's
efforts to apply his vision of Cuchulain to modern Irish heroes.
Blake's claim that 'the British Antiquities are now in the Artist's
hands, – all his visionary contemplations relating to his own country
and its ancient glory, when it was, as it shall be again the source of
learning and inspiration' (II, 374) might have dovetailed neatly in
Yeats's mind with O'Grady and his claims for the Irish antiquities,
both their past greatness and the profound effect they might have
on the future. Blake even listed among the antiquities he possessed
stories of 'the Druid monuments', of 'the Giants of Ireland', and of
the Fairies. 'All these things', according to him, 'are written in Eden.
The Artist is an inhabitant of that happy country, and if everything
goes on as it has begun, the world of vegetation and generation may
expect to be opened again to Heaven, through Eden, as it was in the
beginning' (II, 374). A key part of this project was apparently 'The
Ancient Britons', his painting of the last battle of King Arthur, in
which only three Britons, *'the Strongest Man, the Beautifullest Man
and the Ugliest Man,'* escaped; *'these three marched through the field,
unsubdued, as Gods, and the sun of Britain set, but shall rise again with
tenfold splendour when Arthur shall awake from sleep . . .'* (II, 373). Blake
had taken a Classical statue of Apollo (probably the Apollo Belvedere
(II, 364) as the model for his Beautiful Man, emulating 'those precious
remains of antiquity', perfect and eternal images of Beauty essential
to his plan: 'The Beauty proper for sublime art is lineaments, or forms

and features that are capable of being the receptacles of intellect. Accordingly the painter has given, in his Beautiful Man, his own idea of intellectual Beauty' (II, 375; *IGE* 185). Thus 'The Ancient Britons' and Yeats's 'The Statues' had the same core and purpose. A draft indicates that the statue in Yeats's poem was conceived of as depicting Apollo; it is clearly a receptacle of intellect, an embodiment of the divine archetype of man.[33] Blake said his picture supposes that 'in the fifth century, there were remains of those naked Heroes in the Welch mountains. They are there now. Gray saw them in the person of his Bard on Snowdon . . .' (II, 374). Similarly in 'The Statues' the archetype survives through various historical eras in various incarnate forms. The final lyric of *The Death of Cuchulain* would ask, 'What comes out of the mountain / Where men first shed their blood?' As Blake painted heroes destined to arise again when Arthur should awake as an image of Albion and England resurgent (as he hoped to see them), so Yeats would show the Irish of his day tracing the lineaments of a statue – represented by the poem and companion play – that would inspire them to restore their country to its ancient glory. Thanks to Shelley, Yeats in the late eighties would have been well able to appreciate the implications of Blake's defiance when he wrote 'let it no more be said that empires encourage arts, for it is arts that encourage arts. Arts and artists are spiritual and laugh at mortal contingences. This is their [i.e., empires'] power, to hinder instruction, but not to instruct, just as it is in their power to murder a man but not make a man' and 'let us teach Buonaparte and whomsoever it may concern that it is not the arts that follow and attend upon Empire, but Empire that attends upon and follows arts' (II, 384). Wherever he looked, it seems, Yeats found support for the idea of the artists as makers, their songs potent to work the fall of one nation, the rise of another.

This was true also of yet another contributing influence, the poem 'Ode' ('We are the music makers') by the little-known Árthur O'Shaughnessy (1844–81). Although O'Shaughnessy was of Irish extraction, it is difficult to see his work within any Irish tradition. He was a friend of the painter J.T. Nettleship, whom Yeats also knew.[34] The Pre-Raphaelites and the contemporary French poets, especially Victor Hugo, were dominant influences upon him, and his poems show no concern with Irish subjects. Katharine Tynan published a rather critical article on him in *The Irish Fireside* in 1887, which Yeats praised as 'admirable well written in every way' (*CL1* 12). It did not mention 'Ode'. At what point Yeats first saw the relevance of the poem is not clear. He included O'Shaughnessy in *A Book of Irish Verse* (1895), but chose a different lyric, which Tynan had praised as 'perfect and flawless', to represent his work. His first certain reference to 'Ode' came in 1900 (*IGE* 245). There is an echo also in a contemporary version of *The Speckled Bird* (188).[35] It offered him a passionate assertion *in verse* of the artist's central importance, along with other elements congruent with his own vision:

> We are the music makers,
>   And we are the dreamers of dreams,
> Wandering by lone sea-breakers,
>   And sitting by desolate streams; –
> World-losers and world-forsakers,
>   On whom the pale moon gleams:
> Yet we are the movers and shakers
>   Of the world for ever, it seems.
>
> With wonderful deathless ditties
> We build up the world's great cities,
>   And out of a fabulous story
>   We fashion an empire's glory:
> One man with a dream, at pleasure,
>   Shall go forth and conquer a crown;
> And three with a new song's measure
>   Can trample a kingdom down.
>
> We, in the ages lying
>   In the buried past of the earth,
> Built Nineveh with our sighing,
>   And Babel itself in our mirth;
> And o'erthrew them with prophesying
>   To the old of the new world's worth;
> For each age is a dream that is dying,
>   Or one that is coming to birth.
>
> A breath of our inspiration
> Is the life of each generation;
>   A wondrous thing of our dreaming
>   Unearthly, impossible seeming –
> The soldier, the king, and the peasant
>   Are working together in one,

Till our dream shall become their present,
　　And their work in the world be done.

They had no vision amazing
Of the goodly house they are raising;
　　They had no divine foreshowing
　　Of the land to which they are going:
But on one man's soul it hath broken,
　　A light that doth not depart;
And his look, or a word he hath spoken,
　　Wrought flame in another man's heart.

And therefore to-day is thrilling
With a past day's late fulfilling;
　　And the multitudes are enlisted
　　In the faith that their fathers resisted,
And, scorning the dream of to-morrow,
　　Are bringing to pass, as they may,
In the world, for its joy or its sorrow,
　　The dream that was scorned yesterday.

But we, with our dreaming and singing,
　　Ceaseless and sorrowless we!
The glory about us clinging
　　Of the glorious futures we see,
Our souls with high music ringing:
　　O men! it must ever be
That we dwell, in our dreaming and singing,
　　A little apart from ye.

For we are afar with the dawning
　　And the suns that are not yet high,
And out of the infinite morning
　　Intrepid you hear us cry –
How, spite of your human scorning,
　　Once more God's future draws nigh,
And already goes forth the warning
　　That ye of the past must die.

Great hail! we cry to the comers
　　From the dazzling unknown shore;

> Bring us hither your sun and your summers,
>   And renew our world as of yore;
> You shall teach us your song's new numbers,
>   And things that we dreamed not before:
> Yea, in spite of a dreamer who slumbers,
>   And a singer who sings no more.[36]

The poets of the first stanza are remarkably similar to one of the most prominent masks of the youthful Yeats himself, unworldly dreamers wandering by the sea under the light of the pale moon. It is precisely the juxtaposition of that image of the *apparently* ineffectual artist with the claim that such figures are *really* 'the movers and shakers / Of the world for ever' that would have appealed to the Yeats whose development was so largely a quest for unity through reconciled opposites and whose own early dreaminess coexisted with an intense desire for power.

The second verse not only encapsulated the idea of the artists as the builders of civilisation itself, but offered generic images of their correlative *destructive* force that might well have had a more specifically *national* relevance for an Irish writer concerned with trampling down a particular kingdom, conquering the British crown. In the third stanza O'Shaughnessy began to connect the concept of the power of art with a cyclical movement of history comparable to the one pervading Yeats's oeuvre from *The Wanderings of Oisin* to the last poems and plays. It seems almost certain that Yeats was recalling this stanza in Part VI of 'Vacillation':

> Wheels by milk-white asses drawn
> Where Babylon or Nineveh
> Rose; some conqueror drew rein
> And cried to battle-weary men,
> 'Let all things pass away.' (*VP* 502)

The original title of this section was 'Conquerors'; read in the light of O'Shaughnessy's lines, Yeats's verse reveals its full irony, implying that it is not the generals but the poets who really engineer the rise and fall of the world's great cities. The remainder of Yeats's poem belongs to the singers, from the archetypal bard Homer to the maker of 'Vacillation' itself.

In O'Shaughnessy's fifth verse, the terms 'vision' and 'divine foreshadowing' and the image of the light within the poet's soul represent the transcendental inspiration essential also to Yeats's version of the process; while 'Wrought flame in another man's heart' describes the poet's impact upon the audience with essentially the same image Yeats had used for that impact in the Ferguson piece, 'a fire in the spirit'.

The last three stanzas, in which as gyres run on 'Ceaseless and sorrowless' poets contemplate with equanimity, even with something like a defiant joy, the inevitable destruction of what they have built, evoke in image and even in tone 'Lapis Lazuli'; while 'Once more God's future draws nigh' has many resonances among Yeats's 'apocalyptic' poems of the 1890s. The final verse, hailing 'the comers / From the dazzling unknown shore' and urging them to 'renew our world as of yore', corresponds to the final speech of *The King's Threshold*:

> O silver trumpets, be you lifted up
> And cry to the great race that is to come.
> Long-throated swans among the waves of time
> Sing loudly, for beyond the wall of the world
> It waits and it may hear and come to us. (*VPl* 311–2)

Thus O'Shaughnessy's poem as a whole, with its seemingly powerless poets who are really visionary world-shapers ushering in the future despite the 'human scorning' of their contemporaries, anticipates not only the vision but even the organisation of Yeats's play.

V

The *Irish Fireside* piece on Sir Samuel Ferguson was one of two that Yeats wrote at about the same time shortly after Ferguson's death on 9 August 1886. The other, longer piece was published in the *Dublin University Review* in November 1886 (*UP1* 81, 86–7). From it we can gain further insights into the state of his thought during the composition of *The Wanderings of Oisin*, which he probably began in 1886, and which represented his first major effort to carry his nascent theories into practice (*CL1* xii).

In other obituary articles on Ferguson, Margaret Stokes and J.P. Mahaffy had taken advantage of the occasion of the poet's death to celebrate his loyalty to the Crown (*UP1* 87, 100). Yeats undertook to recover him for the national tradition, boldly asserting that 'Irish singers, who are genuinely Irish in thought, subject and style, must, whether they will or no, nourish the forces that make for the political liberties of Ireland' (*UP1* 100n). The artist's power not only did not require intentional exercise, but could even work *counter* to his conscious purpose. Yeats's claim presumably rested upon the general assumption that any Irish writer who brought his or her Irish readers into vital contact with their indigenous culture would surely lead them towards involvement with it and away from any superficial attraction to the (ultimately) alien English tradition; and that out of national pride would come political patriotism. There were to be plenty of factual instances to establish the legitimacy of such an assumption. More specifically he seems to have had in mind the use of the legendary materials, for later in the essay he wrote that 'of all the many things the past bequeaths to the future, the greatest are great legends; they are the mothers of nations' (*UP1* 104). Again we can see how early Yeats was concerned with the process of casting one's mind on other days in order to inspire a future Irishry. Thus he held it 'the duty of every Irish reader to study those [legends] of his own country till they are familiar as his own hands, for in them is the Celtic heart' (104); O'Grady and Yeats were already of one mind about this. In the next paragraph he turned to direct address, as he would in 'Under Ben Bulben' V:

> If you will do this you will perhaps be saved in their high companionship from that leprosy of the modern – tepid emotions and many aims. Many aims, when the greatest of the earth often owned but two – two linked and arduous thoughts – fatherland and song. For them the personal perplexities of life grew dim and there alone remained its noble sorrows and its noble joys. (*UP1* 104)

The stress upon the primal linkage of fatherland and song was balanced elsewhere in the essay by references to the *universal* element in the legends. But here Yeats was focussing upon an audience of 'those young men clustered here and there throughout our land, whom the emotion of Patriotism has lifted into that world of selfless passion in which heroic deeds are possible and heroic poetry credible' (104). In practice, it might well be the credibility of heroic poetry that would *make* heroic deeds seem possible. One gave the legends new incarnations that one might, as he would write of O'Grady, 'bring back an heroic ideal' (*WB* 70).

Although Yeats's later statement that he had soon turned from the Young Irelanders, whose books O'Leary had put into his hands, back to Homer and 'those that fed at his table' was made apropos of O'Grady, the *Dublin University Review* essay shows that he had seen Ferguson, too, in the Homeric tradition. Davis had given the nation 'a battle call', Mangan 'its cry of despair'; but only Ferguson, 'the one Homeric poet of our time, could give us immortal companions still wet with the dew of their primal world' (*UP1* 90). He was 'like the ancients; . . . like them in nature, for his spirit had sat with the old heroes of his country', and in *Deirdre* 'he has restored to us a fragment of the buried Odyssey of Ireland' (*UP1* 92). Whether Yeats had yet discovered the allegorical Homer of the Neoplatonists, whose poems were epics of the history of the soul, is uncertain; in any case he had already recognised Homer's value as a poetic model of unassailable greatness who could be set up against those his nationalist allies would offer him – not always so sensitively as O'Leary had.

In another paragraph in the essay Yeats praised Ferguson in a way that implies a link between Homer and the oldest native tradition:

> Almost all the poetry of this age is written by students, for students. But Ferguson's is truly bardic, appealing to all natures alike, to the great concourse of the people, for it has gone deeper than knowledge or fancy, deeper than the intelligence which knows of difference – of the good and the evil, of the foolish and the wise, of this one and of that – to the universal emotions that have not heard of aristocracies, down to where Brahman and Sudra are not even names. (*UP1* 101)

Here, of course, his emphasis was upon the archetypal; and the link between *depth* and the 'universal emotions' glosses the reference in the other Ferguson piece to literature 'deepening what is shallow' (*UP1* 84) and links Ferguson to the role of the *visionary* artist. But 'bardic' suggests both Homer and the creators of the legends upon which Ferguson based much of his own poetry. At this early point in his own development Yeats had already discovered the bardic model. Ferguson's own volumes would have been a source, as well as O'Grady if Yeats had yet encountered him. Virtually all he needed was even available in Owen Connellan's essay 'The Bards of Ireland' in the *Transactions of the Ossianic Society*, and in the text to which it was prefixed, *Imtheacht na Tromdhaimhe, The Proceedings of the Great Bardic Institution*, which would be the ultimate source of *The King's Threshold*.

As Connellan was introducing a tale the focus of which was bardic *abuses* of power, he naturally devoted a certain amount of space to supposedly historical instances of such abuses and consequent hostility towards the bards. But he also offered the information that 'the order of Bards is of the very highest antiquity in Ireland' (Connellan xvi) and a chronological account covering many centuries, from Amergin to fairly recent times. He described their high social rank and depicted them participating in the inauguration ceremonies of kings, placing a white wand in the new monarch's hand (xxiii). Equally important was his statement that 'we find a bard often entrusted with the education of a prince' (xviii). (That Yeats considered a modern version of such a role for himself during the hegemony of Parnell is questionable; he would certainly do so during the early years of the Free State.) The bards could play such a role because of their wisdom, linked to their association with Druidism: Druids had been *their* teachers, and the most learned Ollaves 'were sometimes admitted into the Druidic hierarchy' (xx). The one clue Connellan offers as to the substance of that wisdom is a reference to the bards being 'respected by the great for their learning, and reverenced, almost to adoration, by the vulgar, for their knowledge of the secret composition, and hidden harmony of the universe' (xxxi).

A lengthy footnote to the text of the tale may have provided Yeats with his first information about that striking if grotesque example of artistic power, the bards' ability to rhyme rats and even humans to death (76–80). The note cites the well-known passage in *As You Like It* (III, ii, 85) as well as occurrences in numerous other authors, including Sidney and (one that at this stage in his life Yeats was probably not particularly excited about) Jonathan Swift. In 'Advice to a Young Poet' Swift had cited Sidney's reference: 'Our very good friend (the knight aforesaid), speaking of the force of poetry, mentions rhyming to death, which (adds he) is said to be done in Ireland; and truly, to our honour be it spoken, that power in a great measure continues with us to this day.'[37] Much later Yeats would envy Swift's own power and explore the possibility that he himself could play as powerful a role in an independent Ireland.

Yeats's longer essay on Ferguson had argued that he was 'the greatest poet Ireland has produced, because the most central and most Celtic' (*UP1* 103). Like O'Grady, Yeats predicted an imminent Irish literary movement:

> Whatever the future may bring forth in the way of a truly great and national literature – and now that the race is so large, so widely spread, and so conscious of its unity, the years are ripe –

will find its morning in these three volumes of one who was made by the purifying flame of National sentiment the one man of his time who wrote heroic poetry –. (*UP1* 103)

Given the fact that he was writing these words even as he was composing *The Wanderings of Oisin*, it is hard not to see them as applicable to his own situation. As he set out to provide the new movement with its first major poem, *he* was finding inspiration in Ferguson's volumes. According to the argument he used in 'claiming' Ferguson for Nationalism, *anything* Yeats might write that was Irish 'in thought, subject and style' would help shape the political future of the country; but both Ferguson essays stress the use of the legends and legendary texts, Ireland's living past. The power of such materials to inspire political action and their power to rescue readers from 'that leprosy of the modern' and lift their 'souls away from their selfish joys and sorrows to be the companions of those who lived greatly among the woods and hills when the world was young' *might* work in contradictory directions, the latter suggesting that *all* political action was insignificant when compared to the making of one's soul and could even retard that process. These early essays take no notice of the potential problem, but arguably it manifests itself in *The Wanderings of Oisin*, in the conflict between the attraction of the paradisal realms to which Niamh would lead the hero and the pull of the fallen world that in various forms draws him back to Ireland. Many years later, surveying the literary productions of a lifetime, he would observe that 'the swordsman throughout repudiates the saint, but not without vacillation' (*L* 798). Whatever the outcome of Yeats's personal debate, whichever way the reader might be drawn, to God or to the barricades, the poem itself would be an exercise of power.

In *The Wanderings of Oisin* Yeats was himself playing the bardic role, passing on a traditional story as his predecessors had done for centuries. There was, to be sure, a strong subjective element. In 1892 Yeats would write that *The Countess Kathleen* was 'an attempt to mingle personal thought and feeling with the beliefs and customs of Christian Ireland; whereas [*The Wanderings*] endeavoured to set forth the impress left on my imagination by the Pre-Christian cycle of legends' (*VPl* 1288). For the modern bard, using the legends was part of a delicate balancing act: 'Emotions which seem vague or extravagant when expressed under the influence of modern literature, cease to be vague and extravagant when associated with ancient legend and mythology, for legend and mythology were born out of man's longing for the mysterious and the infinite' (*UP1* 423). However personal the bard might be, his poems still brought readers into contact with the 'great impersonal emotions' with which the 'Pagan cycle' dealt (*VPl* 1288).[38] The particular tale he chose to reanimate in *The Wanderings* might have been appealing partly because neither Ferguson nor O'Grady had made it his own, and certainly it offered a correlative for some of his own romantic concerns and occult explorations. Most importantly, perhaps, its hero had been *both* bard and great warrior, and thus an emblem of the *fusion* of art and power.

Having said so much, however, we must admit, too, that Yeats does not stress the power of Oisin's art in the way we might expect. Instead of making verses in which the eternal is brought to bear upon the fallen world, Oisin in Book I sings to the Immortals 'of earthly lands' until they are overcome by sadness and fling his harp away (*VP* 17, l.233 1889 version). The huge stone statues flanking the stairs of the castle in Book II remain mere stage scenery (*VP* 31, ll.35–37 1889 version). Moreover, the framestory of the poem focusses upon Oisin at precisely the point when the warrior bard himself appears *least* powerful:

Ah me! to be old without succour, a show unto children, a stain,
Without laughter, a coughing, alone with remembrance and fear,
All emptied of purple hours as a beggar's cloak in the rain,
As a grass seed crushed by a pebble, as a wolf sucked under a
weir.

(*VP* 63)

Neither his final expression of heroic defiance, nor the prospect of the return of power such as his that might be expected from the cyclical vision of history implicit in the poem, can quite efface this impression. In the poem, Oisin blames the Church for weakening the bardic tradition – 'Patrick, before thy craft dies each old song' (*VP* 42, l.96 1889 version). That Yeats himself in the late 1880s saw Catholic power and artistic power as deadly antagonists is possible; but his decision to focus upon so inauspicious a point in his protagonist's career could in any event reflect (perhaps unconscious) doubts and uncertainties constituting a less sanguine countertruth to the tone he generally adopted in his programmatic writings of the same period.

Similar manifestations of such concerns appear in other early texts. In 'Fergus and the Druid' (published 1892), the Druid figure shares Oisin's physical infirmities, and wisdom and power seem incompatible – opposed desires in the psyche of the poem's creator. When Fergus casts *his* mind on other days, the result is disasterous for his sense of self. *The Countess Kathleen* (1892) offers another striking instance. The bard Kevin was not in Yeats's source, and he did not figure in the early drafts of the play, appearing only in 1891, after Yeats had been refused by Maud Gonne.[39] Although the events of the play take place in the sixteenth century, when the power of the bardic order was still intact and the bards were often vociferous defenders of the traditional Gaelic social system, Yeats made no effort to connect Kevin with the historical milieu; he has no lord or patron, unless the Countess is to be thought of as playing that role, but his attachment to her seems rather to be based on the romantic bond of his unrequited love.[40] He is a visionary, and his imagination is, significantly, haunted by the old legends (*VPl* 150, l.748). However, not only is he ludicrously ineffectual in action, but he and his songs are depicted as *escapist alternatives* to significant action (*VPl* 60–2); there is absolutely no suggestion that his art might be brought to bear upon events in the public world. Driven crazy by love, he does not even appear in the climactic final scene. Undoubtedly his limited role reflects his late introduction; according to Michael Sidnell, Yeats 'seems to have had neither the time nor the desire completely to revise the structure of the play to accommodate the new character' (186). It remains clear, though, that Yeats did not automatically project himself as a figure of artistic power. As the nineties progressed, Yeats's engagement with the problem remained intense and complex. His essays and organisational activities continue to develop and emphasise the concept, while the literary texts reveal lingering personal uncertainties but also a movement towards presentation of genuinely powerful artist figures.

VI

The assumption of art's shaping power pervades virtually every facet of Yeats's efforts during the 1890s to expand and direct the course of the growing Irish literary movement. Thus in October, 1891 he attempted to revive moribund Young Ireland Societies and to open reading rooms in the small towns in connection with them.

The reading-room libraries were to contain 'before all else ... the books that feed the imagination. ... Imagination, and not learning, is the centre of life, and from the direction it takes spring thought and conduct' (*UP1* 208). This stress on imagination undoubtedly reflects not only Blake, but also O'Grady's perception that the imagined history of a country represents its heart, its deepest desires, and thus is crucially important in shaping its development. Yeats almost at once formulated a plan to ensure the availability of appropriate books by starting a new 'Library of Ireland', inspired by the one so successfully developed by Young Ireland in the 1840s but intended to feature work generally more imaginative and higher in quality than the books in the earlier series (*YBIR* 79–103). After the bitter struggle in which he lost control of the series to Gavan Duffy, Yeats in 1894 vigorously attacked the first volumes: 'Believing, as I do, that literature is almost the most profound influence that ever comes into a nation, I recognise with deep regret, and not a little anger, that the "New Irish Library" is so far the most serious difficulty in the way of our movement, and that it drives from us those very educated classes we desire to enlist, and supplies our opponents with what looks like evidence of our lack of any fine education, of any admirable precision and balance of mind, of the very qualities which make literature possible' (*CL1* 397–8).

The Dowden controversy of the following year, in which the urbane cosmopolitan scholar levelled just such criticisms at the current national literary movement (*YBIR* 104–21), led Yeats to offer his own *precise* and *balanced* survey of 'Irish National Literature' in a series of four articles in the *Bookman*. In the first of them he criticised the Young Irelanders as primarily 'orators' rather than 'poets or romance-writers, priests of those Immortal Moods which are the true builders of nations, the secret transformers of the world, and need a subtle, appropriate language or a minute, manifold knowledge for their revelation' (*UP1* 361). The passage incorporates another echo of Blake ('minutely appropriate words'); and the Ellis-Yeats edition had included also an exploration of the concept of the 'Moods', which correspond to the archetypes.[41] 'Secret transformers of the world' obviously paraphrases Shelley's *Defence*. In order to forge the necessary vehicles, the modern Irish writers would need not the slipshod 'rhetoric' of the writers of *The Nation* but rather a sophisticated artistry comparable to that of the bardic tradition.[42] In the third essay, AE was especially praised for having 'a subtle rhythm, precision of phrase, an emotional relation to form and colour, and a

perfect understanding that the business of poetry is not to enforce
an opinion or expound an action, but to bring us into communion
with the moods and passions which are the creative powers behind
the universe; that though the poet may need to master many opinions,
they are but the body and the symbols for his art, the formula of
evocation for making the invisible visible '(*UP1* 380). In quoting one
of AE's own allusions to Blake – 'Every word which really inspires
is spoken as if the golden age had never passed away' – and adding
the observation that 'surely criticism, even criticism of life, is of the
fall and the fatal tree', Yeats was repeating the rejection of Arnold,
and the assertion of the power of heroic literature to help us
recapture the pre-lapsarian past, in the first article on Ferguson.[43]
Consequently, at the end of this 1895 piece he noted with approval
that 'even A.E. has begun to dig for new symbols in the stories of
Fin and Oisin' (*UP1* 382).

Yeats's national concerns had encouraged AE to direct his attention
to the matter of Ireland; once he did so he in turn was able, because
his visionary powers were more constant than Yeats's and because
he believed in them far more unquestioningly, to stimulate his
friend's own already great enthusiasm. In 1896 he wrote to Yeats to
inform him of

some things about the Ireland behind the veil. You remember my
writing to you about the awakening of the ancient fires which I
knew about. Well, it has been confirmed from other sources and
we are likely to publish it. The gods have returned to Erin and
have centred themselves in the sacred mountains and blow the
fires through the country. They have been seen by several in
vision, they will awaken the magical instinct everywhere, and the
universal heart of the people will turn to the old druidic beliefs. I
note through the country the increased faith in faery things. . . .
Furthermore, we were told that though now few we would soon
be many, and that a branch of the school for the revival of the
ancient mysteries to teach real things would be formed here soon.
Out of Ireland will arise a light to transform many ages and peoples.
There is a hurrying of forces and swift things going out and I
believe profoundly that a new Avatar is about to appear and in all
spheres the forerunners go before him to prepare. It will be one
of the kingly Avatars, who is at once ruler of men and magic sage.
I had a vision of him some months ago and will know him if he
appears. America is on fire with mysticism just now and the new

races are breaking the mould of European thought and psychics abound. Their light reflects itself in Ireland, and the path of connection has been seen. Now I wish you could come over to this county Sligo or wherever you like and absorb this new force. To me enchantment and fairyland are real and no longer dreams.[44]

The correspondence here with Yeats is very close, with the 'ancient mysteries', the 'old druidic beliefs', being brought to bear upon the nation (and the larger world as well) and effecting there a profound spiritual transformation. For Yeats, the 'masters' in that 'school for the revival of the ancient mysteries' would be the artists. (AE does not say that here, but before long – perhaps again at least in part because of Yeats – he was to do so.)

By 1897 Yeats had come to see AE as the center of a 'spiritual group' among contemporary Irish writers. He claimed about this group, in which he included also Nora Hopper and Lionel Johnson, that although unlike many of their predecessors not always exclusively nationalistic, they were nevertheless 'speaking with ... the truest voice of the Celt' – a merit he had earlier discerned in Ferguson. They were 'spiritual' because they all believed that 'a beauty, not a worldly beauty, lives in worldly things' (*UP2* 71). He expressed confidence that the group would exert a powerful influence, but with a more explicit account than AE's of how the few would become many:

> This new school cannot fail to influence Irish thought very strongly, for it is full of the dreams that we dream in our most exalted moments. Few who have not read deeply in the history of literary movements, know how strong is the influence of the highest kind of poetry, for it does not directly influence many minds, but it influences the finest minds and through them many minds. This new school, and the ever increasing knowledge of the old poetry in Gaelic, must in time make many strong and delicate minds spend themselves in the service of Ireland that would else have spent themselves in alien causes, and Ireland may become again a spiritual influence in the world. (*UP2* 73)

He said of his own contemporary volume *The Secret Rose* that it was 'an honest attempt towards that aristocratic esoteric Irish literature, which has been my chief ambition. We have a literature for the people but nothing yet for the few' (*L* 286). In fact he had at times hoped to reach a wide audience more quickly and directly, and would periodically feel such an urge again. The theatre movement was a virtually contemporary manifestation of that urge; before long, however, it too would force him to fall back on the paradigm of a slower, indirect process.

In 1896, AE had proposed to Yeats a collaborative book of essays (to contain a contribution by O'Grady) on 'the renewal in Ireland of the heroic figures of our own dawn.' This proposal was eventually realised in the controversy about the legendary materials in which Yeats and John Eglinton and others engaged in 1898.[45] In one of AE's own contributions he argued that Irish culture was in a period comparable 'to Greece before the first perfect statue had fixed an ideal of beauty which mothers dreamed of to mould their yet unborn children' and that modern Ireland thus needed 'the creation of heroic figures, types, whether legendary or taken from history, and enlarged to epic proportions by our writers, who would use them in common, as Cuculain, Fionn, Ossian, and Oscar, were used by the generations of poets who have left us the bardic history of Ireland. . . . [F]rom iteration and persistent dwelling on a few heroes their imaginative images found echoes in life, and other heroes arose continuing their tradition of chivalry. ¶ That such types are of the highest importance and have the most ennobling influence on a country, cannot be denied'.[46] AE, too, had read his O'Grady, and presumably also his Wilde; the conclusions he drew were, in this case, identical to Yeats's own.

VII

The figure of the poet in *The Countess Kathleen* undergoes a significant transformation in the version Yeats published in 1895. When first mentioned, Aleel (as the bard is now called) sounds quite as ineffectual as his predecessor, 'so wrapped up in dreams of terrors to come / That he can give no help' (*VPl* 21, ll.118d–e); and he still represents an escapist alternative to public responsibility. In one scene early in the play, the Countess actually *leaves* the stage 'While he is singing' (*VPl* 23, l.127 directions). Although his later effort to deter her from sacrificing herself fails in the revised version, too, there is a suggestion that he develops strength during the course of the play. In 1892 he had been absent from the final scene, while in 1895 he is perhaps the central figure there. Cathleen's final speech is addressed to Oona and to him; following Cathleen's death he violently shatters the looking glass and then, standing up while almost all the other characters on stage are kneeling, he curses 'Time and Fate and Change' and longs for 'the great hour / When you shall plunge headlong through bottomless space' (*VPl* 165). His creator would similarly 'await / The hour of thy great wind of love and hate' in the apocalyptic verses of 'The Secret Rose' (*VP* 170). With a boldness inconceivable from Kevin, Aleel even seizes one of the angels and forces it to reveal Cathleen's fate.

Aleel's smashing of the looking glass was a splendid *coup de théâtre*, and of course an appropriate gesture for the romantic lover in despair. In light of Yeats's later fondness for identifying realistic art with an epigraph in *Le Rouge et le Noir* defining the novel as a mirror dawdling down a laneway, it is tempting to see Aleel's act as involving also symbolic implications about artistic mimesis.[47] Joyce may have seen it so; in *A Portrait* he had Stephen Dedalus recall the scene, then in *Ulysses* toss off a *mot* about 'Irish art' as 'the cracked lookingglass of a servant' that seems to fuse Yeats's scene with passages from Oscar Wilde.[48] Stephen's remark, of course, could be consistent with a mimetic aesthetic giving primacy to nature; the implication in *The Countess Cathleen*, however, would be quite different – a defiant reversal. In combination with Aleel's new-found confidence and assertiveness, that gesture might in turn imply an art that would not be identified, as Aleel's has up to this point in the play, with impotence. The act remains only emblematical: there is no *dramatisation* of artistic power. The suggestion is there, however, of an alternative to the potentially self-destructive form of political activism in which Yeats felt Maud Gonne to be engaged. For more than this suggestion, the fable that constituted Yeats's donnée offered no real place.

The Shadowy Waters was another text that during its development registered the impact of Yeats's thoughts about the nature and function of art. In the earliest surviving version we can already discern elements associated with the aesthetic of a life-moulding art. In a manuscript prologue that may date from the 1880s, an old man holds up before the audience a crystal globe that he identifies as 'the globe of realistic / art'.[49] At first the 'children of time' will see the world and their own faces reflected in it, but then they will appear 'transformed ... by the light of / the interior spirit change into / types & symbols. ...' Yeats was here anticipating Wilde's famous epigrams about realistic and romantic art, as well as his own Shelleyan epithet for artists, 'secret transformers of the world'. The old man then speaks of carrying 'the globe of ideal / art' until ~~the day when all~~ / Behind all life burns [?] the archetypal / life & to the archetypes do all / things return, knocking again & again / at the ~~Eternal~~ [?] doors windy [?] doors'. This prologue, which, as the editors of the manuscript versions have noted, anticipates closely the Old Man's speech (similarly an attack upon realist art) at the beginning of *The Death of Cuchulain*, does not appear in subsequent drafts; but the metaphysical vision involved is embodied in the basic plot of all versions of the work, Forgael's visionary guest. Forgael himself is a man of action, but in the version composed in 1894 he is also identified as a 'Druid' (*DC* 52). He has 'learned all / The wisdom druids ... wrote upon their boards / Of hazel wood, oak wood & apple wood / And all that prophesying images / Made out of dim gold rave out in secret tombs' (*DC* 94); but as in 'Fergus and the Druid' the wisdom proves a heavy burden.

Druidism has also been a source of his *power* (*DC* 124). In one passage he even speaks of playing upon the harp 'Druidic songs that awake the winds / Or cradle them to sleep' (*DC* 120). Yet it was not Forgael who was literally the poet of the text. That role fell to Dectora's consort, a shadowy figure at first, who emerges more prominently during the same period in which Yeats was carrying out his first rewriting of *The Countess Kathleen*; he, too, is then given the name Aleel (*DC* 107–8). In one of the drafts, the music from *his* harp has its origin in 'the moods, builders of night & day' (*DC* 130). That both Forgael and Aleel correspond to aspects of their creator is obvious, and their interplay thus becomes a psychomachia. At one point Forgael speaks with scathing contempt of his rival, 'this foam light reed limb man'; killing him and taking his harp to play upon are symbolic gestures (*DC* 120, 187–9). A draft dating from 1897 expands Aleel's part to the point that he trespasses upon Forgael's role 'and the two figures lose their distinctness' (*DC* 201). At this stage Aleel expresses apocalyptic yearnings reminiscent of those voiced by his namesake in the face of Cathleen's death:

> I cry to you who wait, trembling with hope,
> The hour when all things shall be folded up
> Finding no help in any thing that lives.
> O reaper come from the grey stones, heap up
> The threshing floor, pluck out the stars
> Beat down the hills & bid all be at an end. (*DC* 203)

In such a context, Forgael's own use of the harp to divert Dectora's love onto himself can be seen as an alternative version of *The Countess Cathleen* (1895), in which the lover's songs had *failed* to weaken the heroine's resolve. Aleel himself was to drop out of *The Shadowy Waters* (*DC* 270), but the harp became increasingly prominent, eventually requiring a spectacular stage prop. As an image of the power of art its positive force was undercut to a considerable extent by the unpalatability of the idea of winning *love* by its means. In no version does Forgael use it to shape future civilisations; it remains always a device capable of making Dectora a companion in a *flight from* all human life. In one of Yeats's 'Irish National Literature' essays of 1895 he had expressed his hope 'some day, in the maturity of our traditions, to fashion out of the world about us, and the things that our fathers have told us, a new ritual for the builders of peoples, the imperishable moods' (*UP1* 373). The persistence of the escapist element in *The Shadowy Waters* suggests an ambivalence not discernible in the essay between the artist as 'builder' in the service of the Moods and the artist as agent of cosmic deconstruction.

In assembling *The Secret Rose* (1897), Yeats produced not a mere collection of stories but rather a volume with the sort of coherence and cumulative effect that would later characterise Joyce's *Dubliners*. In a dedicatory note to AE, Yeats identified the unifying concern of the volume as 'the war of spiritual with natural order' (*VSR* 233).[50] Such a book, he was well aware, was not likely to satisfy those of his Irish friends who were wont to ask him when he was 'going to write a really national poem or romance', meaning one 'founded upon some moment of famous Irish history, and built up out of the thoughts and feelings which move the greater number of patriotic Irishmen.' The *pressure* to move such an audience is easily detectable behind these lines, and Yeats knew this book would not do *that*, but he imagined an impact for it no less important for being more narrow. Writing it was part of his self-proclaimed mission to provide an 'aristocratic esoteric Irish literature . . . for the few'. As the dedicatory note went on to stress, he could only be true to the dictates of his inner vision, but that did not mean he would be any less a part of the national tradition: 'So far . . . as this book is visionary it is Irish; for Ireland . . . has preserved with some less excellent things a gift of vision, which has died out among more hurried and more successful nations. . . .' By arranging the stories according to the chronological order of the action, Yeats did in fact engage Irish history, which emerges as itself the story of that ongoing battle between spiritual and natural orders (*YBIR* 49–50). It is within that pattern that his concern with the power of art appears. *The Secret Rose* begins with a story focussing upon such power at the prehistoric dawn of Irish civilisation, and ends with stories foreshadowing the resurgence of that power in Yeats's own day.

Aodh, the bard in 'The Binding of the Hair', sings of past wars in order to inspire the warriors of his beloved queen and achieves direct, immediate success, the 'vehement passages' of his tale making them 'clash their swords upon their shields and shout an always more clamorous approval' (*VSR* 178). Such influence obviously comes closer to the Young Ireland model than to Yeats's own; and Aodh himself participates in the fighting , and dies at the hands of the enemy. But the most dramatic manifestation of his power, the song of his severed head, links him also to the occult tradition and to visionary art. Many years later Yeats suggested how the story relates to that tradition when he associated his play *The King of the Great Clock Tower*, a reworking of 'The Binding of the Hair', with 'the old ritual of the year: the mother goddess and the slain god' (*VPl* 1010).[51] Such rituals, as Frazer had made clear in *The Golden Bough* (1890), were sacrifices intended to restore the fertility of the land or the spiritual health of the polity, and as esoteric allegories could represent the purification and regeneration or resurrection of the soul.[52] Robert Graves was to see the same pattern also as an allegory of the creative process. It is significant that in the story Dectira's husband is depicted as 'old and foolish', like one of those monarchs in primitive societies with whose own health the state of the land was inextricably connected and whose dotage was the signal that sacrifice was once again required. The biographical model for the queen may have been the unhappily married Olivia Shakespear, and she owes something also to Maud Gonne, and to the *fin de siècle* obsession with the femme fatale, but archetypally she embodies aspects of the fertility deity, Graves's White Goddess, and the occult figure of Sophia or Wisdom central in the poems of *The Wind Among the Reeds*.[53] Frequently the impotent, superannuated monarch was supplanted by a younger, more virile male who would become the consort of the goddess, their sexual union the source of renewed fertility. During the nineties, however, Yeats's imagination dwelt ever more intensely upon esoteric apocalyptic versions of the paradigm, in which the emphasis was upon *transcendence* of the 'natural order'. The apocalyptic lyric 'The Secret Rose' comes just before 'The Binding of the Hair' in the volume. It is not necessary to deny a psychosexual level to the story to establish that mythically the text has a far more positive import: though at the end of the story the bard is dead, he has achieved a spiritual union with the divine Mother-Lover-Muse and his poem celebrating her survives, an instance of what in 'The Tables of the Law' (a story Yeats intended to include in *The Secret Rose*) is called ' "that supreme art which is to win us from life and gather us into eternity like doves into their dove-cots" ' (*VSR* 158).[54] In a sense, then, in 'The Binding of the Hair' Yeats has it both ways, his bardic persona's art strengthening the valor of armies and, by implication, bringing souls to God. The first story in the 1897 volume, it gave concrete form to Yeats's claims in the dedicatory note. It was in fact also another version of the 'Apologia'. As the speaker there asked to be counted a 'true brother' of the company of Ireland's patriotic poets, so Aodh 'claimed to be descended from the bard for whom the nations of Heber and Heremon cast lots at the making of the world';[55] and in both cases the 'national' element is fused with the occult. The reference to Aodh's 'Druid sleep' (*VSR* 179) suggests that fusion as 'druid tune' does in the 'Apologia'. Queen Dectira corresponds precisely to the female figure in the 'Apologia', as verbal similarities between the poem and Aodh's lyric make clear:

'Apologia'	'Binding'
For in the world's first blossoming age	You need but lift a pearl-pale hand,
The light fall of her flying feet	And bind up your long hair and sigh;
Made Ireland's heart begin to beat,	And all men's hearts must burn and beat;
And still the starry candles flare	And candle-like foam on the dim sand,
To help her light foot here and there,	And stars climbing the dew-dropping sky,
(*VP* 138; 1892 version)	Live but to light your passing feet. (*VSR* 181)

Appropriately the story, like the 'Apologia', even foreshadows Yeats's most famous later assertion of art's shaping power, for it is set in Sligo and Aodh's head sings from beyond the grave in a landscape dominated by 'the mountain of Gulben' (*VSR* 177). The organisation of *The Secret Rose* thus anticipates that of *Last Poems and Two Plays*, which Yeats arranged so that the contents of the volume unfold from 'Under Ben Bulben' and the poet's own epitaph, and end in a modern world at cycle end awaiting apocalypse.

'The Binding of the Hair' is further linked to Yeats's aesthetic of artistic power by the lyric 'Aedh thinks of those who have Spoken Evil of his Beloved', originally published as one of a group collectively titled 'Aodh to Dectora / Three Songs':

> Half close your eyelids, loosen your hair,
> And dream about the great and their pride;
> They have spoken against you everywhere,
> But weigh this song with the great and their pride;
> I made it out of a mouthful of air,
> Their children's children shall say they have lied. (*VP* 166)

In using the bardic persona here Yeats in effect identifies himself as a contemporary incarnation of the tradition: he speaks *as* bard; and his claim that his apparently fragile song will eventually give the lie to his beloved's detractors assumes the long-term process of influence imaged for him by the statues in Greek bridal chambers. The final lines will be echoed in the passage in 'To a Shade' concerning Hugh Lane, another victim of slander, whose pictures, rejected by Dubliners, would have brought 'their children's children loftier thought, / Sweeter emotion, working in their veins like gentle blood....' (To these lines, part of a poem the gloomy vision of which reveals that Yeats would not always be able to maintain the confident tone that characterises the earlier lyric, we shall return in Chapter 3.)

The tension between wisdom and power, muted in 'The Binding of the Hair', becomes central in the second story, 'The Wisdom of the King'. Its protagonist is not a bard, but his mother was a queen – a link back to 'The Binding of the Hair' – and the 'wisdom' the king pours at the feet of his beloved is virtually identical with that expressed by Yeats himself in the contemporary 'Irish National Literature' essays. The King tells of

> the great Moods, which are alone immortal, and the creators of mortal things; and how every Mood is a being that wears, to mortal eyes, the shape of Fintain, who dwells, disguised as a salmon, in the floods; or of the Dagda, whose cauldron is never empty; or of Lir, whose children wail upon the waters; or of Angus, whose kisses were changed into birds; or of Len, the goldsmith, from whose furnace rainbows break. (*VSR* 31)

For the central irony of the story Yeats returns to the advice he offered in his first Ferguson piece, that art should spurn Arnoldian canons and be 'a fire in the spirit'. When the king attempts to advise his retainers, the results are disastrous: those who follow his advice function less well than before, and some 'remembered words and sentences that became like a fire in their hearts, and made all kindly joys and traffic between man and man as nothing, and went different ways, but all into vague regret' (*VSR* 30). The king, concluding that 'wisdom the gods have made, and no man shall live by its light' (*VSR* 33), disappears from the world, making the story seem far less positive than its predecessor as well as answering proleptically the question that would end Yeats's famous later text about the results of a similar coupling between a human woman and a bird-like divine being, 'Leda and the Swan'.

The next several stories offer glimpses of the fortunes of the bardic order from the Christian Middle Ages to its near extinction during the seventeenth and eighteenth centuries. In 'Where there is Nothing, there is God' one of the Brothers suspects the suddenly intelligent young boy of 'trafficking with bards, or druids, or witches . . .' (*VSR* 52). The gleeman in 'The Crucifixion of the Outcast' is condemned by the abbot because, like the poets in O'Shaughnessy's ode, he threatens to upset the status quo: 'Who can eat and sleep in peace while men like him are going about the world?' The bards and gleemen, he asserts, 'are an evil race, ever cursing and ever stirring up the people, and immoral and immoderate in all things, and heathen in their hearts . . .' (*VSR* 11). Their songs praise 'the Son of Lir, and Angus, and Bridget, and the Dagda, and Dana the Mother, and all the false gods of the old days' as well as fairy queens such as Cleena of the Wave (who will be Red Hanrahan's muse) and Aoibhell of the Grey Rock (the muse figure in one of Yeats's own later poems about his refusal to sacrifice artistic merit in order to produce politically expedient verse). As the gleeman is about to be crucified, he reveals that he has heard in his heart 'the rustling of the rose-bordered dress of her who is more subtle than Angus the Subtle-Hearted, and more full of the beauty of laughter than Conan the Bald, and more full of the wisdom of tears than White-Breasted Deirdre' (*VSR* 15): the Wisdom figure of the 'Apologia', whose 'red rose bordered hem . . . / Trails all about the written page. . . .'

The poets appear less favourably in 'The Old Men of the Twilight', in the form of ollamhs or 'men of learning' whose absorption in purely technical disputes concerning prosody represents a sterile forsaking of their visionary function; and their indifference to the question of how Patrick's theology relates to traditional Druidic doctrines seems to implicate them in the triumph of the new religion. (In this story Yeats may have had one eye on his fellow Rhymers (see *Au* 165–7), or TCD scholasticism, or both.) In 'Proud Costello. . . .', set in the seventeenth century, the protagonist is attacked on the Eve of Saint John (a reminder of 'The Binding of the Hair') by 'a story-teller and poet, a last remnant of the bardic order', whose patron is Costello's enemy MacNamara (*VSR* 71; see also *Ex* 283). But if, as Yeats had suggested in *A Book of Irish Verse*, 'the great bardic order . . . had gone down in the wars of the seventeenth century, . . . poetry had found shelter amid the turf-smoke of the cabins'; and in the group of stories devoted to Red Hanrahan Yeats explored the survival of the tradition and its power in the Hidden Ireland.

'The Book of the Great Dhoul and Hanrahan the Red', the first story in the group of six devoted to the peasant poet, is set in Cork; but at the beginning of the second story we see Hanrahan travelling to the West, 'for Gaelic Ireland was still alive, and the Gaelic poets were still honoured in the West' (*VSR* 198). Hanrahan sees himself as 'the last of that mighty line of poets which came down unbroken from Sancan Torpeist . . . and mightier Oisin' (*VSR* 198) – both key bardic personae used by Yeats himself, of course; but though bards might still be revered, the old Gaelic socio-economic order had been destroyed, and with it the system of aristocratic patronage that would have supported figures like Hanrahan, reduced as a consequence to keeping a hedge school and even occasionally working as a day labourer (*VSR* 198). Yeats makes it clear, however, that even in this humble condition Hanrahan is in touch with 'the Powers that have never lived in mortal bodies' (*VSR* 199). He has, in fact, his own version of the Wisdom figure, of the White Goddess, in the form of Cleena of the Wave, Queen of the Munster fairies and a 'Lianaan Shee or Fairy-mistress' (*VSR* 197). Their relationship instances those romances between supernatural beings and mortals that fascinated Yeats from Niamh and Oisin to Cuchulain and Fand and, at the end of his life, Cuchulain and the Morrigu. ('The Grey Rock' and 'The Two Kings' are other texts in which this concern figures prominently.) It is clear that Cleena is the ultimate source of Hanrahan's power, but also that their relationship is a fatal one for him, because it condemns him never to be satisfied with any earthly love. In contrast with Aodh, he tries to reject his role, but unsuccessfully, for at the moment of his death he hears her voice whispering 'you will seek me no longer upon the breasts of women' and claiming him as hers 'until the world is melted like wax' (*VSR* 226). Consequently, although in 'The Twisting of the Rope and Hanrahan the Red' he seems a common seducer of innocent peasant maidens, he courts the girl in the story among May Eve fertility rituals, including 'the serpent dance, the dance made by the wise Druids' and his blarneying flattery is full of references to Irish myth and legend and to the occult symbolism of the antinomy of sun and moon (*VSR* 201).

While living briefly a settled life with comfortable if slovenly peasant mistresses, he experiences a period of great literary productivity, including not only love songs but also 'songs of penitence' and even 'poems disguising a passionate patriotism under the form of a love-song addressed to the Little Black Rose or Kathleen the Daughter of Hoolihan or some other personification of Ireland' (*VSR* 207; see also *Ex* 283). 'Kathleen the Daughter of Hoolihan and Hanrahan the Red' gives a poem of the last type in its entirety, dramatising the appeal of its strategy:

O tufted reeds, bend low and low in pools on the Green Land,
Under the bitter Black Winds blowing out of the left hand!
Like tufted reeds our courage droops in a Black Wind and dies:
But we have hidden in our hearts the flame out of the eyes
    Of Kathleen the Daughter of Hoolihan.

O tattered clouds of the world, call from the high Cairn of Maive,
And shake down thunder on the stones because the Red Winds rave!
Like tattered clouds of the world, passions call and our hearts beat:
But we have all bent low and low, and kissed the quiet feet
    Of Kathleen the Daughter of Hoolihan.

O heavy swollen waters, brim the Fall of the Oak trees,
For the Grey Winds are blowing up, out of the clinging seas!
Like heavy swollen waters are our bodies and our blood:
But purer than a tall candle before the Blessed Rood
    Is Kathleen the Daughter of Hoolihan. (*VSR* 208–9)

Such poems, in which political passion is expressed as romantic passion, allow the poet to have it both ways, implying a political statement without using the overtly political language that Yeats felt so often degenerated into 'rhetoric'. [56] 'The Immortal Moods', he wrote about this time, 'are so impatient of rhetoric' (*UP1* 363).

The Gaelic poem about Kathleen ni Houlihan by William Dall Heffernan, Mangan's translation of which Yeats knew, had itself been overtly Jacobite.[57] We can appreciate Yeats's tactics by comparison with it:

> Sore disgrace it is to see the Arbitress of thrones,
> Vassal to a *Saxoneen* of cold and sapless bones!
> Bitter anguish wrings our souls – with heavy sighs and groans
>   We wait the young Deliverer of Kathaleen Ny-Houlahan!

and with Thomas Davis's 'The West's Asleep', one of the most famous Young Ireland songs, still sung by Irish patriots at the *Playboy* riots in 1907:[58]

> When all beside a vigil keep,
> The West's asleep, the West's asleep –
> Alas! and well may Erin weep,
> When Connaught lies in slumber deep.
> There lake and plain smile fair and free,
> 'Mid rocks – their guardian chivalry –
> Sing oh! let man learn liberty
> From crashing wind and lashing sea.
>
> That chainless wave and lovely land
> Freedom and Nationhood demand –
> Be sure, the great God never plann'd,
> For slumbering slaves, a home so grand.
> And, long, a brave and haughty race
> Honoured and sentinelled the place –
> Sing oh! not even their sons' disgrace
> Can quite destroy their glory's trace.
>
> For often, in O'Connor's van,
> To triumph dash'd each Connaught clan –
> And fleet as deer the Normans ran
> Through Coirrsliabh Pass and Ard Rathain.
> And later times saw deeds as brave;
> And glory guards Clanricarde's grave –
> Sing oh! they died their land to save,
> At Aughrim's slopes and Shannon's wave.
>
> And if, when all a vigil keep,
> The West's asleep, the West's asleep–

> Alas! and well may Erin weep,
> That Connaught lies in slumber deep.
> But – hark! – some voice like thunder spake:
> *'The West's awake, the West's awake'* –
> Sing oh! hurra! let England quake,
> We'll watch till death for Erin's sake!'[59]

Davis, like Hanrahan, had moralised a Western landscape to rouse a demoralised people (and even, in the third stanza, cast *his* mind on other days), but in the absence of a central symbolic figure such as Kathleen had had to resort to the hackneyed coinage of 'Freedom and Nationhood', of chains and slaves. In Yeats's poem, of course, the intensity was heightened because the romantic passion, instead of being a mere vehicle for nationalist feeling, itself reflected genuine personal emotion. When Yeats later wrote his famous play about Kathleen ni Houlihan he moved away from this strategy somewhat, for there, although the figure of the Poor Old Woman is still irradiated by his passion for Maud Gonne, the play itself (like *The Countess Cathleen*) sets love and patriotism in *opposition* to each other. The popular success of the play was to replicate that of Hanrahan's song. Although Hanrahan's immediate audience is composed of a few 'ragged peasants' and 'beggars', they spread his compositions 'throughout Connaught', presumably at least helping to sweeten Ireland's wrong if not sending out anyone to be shot. Thus, despite the homely surroundings, he seems 'a king of the poets of the Gael and a ruler of the dreams of men' (*VSR* 207, 209).

The farm wives in 'The Twisting of the Rope ...' recall another traditional aspect of the poet's power, connecting it, too, to fertility: 'In old days a poet's curse could wither the corn in the earth and make the milk dry in the udders of the cows ...' (*VSR* 202–3). Hanrahan's own curse upon them seems totally ineffectual, however; and later, when he puts a 'threefold curse of Druid power' on the old men who wish to marry young girls, the effect is merely ludicrous (*VSR* 213–15). But his visionary gift is reaffirmed in 'The Vision of Hanrahan the Red'. Interestingly, the spirits he sees in that story include 'Dervadilla', who, unlike the others, has been 'sung by no bards' (*VSR* 220); the artistic, political, and occult implications of such an encounter were to be explored more fully in *The Dreaming of the Bones*.

Hanrahan's own death takes place in the most squalid surroundings, but, as with Aodh, involves a union with his femme fatale Muse; so it seems appropriate and even touching that the turf cutters who found his body, 'gathering a concourse of mourners and of keening women gave him burying worthy of so great a poet' (*VSR* 227).

In 'The Rose of Shadow', which came immediately after the Hanrahan group in *The Secret Rose*, we see the power of Hanrahan's verse in its most frightening form. For Oona, the young girl in the story, one of his songs is associated with her dead lover. Her father forbids her to sing it, because 'Hanrahan the Red sang it after he had listened to the singing of those who are about the faery Cleena of the Wave, and it has lured, and will lure, many a girl from her hearth and from her peace' (*VSR* 229). As the lover was renowned for 'his violence and brutality', the reader might feel some sympathy with the father's point of view here (*VSR* 228); the mother's objections, though, cast the situation into quite a different light:

> "The host of Cleena sang of a love too great for our perishing hearts , and from that night Hanrahan the Red is always seeking with wild tunes and bewildered words to answer their voices, and a madness is upon his days and a darkness before his feet. His songs are no longer dear to any but to the coasting sailors and to the people of the mountain, and to those that are ill-nurtured and foolish. Look, daughter, to the spinning-wheel, and think of our goods that, horn by horn and fleece by fleece, grow greater as the years go by, and be content". (*VSR* 229–30)

As agent of apocalyptic forces that threaten to destroy a materialistic society, Hanrahan's verse play a positive role. Yet the final picture of the roof of the house consumed in flame. revealing the 'heavy and brutal face' of the demon-lover, shows also the more troubling face of artistic power (*VSR* 231).

The next story was 'The Old Men of the Twilight'; although its images of a completely detached aestheticism come from the era of Saint Patrick, the story itself is set in the eighteenth century and, in combination with 'The Rose of Shadow', was perhaps meant to create an atmosphere of decadence appropriate as an introduction to the apocalyptic final movement of the volume, the stories set in the present: 'Rosa Alchemica' and also 'The Tables of the Law' and 'The Adoration of the Magi' (the omission of which had been demanded by the publisher).[60]

Michael Robartes, who though not himself an artist seems in many ways a reincarnation of Hanrahan, describes the return of the old gods in terms that stress visionary artistic *power*:

The more a man lives in imagination and in a refined understanding,
the more gods does he meet and talk with, and the more does he
come under the power of Roland, who sounded in the Valley of
Roncesvalles the last trumpet of the body's will and pleasure;
and of Hamlet, who saw them perishing away, and sighed; and
of Faust, who looked for them up and down the world and could
not find them; and under the power of all those countless
divinities who have taken upon themselves spiritual bodies in
the minds of the modern poets and romance writers, and under
the power of the old divinities, who since the Renaissance have
won everything of their ancient worship except the sacrifice of
birds and fishes, the fragrance of garlands and the smoke of
incense. The many think humanity made these divinities, and
that it can unmake them again; but we ... know that they are
always making and unmaking humanity.[61]

Later in the story these divinities are explicitly identified as 'the
moods', which

worked all great changes in the world; for just as the magician or
the artist could call them when he would, so they could call out
of the mind of the magician or the artist, or if they were demons,
out of the mind of the mad or the ignoble, what shape they
would, and through its voice and its gestures pour themselves out
upon the world. In this way all great events were accomplished; a
mood, a divinity, or a demon, first descending like a faint sigh
into men's minds and then changing their thoughts and their
actions until hair that was yellow had grown black, or hair that
was black had grown yellow, and empires had moved their
border, as though they were but drifts of leaves. (*VSR* 143)

The 'empires' may owe something to O'Shaughnessy, and seem to
hint also at a nationalistic level, though Robartes' apparent fate at
the hands of irate Connemara peasants makes any suggestion in the
latter of a successful *Irish* revolution appear ironically premature
(*VSR* 126). In 'The Tables of the Law' Owen Aherne, 'half monk,
half soldier of fortune', is said to have held the paradoxical belief
'that the beautiful arts were sent into the world to overthrow
nations, and finally life herself, by sowing everywhere unlimited
desires, like torches thrown into a burning city'. Subsequently he
returned to Ireland and experienced 'the fermentation of belief

which is coming upon our people with the reawakening of their imaginative life' (*VSR* 151). But although the aesthetic concept appears in both stories, neither contains the actual artist who will give it life. Perhaps, however, it may not be too far-fetched to see an anticipation of such a figure in the childbed scene in the final story, 'The Adoration of the Magi'. The woman who has given birth is a harlot, for ' "when the Immortals would overthrow the things that are to-day and bring the things that were yesterday, they have no one to help them, but one whom the things that are to-day have cast out" ' (*VSR* 168–9). In the closing lyric of *The Death of Cuchulain*, Yeats's last celebration of art's shaping power, it is a harlot who sings of how the Old Man, finding no body like Cuchulain's in the modern world, turned to the past for a model. The harlot in the story gives birth to a unicorn-like figure who is presumably to be the avatar of a new historical era. While Yeats was seeing these stories through the press he was also at work on his *Bildungsroman*, *The Speckled Bird*, which traces the early life of a character destined to become an artist. That character, Michael Herne, may represent the *modern* bard present only by implication in *The Secret Rose*.

As a child, Michael feeds his imagination on legend and mythology, his two favorite books being *The Mabinogion* and the *Morte d'Arthur* (*SB* 9). In a variant passage Yeats had him also reading Shelley, who 'called[?] the arts "wandering voices" "of all man becomes" and even held that the thoughts that come to us in our highest moments are truly the souls of the dead become a part of that ideal loveliness that was some day to take us to its heart' (*SB* 244–5). When Yeats was first planning the novel he wrote O'Leary that it was 'to be among other things my first study of the Irish Fairy Kingdom and the mystical faith of that time, before I return to more earthly things. There are certain preliminary studies in my new book *The Secret Rose . . .*' (*L* 268). Michael comes into contact with such lore through the peasant lads with whom he plays, and, in a scene that except for the Galway setting will reappear in Part I of 'Under Ben Bulben', one of the boys points to Cruachmaa and tells him 'of the invisible horsemen that came out of the hill and rode hither and thither through all Ireland' (*SB* 10–11). Michael, recalling the heroes of *The Mabinogion*, senses that ' "they are not dead. They are living like Finvarra and his horsemen. Maybe they are quite near us. Does not everybody who does not say that Finvarra's people are fallen angels say that they are the old ancient inhabitants of the country?" ' Within a few years he has grasped the gist of what such figures mean: he has decided to devote his life to serving the 'divine essences' (*SB* 52) and has a conception of art's role in the process that seems to reflect Shelley and O'Shaughnessy, for he writes Margaret that 'we will only make a beginning, but centuries after we are dead cities shall be overthrown, it may be, because of an air that we have hummed or because of a curtain full of meaning that we have hung upon a wall' (*SB* 53; cf. 'o'erthrew them', p. 34.) A *fin de siècle* sense of apocalypse has taken hold of his imagination, so that 'the fantastic lights and colours of the eastern skies suggested to his imagination armed figures gathering to overturn the present order of the world'. Seeking in such thoughts an omen, he meets that same day an old tinker with whom he discusses Raftery, whose poetry he has already encountered and who provides him with a further link to the bardic tradition as well as balancing the apocalyptic implications of his vision of 'armed figures' with more mundane national ones (*SB* 55–6).

Michael's occultist friend Maclagan was based on MacGregor Mathers, but his story of how he first encountered spirits –

> I went through a ceremony I read of in a book. I wrote something with the blood of a bat and made a circle (and) after waiting many hours in the dark I believed that I saw the white moon, a little way from me, but I was afraid and covered my face. . . . (*SB* 21)

– links him also with the Hanrahan of 'The Book of the Great Dhoul . . .' (*VSR* 188–91). Michael had already defined it as his purpose 'to remake everything in a more ancient pattern '(*SB* 52); now, as he and Maclagan were looking at the statues in the Greek Room of the British Museum, his new friend spoke to him of 'the contrast between the form of Greek statues and the men and women who were looking at them. He said, "Men were once like that and now they are getting more and more miserable looking. But for them the world would get much worse, for everybody is trying, though half-heartedly enough, to become a little like them, but their endeavour gets fainter and fainter. . . . The old gods are still worshipped in secret and what we have to do is to make their worship open again"' (*SB* 59–60). Once again Yeats's own later work enables us to make explicit a connection only implied: the people of Michael's time are 'All out of shape from toe to top' and to reverse the trend artists such as himself must turn to the past, to the 'old gods', for images to embody in a modern art that will restore society to its former greatness. In one of the earlier versions of the novel Michael had written, 'Do [you] think that men would let all[?] grow ugly and their[?] own bodies become mis-shapen and their voices become unmusical if they understood that to do thus was to deny God and condemn to perpetual [? perhaps purgatorial ?] torture that which outlives the grave?' (*SB* 207). There he had already envisaged the founding of an occult Order the rituals of which, drawing upon art and in turn inspiring 'painters and poets', would be the primary force for reversing the decadent trend. In the final version the rituals Michael envisaged for the Order 'must not be founded on Egypt or on Greece, but they must make the land in which they lived a holy land. He proposed the Grail stories as their foundation' (*SB* 63–4). This plan was treated more fully in passages that Yeats eventually discarded. Such rituals were to 'describe the history of the soul through the symbolism of the quest of the Grail and the coming to the castle of the Grail, which is to us the country of the dead and of all Wisdom' (*SB* 202–3). (Years later, in the first edition of *A Vision*, Yeats was to rejoice that 'the system' left his imagination free to create as it chose and yet made 'all that it created, or could create, part of the one history, and that the soul's [xi].) Michael felt it certain that the Grail story had been created by the Moods, that it 'has behind it immense[?] beings and powers who shape it in the minds of poets and artists, for the great myths are images cast upon our minds from the wars and loves of the beings and powers who have built[?] up all things.... They never pass away' (*SB* 203). Embodied in the rituals of the Order, the Grail legends would become 'to many what the myth of Dionysus was to the ancient world' (*SB* 202).[62] Maud Gonne has recorded how Yeats himself 'loved to trace to Ireland' the symbolism of the Grail;[63] but Michael was somewhat equivocal about the national element in the Order, writing to his beloved that 'poets and artists should be known less by their nationality than by the mythology or cycle of legends that they chose to be their expression of the transcendent life' (*SB* 206). In the rather abrupt last scene of the 'final' version of the novel Michael even seems to have given up the idea of using the Grail material and speaks of going to the East to seek 'some lost doctrine' that would 'reconcile religion with the natural emotions' – a need newly felt since he had himself come to experience 'sexual love' (*SB* 106). But the Grail material was to resurface before long and be reconnected with the artist figure in Yeats's early work, for when with Lady Gregory's help he revised the Hanrahan group he substituted for 'The Book of the Great Dhoul ...' a new opening story based on the Grail quest, with Power and Knowledge being attributes of two of the talismans, the Grail Maiden being like Cleena a sort of Muse, and the quest an allegorical fertility ritual (*VSR* 92).

Hanrahan failed in the quest, as he had failed in the earlier version with Cleena. Whatever the personal reasons for his failure, he was born at a phase of the Irish historical gyre that would virtually ensure only the most limited success for his art as a social force. Such would not be true of Michael, whose development towards maturity coincides with a historical moment at which the current order of things seemed ready for reversal. Yet despite his confidence he falls far short of actually becoming the figure of the powerful artist. Although Maclagan accuses him of being 'some kind of an artist' rather than a 'magician' (opposites an aesthetic such as Yeats's own would allow him to reconcile), Michael's own sense of vocation seems unfocused (*SB* 92). Early in the novel he had had an experience suggesting a supernaturally controlled destiny:

> Michael sat looking out over the bulwark. He was tired and watched the grey waters wearily. . . . Suddenly it was as if the grey waters had been torn away, it was as if they had been painted on paper which somebody was tearing, and he saw in their stead a sea of an intense brightness, and on this sea a girl, in a deep olive dress and with heavy, bronze-like hair and a beautiful, mild, almost expressionless face, stood on the water or floated with her feet a few inches above it. He saw her with a curious minuteness[?] and distinctness, as though every detail of her dress was in as full a light as every other, as if the air had grown clearer than in our ordinary moments. The girl began to speak: 'When are you going to begin the work? Michael, you are a man now and it is time to begin the work. [CANCELLED: We have brought you here that we might tell you what is going to happen. You are to begin the work you have so long thought of, and you will go far away from this. You are going away at once for our first teaching of you is at an end. We have been always near.]' (*SB* 37)

There are resonances here not only with Hanrahan's encounter with his Muse, but also with the famous scene in *A Portrait* in which Stephen encounters the bird-girl, an emissary from the fair courts of life. Yeats and Joyce emphasise precisely opposite values, Joyce's figure *in* the water, an emblem of 'mortal youth and beauty', while Yeats's is clearly a divine being; but in both cases the appearance of the character seems to point a definite direction for the protagonist. In *The Speckled Bird*, however, we never see Michael produce a work of art. In this regard he lags behind even Stephen, who at least writes his 'Villanelle of the Temptress', derivative though it may be of the work of others, including Yeats's own early poetry. It is not unusual, of course, for the protagonists of *Bildungsromane* to fail where their creators have succeeded, but that was not necessarily to be Michael's fate (see *Au* 376). Yeats, as we know, never did in fact succeed in finishing *The Speckled Bird*, laying it aside for good by 1903. Perhaps this was because his own literary talents just were not suited to 'real novel writing' (*L* 345). Perhaps, though, the problem was at least in part one of distance; the novel had brought his fictional alter ego up to what was in effect the present moment of the author's own life, full of unfinished business such as the Literary Revival, the founding of the occult Order, and the relationship with Maud Gonne, the precise outcome of which Yeats himself could not clearly see. With the benefit of hindsight we can surmise for Michael the future his creator could not: his literary aspirations and his efforts to found an occult order might come together – as Yeats's own were doing – in the founding of a theatre movement, drama being as Yeats called it 'the ritual of a lost faith' (*LTSM* 156). *Bildungsroman* heroes are famously idealistic and naive; in reality success would be extraordinarily hard to achieve. At times Yeats himself was to feel an optimism his experience might have warned him was unwarranted. As one by one his new hopes were rudely thwarted, he found more and more necessary the faith that, however indirectly and gradually, in the fullness of time at least, his art would still shape his 'fool-driven land'. But that takes us into a new century and a new chapter.

3

1899–1917

I

During the nineties, Yeats's creative work had grown increasingly preoccupied with that ultimate reality of which this vegetable world was merely a shadow.[1] This preoccupation, epitomised by the use as one of the epigraphs for *The Secret Rose* of the famous speech from *Axël*, 'As for living, our servants will do that for us' (*VSR* 5) and by Forgael's quest in *The Shadowy Waters* for a perfection beyond all human life, would be succeeded at the turn of the century by an opposite emphasis. As Yeats himself described the change in 1903,

> I have always felt that the soul has two movements primarily, one to transcend forms, and the other to create forms. Nietsche ... calls these the Dionysic and the Apollonic respectively. I think I have to some extent got weary of that wild God Dionysius, and I am hoping that the Far-Darter will come in his place. (*L* 403)

There was no renunciation here of his commitment to a spiritual reality: 'the soul' was still supreme. He was merely focusing now upon its movement 'downward', *into* forms – a movement that could be effected by the visionary artist. In a second letter written at this period he yoked Christian with Nietzschean language to describe the process:

> ... I think I mistook for a permanent phase of the world what was only a preparation. The close of the last century was full of a strange desire to get out of form to get to some kind of dis-embodied beauty and now it seems to me the contrary impulse has come. I feel about me and in me an impulse to creat form, to carry the realization of beauty as far as possible. The Greeks said that the Dionysisic enthusiasm preceeded the Apollonic and that the Dionysisic was sad and desirous, but that the Apollonic was joyful and self sufficient. Long ago I used to define to myself

.these two influences as the transfiguration on the mountain and the incarnation, only the Transfiguration comes before the Incarnation in the natural order. (*L* 402)[2]

The figure of Incarnation was appealing precisely as a metaphor for the creative act in which the artist gave human form to the Divine, brought the supernatural into the natural order and thereby reshaped that order; yoked with Apollo, it represented a new version of Wilde's Greek statues in bridal chambers. 'The Adoration of the Magi' had proleptically made Incarnation the sign that a new era was beginning. Apollo, the creation of forms, and cyclical change coalesce in Yeats's sense of his own direction as the twentieth century began – and would memorably reappear in 'The Statues'.

In a meditation recorded in his journal in 1909, Yeats made overt the connection between Incarnation and power (and between both and the opposition of East and West that informs 'The Statues'):

By implication the philosophy of Irish faery lore declares that all power is from the body, all intelligence from the spirit. Western civilization, religion and magic alike insist on power and therefore body and these three doctrines – efficient rule, the Incarnation, and thaumaturgy. Eastern asceticism answers to these with indifference to rule, scorn of the flesh, contemplation of the formless. Western minds who follow the Eastern way become weak and vapoury because they become unfit for the work forced upon them by Western life. Every symbol is an invocation which produces its equivalent expression in all worlds. The Incarnation involved modern science and modern efficiency and also modern lyric feeling which gives body to the most spiritual emotions. It produced a solidification of all things that grew from the individual will. . . . The historical truth of the Incarnation is indifferent, though the belief in that truth was essential to the power of the evocation. (*Mem* 166)

Applying this distinction to Yeats's own career, we might say that his early work had been moving increasingly in an 'Eastern' direction, towards 'scorn of the flesh, contemplation of the formless'; and that just as it was reaching that extreme he felt the urge to direct it back more towards the 'West', giving 'body to the most spiritual emotions'. Although he wrote here of 'modern *lyric* feeling', another passage from the same journal, implicitly concerned with Incarnation, enables us to see his developing immersion in the theatre movement as part of the same impulse:

> In Christianity what was philosophy in Eastern Asia became life – biography, drama. A play passes through the same process in being written. At first, if it has psychological depth, there is a bundle of ideas, something that can be stated in philosophical terms; my *Countess Cathleen*, for instance, was once the moral question, may a soul sacrifice itself for a good end? – but gradually philosophy is eliminated more and more until at last the only philosophy audible, if there is even that, is the mere expression of one character or another. When it is completely life it seems to the hasty reader a mere story. Was the *Bhagavad Gita* the 'scenario' from which the Gospels were made? (*Mem* 150)[3]

Not only could drama incarnate what might otherwise remain abstract 'philosophy', but actual performance of plays offered a second incarnation, literally gave body to the words.

At the moment when Yeats first set out to found a national theatre, he may not yet have fully recognised the relationship between that project and the larger pattern he was acting out; but from the beginning of the theatre movement, in the public announcement he and Lady Gregory composed at Coole in 1897, he consciously looked upon the stage as a vehicle for his aesthetic:

> We propose to have performed in Dublin, in the spring of every year certain Celtic and Irish plays, which whatever be their degree of excellence will be written with a high ambition, and so to build up a Celtic and Irish school of dramatic literature. We hope to find in Ireland an uncorrupted and imaginative audience trained to listen by its passion for oratory, and believe that our desire to bring upon the stage the deeper thoughts and emotions of Ireland will ensure for us a tolerant welcome, and that freedom to experiment which is not found in theatres of England, and without which no new movement in art or literature can succeed. We will show that Ireland is not the home of buffoonery and of easy sentiment, as it has been represented, but the home of an ancient idealism. We are confident of the support of all Irish people, who are weary of misrepresentation, in carrying out a work that is outside all the political questions that divide us.[4]

The claim that Ireland was 'the home of an ancient idealism' reflects the gospel according to O'Grady, whom Yeats was actually at this time trying to get to write a play for the theatre;[5] and the 'high ambition', unspecified here, was none other than to mould Ireland in the new century. In an essay published only a few months before the inaugural performances, Yeats made it explicit that the purpose of thus looking back to the past was to shape the Irish future: 'Victor Hugo has said that in the theatre the mob became a people, and, though this could be perfectly true only of ancient times when the theatre was a part of the ceremonial of religion, I have some hope that, if we have enough success to go on from year to year, *we may help to bring a little ideal thought into the common thought of our times*' (*UP2* 141; emphasis added. In a lecture he began giving in 1902 Yeats interpreted Hugo's statement to mean that 'it is the Theatre which takes up the traditions of the past and shapes them into such a form that they can become the ideals of the Present and the substance of the future.'). The writers on whom the new movement would depend, he suggested, 'have laboured to be citizens ... of that eternal and ancient Ireland which has lived from old times in tender and heroic tales' and 'to write of Irish and all other things, as men should write who have never doubted that all things are shadows of spiritual things, and that men may come to the gates of peace by beautiful and august thoughts' (*UP2* 141–2). The national element here is balanced by residual nineties Dionysianism, the image of the artist leading men to the gates of peace another anticipation of the passage in 'Under Ben Bulben' in which the artists are urged to 'Bring the soul of man to God'. Seeing his own plays as 'the ritual of a lost faith' (*LTSM* 156) implied a hope of bringing back that faith. 'Has not the long decline of the arts been but the shadow of declining faith in an unseen reality?' he would ask in *Samhain* in 1904, making such a faith the foundation of his theory of drama; 'our next art', he argued, will feature 'the soul rejoicing in itself.... We, who are believers, cannot see reality anywhere but in the soul itself, and seeing it there we cannot do other than rejoice in every energy, whether of gesture, or of action, or of speech, coming out of the personality, the soul's image....'[6]

Yeats's fascination with drama went back to his earliest days as a writer, of course. It may have been his efforts in the nineties to found an Irish mystical order that made him particularly interested in the origins of drama in religious ritual (*IGE* 266). The theatre may also have become increasingly attractive because as 'the most immediately powerful form of literature' it might more certainly affect the audience – especially an audience that, he liked to think, had behind it a long oral literary tradition as well as a passion for political oratory.[7] The public announcement in fact reveals a preoccupation with precisely the question of audience. In the light of the opposition Yeats had encountered earlier in the decade from Nationalists and Unionists alike, the claims about an 'uncorrupted and imaginative audience' and 'the support of all Irish people' may seem disingenuous; but the former could be expected to approve of a theatre that promised to substitute Cuchulain and Finn for the stage Irishman, Handy Andy, and the rollicking officers of Charles Lever; while the latter, though disdainful as a class, had produced, as Yeats noted, individuals extraordinarily fruitful in imagination (*UP2* 141).[8] And the guarantors and supporters of the initial project did actually include the Fenian O'Leary, Maud Gonne, the leaders of all factions of the splintered Parliamentary Party; and Unionists from Horace Plunkett to Mahaffy and Lord and Lady Ardilaun.[9] Nevertheless, prior to the opening performances on 8 May, 1899, Yeats made it clear that his immediate hope was that the new dramatists might merely appeal to 'that limited public which gives understanding, and not to that unlimited public which gives wealth; and if they interest those among their audience who keep in their memories the songs of Callanan and Walsh, or old Irish legends, or who love the good books of any country, they will not mind greatly if others are bored' (UP2 159–60). In another piece he pointed to the example of John Todhunter in the early nineties as a clear sign that 'we must make a theatre for ourselves and our friends, and for a few simple people who understand from sheer simplicity what we understand from scholarship and thought. We have planned the Irish Literary Theatre with this hospitable emotion, and, that the right people may find out about us, we hope to act a play or two in the spring of every year', and that the right people may escape the stupefying memory of the theatre of commerce which clings even to them, our plays will be for the most part remote, spiritual, and ideal.'[10] 'Ideal' here seems to suggest not only the 'idealism' of the preliminary manifesto but also the Platonic Ideas and perhaps an opposition to realism. (As he wrote in 'At Stratford-on-Avon' in 1901, '"Art is art, because it is not nature!" It brings us near to the archetypal ideas themselves, and away from nature, which is but their looking-glass.')[11] By this point

Yeats had come to use certain images and allusions as a sort of shorthand way of referring to his aesthetic, and he used a reference to Blake in that way in the second of the *Beltaine* pieces of 1899, linking it with the key concept that through the few one might reach the many:

> Blake has said that all Art is a labour to bring again the Golden Age, and all culture is certainly a labour to bring again the simplicity of the first ages, with knowledge of good and evil added to it. The drama ... has one day when the emotions of cities still remember the emotions of sailors and husbandmen and shepherds and users of the spear and the bow; ... and it has another day, now beginning, when thought and scholarship discover their desire. In the first day, it is the Art of the people; and in the second day, like the dramas acted of old times in the hidden places of temples, it is the preparation of a Priesthood. It may be, though the world is not old enough to show us any example, that this Priesthood will spread their Religion everywhere, and make their Art the Art of the people.[12]

When the first season's plays were actually performed, the response of the audience presaged the magnitude of the task ahead.

The *Countess Cathleen* was particularly appropriate for the inaugural program because it dealt with some of the very questions that Yeats himself was addressing in attempting to create a national theatre in the first place. The opposition that developed lent itself to various interpretations. James Joyce, presumably an exemplar of at least one portion of the audience Yeats had hoped to reach from the beginning, admired Yeats's initial resolution to fight for art of the highest quality but condemned him for supposedly yielding to the 'rabblement' in ensuing seasons; in *A Portrait* Stephen recalls the inaugural performance as evidence that it was impossible to find in Ireland an audience for great art and thus sees in the play's conclusion a 'symbol of departure', a sign that he must leave his country.[13] Lady Gregory, committed to staying and fighting, offered advice more congruent with Yeats's own principles: 'Clearly just now your work is not directly with the masses, which would be the most directly interesting work, but that matters less as the Gaelic movement has taken up their education, and any of the fine work you do, besides having an influence on the best

minds, is there ready for the time when your countrymen will dare
to praise it.'[14] Yeats was to make similar observations, as well as
learning an important lesson: 'In using what I considered traditional symbols I forgot that in Ireland they are not symbols but
realities' (*AU* 416). During the next several years, the tension
between the symbolic art crucial to his aesthetic and demands for
theatrical realism (demands often coming, paradoxically, from
ultra-Nationalist audiences committed to an idealised vision of
Ireland) was to be an ongoing and increasing problem.

In essays published in 1900, Yeats invoked his aesthetic in
connection with both the Gaelic movement and symbolic art. 'Irish
Language and Literature' was addressed to D. P. Moran, whose
passionate support of the language revival and of Irish cultural and
economic self- reliance left him with virtually no sympathy for the
idea of an Irish literature in English. Yeats, writing at a moment
when the bitterness of the quarrels between Parnellites and anti-
Parnellites had tarnished parliamentary nationalism and the land
question seemed on the verge of settlement, suggested that 'we
must be prepared to turn from a purely political nationalism with
the land question as its lever, to a partly intellectual and historical
nationalism ... with the language question as its lever.... We will
always have politics of some kind, and we may have to send
members of Parliament to England for a long time to come, but our
politics and our members of Parliament will be moved, as I think,
by a power beyond themselves ...' (*UP2* 237). He professed himself
glad to recognise the 'political power' of the Irish language, but
asserted also, perhaps with Lady Gregory's advice in mind, that

> side by side with the spread of the Irish language, and with much
> writing in the Irish language, must go on much expression of
> Irish emotion and Irish thought, much writing about Irish things
> and people, in the English language ... and this writing must for
> a long time to come be the chief influence in shaping the opinions
> and the emotions of the leisured classes in Ireland in so far as
> they are concerned with Irish things, and the more sincere it is,
> the more lofty it is, the more beautiful it is, the more will the
> general life of Ireland be sweetened by its influence, through its
> influence over a few governing minds. It will always be too
> separate from the general life of Ireland to influence it directly,
> and it was chiefly because I believed this that I differed so strongly
> in 1892 and 1893 from Sir Charles Gavan Duffy and his supporters,

who wished to give such writing an accidental and fleeting popularity by uniting it with politics and economics. (*UP2* 238)

Yeats was rewriting history here, for all other evidence indicates that he and Duffy had both hoped to reach a large audience directly, the contention arising because Duffy had wanted to fill the series with volumes in the Young Ireland tradition while Yeats had fought for contemporary work of the highest possible quality; the distortion suggests how strongly now the process of a more gradual influence through the few to the many was establishing itself in his mind. This passage was also a sort of ur-scenario for 'To a Shade', in which he would assail his enemies for failing to see that the Lane pictures would have 'given their children's children loftier thought, / Sweeter emotion, working in their veins / Like gentle blood . . . .'

In 'The Symbolism of Poetry' Yeats's concerns were more universal: a 'spiritual' reality and the literary devices by which the artist brings an audience into contact with that reality. Sounds, colours, and forms 'call down among us certain disembodied powers, whose footsteps over our hearts we call emotions . . .' (*IGE* 243). The process might seem rarified and insignificant, but

> It is indeed only those things which seem useless or very feeble that have any power, and all those things that seem useful or strong, armies, moving wheels, modes of architecture, modes of government, speculations of the reason, would have been a little different if some mind long ago had not given itself to some emotion, as a woman gives herself to her lover, and shaped sounds or colours or forms, or all of these, into a musical relation, that their emotion might live in other minds. A little lyric evokes an emotion, and this emotion gathers others about it and melts into their being in the making of some great epic; and at last, needing an always less delicate body, or symbol, as it grows more powerful, it flows out, with all it has gathered, among the blind instincts of daily life, where it moves a power within powers, as one sees ring within ring in the stem of an old tree. (*IGE* 244–5)

The repeated references to 'power' link the essay with the specially national preoccupations of the piece addressed to Moran, and the reference to lyrics coalescing into epic anticipates, as we shall see, a key preoccupation of his own in the near future, when Lady

Gregory's 'canonical books' *Cuchulain of Muirthemne* and *Gods and Fighting Men* would largely supplant O'Grady's 'Histories' as primary repositories of the 'heroic ideal' Yeats would seek to revive in this unheroic decade. In support of his claims in this passage Yeats specifically brought in O'Shaughnessy as well as echoing Wilde:

> This is maybe what Arthur O'Shaughnessy meant when he made his poets say they had built Nineveh with their sighing; and I am certainly never certain, when I hear of some war, or of some religious excitement, or of some new manufacture, or of anything else that fills the ear of the world, that it has not all happened because of something that a boy piped in Thessaly. I remember once asking a seer to ask one among the gods ... what would come of a charming but seemingly trivial labour of a friend, and the form answering, 'the devastation of peoples and the over-whelming of cities'.... Solitary men in moments of contemplation receive, as I think, the creative impulse from the lowest of the Nine Hierarchies, and so make and unmake mankind, and even the world itself.... (*IGE* 245-7)

Yeats was soon to declare about *Ideas of Good and Evil*, the volume in which 'The Symbolism of Poetry' was collected, that it reflected a mood with which he was no longer in full sympathy, 'too lyrical, too full of aspirations after remote things, too full of desires', whereas now he looked upon the world with 'somewhat more defiant eyes' (*L* 402–3). But the aesthetic of artistic power under-lying the essay actually mediated between the longing for contact with the realm of 'remote things' and the defiance with which he would be defending against enemies on all sides his own role in directing the future of his country.

A brief controversy of 1901 concerning the theatre showed him stressing the desirability even of a disruptive art. George Moore had proposed clerical censorship of the theatre. Yeats, attempting to make the best of the opposition several of the early plays had encountered, welcomed the new debate: 'We cannot have too much discussion about ideas in Ireland. The discussion over the theology of *The Countess Cathleen*, and over the politics of *The Bending of the Bough*, and over the morality of *Diarmuid and Grania* set the public mind thinking of matters it seldom thinks of in Ireland, and I hope the Irish Literary Theatre will remain a wise disturber of the peace' (*L* 356). (His own Seanchan would soon echo these words yet more defiantly.) He could not himself accede to Moore's proposal because he believed 'that literature is the principal voice of the conscience, and it is its duty age after age to affirm its morality against the special moralities of clergymen and churches, and of kings and parliaments and peoples'. When Fred Ryan objected to Yeats's claims for literature, Yeats replied that he had been echoing a sentence of Verhaeren's to the effect that 'a masterpiece is a portion of the conscience of the world'. To support his case he cited Shelley's *Defence* and 'certain essays by Schopenhauer' as 'probably the best things that have been written on the subject by modern writers' and recommended George Santayana's T*he Sense of Beauty* (1896), 'which deals profoundly with the whole philosophy of aesthetics' (*UP2* 262–4)

II

Encounters like this one, of course, were secondary to his main task, the actual creation of such 'masterpieces'. Yeats presented his program for the task in the contemporary essay 'Ireland and the Arts' (1901). Although he was concerned there to reach 'those who, while moved in other things than the arts by love of country, are beginning to write, as I was some sixteen years ago, without any decided impulse to one thing more than another, and especially to those who are convinced, as I was convinced, that art is tribeless, nationless, a blossom gathered in No Man's Land', he was (as the personal references suggest) simultaneously reaffirming for himself at a crucial moment principles that would inform his current creative work (*IGE* 324). The arts might seem to have failed, and those who cared for them found themselves 'the priesthood of an almost forgotten faith', but it was possible to 'win the people again' (*IGE* 320). (Links between this essay and the second of the *Beltaine* pieces of 1899 are obvious and pervasive.) To achieve such a goal, the writer must choose Irish subjects, especially legends and history, and choose them under 'that belief in a spiritual life which is not confined to one Church' (*IGE* 328). And though the ultimate goal might be popular influence, 'no artist ... should try to make his work popular. Once he has chosen a subject he must think of nothing but giving it such an expression as will please himself ....

He must make his work a part of his own journey towards beauty and truth' (*IGE* 326-7). Such artists

> would give Ireland more than they received from her, for they
> would make love of the unseen more unshakeable, more ready to

plunge deep into the abyss, and they would make love of country more fruitful in the mind, more a part of daily life. One would know an Irishman into whose life they had come – and in a few generations they would come into the life of all, rich and poor – by something that set him apart among men. He himself would understand that more was expected of him than of others because he had greater possessions. The Irish race would have become a chosen race, one of the pillars that uphold the world. (*IGE* 331–2)

Their work would impart both Dionysiac ('love of the unseen') and Apollonic ('love of country') values and gradually they would infuse the people as a whole with both sacredness and strength.

The lyric 'Old Memory', though it might seem at first merely a personal love poem, not only shows Yeats putting such principles into practice but is in fact *about* the process:

> O thought fly to her when the end of day
> Awakens an old memory, and say
> 'Your strength, that is so lofty and fierce and kind
> It might call up a new age, calling to mind
> The queens that were imagined long ago,
> Is but half yours; he kneaded in the dough
> Through the long days of youth, and who would have thought
> It all and more than it all would come to naught
> And that dear words meant nothing?' . . .

> (*VP* 201; *Wayfarer's Love* version, 1904)

This poem seems to presume awareness of the recently published *The Old Age of Queen Maeve*, in which the telescoped relationship between modern beloved and epic counterpart leads the poet to upbraid himself:

>   O unquiet heart,
> Why do you praise another, praising her,
> As if there were no tale but your own tale
> Worth knitting to a measure of sweet sound?
> Have I not bid you tell of that great queen
> Who has been buried some two thousand years? (*VP* 181)

Near the end of that text he addresses the beloved directly:

> Friend of these many years, you too had stood
> With equal courage in that whirling rout;
> For you, although you've not her wandering heart,
> Have all that greatness, and not hers alone.
> For there is no high story about queens
> In any ancient book but tells of you.... (*VP* 186)[15]

Here the intensity of the poet's feeling threatens to break down the delicate balance of objective and subjective, paradigm and example, story and personal feeling. In 'Old Memory', by contrast, the argument is that the poet's own work, inspiring the beloved with heroic images, helped make her what she is – a *living* symbol of the past who can serve to evoke a 'new age' modelled upon the virtues she shares with ancient queens. (Those queens themselves were 'imagined', the creation of earlier artists.) Her lofty strength yokes Dionysiac and Apollonic elements like the powerful national art described in the concluding paragraph of 'Ireland and the Arts'. Verbally as well as conceptually 'Old Memory' is another early work that anticipates 'Under Ben Bulben'. It is tempting to assume that between the composition of the first poem and the second Maud Gonne's marriage on February 21, 1903 had given a bitter irony to the lines in *The Old Age of Queen Maeve* about the steadfastness of *her* heart. Although the later poem obviously has its roots in deeply painful personal experiences, Yeats wrote it while on his first lecture tour in America and in sending it to the Duchess of Sutherland revealed that he meant for it to have broader implications:

> I am lecturing to colleges & beleive I am setting a good many people reading our Celtic books & it was for that I came here – & our Celtic books mean to me not in the end books but in the end a most passionate kind of life – a present revery 'calling up a new age, calling to mind the queens that were imagined long ago' as I say in the poem of a fair woman.[16]

From this more general perspective the art of today becomes the life of tomorrow and the beloved's power to shape coming days becomes synechdotal; that strength of hers would become the indomitability of a nation.

Yeats's concurrent experiments with the speaking of verse to the psaltery represent among other things a way of making lyric poetry performative and thus lending it some of the same heightened power to affect audiences offered by drama on stage. On the back of a letter of 1903 dealing with the experiments, Yeats jotted down some notes on the subject, including 'movement against the external. / Future of Art / Unnaturalness of print / Poetry will recover power / All but a few too busy to read.'[17] He felt spoken verse would be especially effective in reaching country audiences, for 'the player rose into importance in the town, but the minstrel is of the country';[18] accordingly he even formulated a scheme for sending trained 'reciters' into rural areas. Ronald Schuchard has convincingly demonstrated the centrality of these Yeatsian experiments, which have often been dismissed as embarassingly quixotic.[19] They were, in fact, an essential part of Yeats's larger plans for affecting the direction of Ireland in the new century. He clearly conceived of the performers as carrying on a facet of the bardic tradition: 'They will have by heart, like the Irish *File*, so many poems and notations that they will never have to bend their heads over the book to the ruin of dramatic expression and of the wild air the bard had always about him in my childish imagination' (*IGE* 27).[20] Yeats's enthusiasm for this aspect of bardic literature had been stimulated by his presence in August of 1901 at a *Gorsedd* or Convocation of Bards in Dublin that as he noted drew large crowds 'with its picturesque ceremonial & traditional chanting';[21] and especially by the blind bard Raftery, whose songs were kept in memory by people who had actually heard him sing them and were still living in Yeats's day. An old peasant woman sang one for him in Irish, and 'every word was audible and expressive, as the words in a song were always, as I think, before music grew too proud to be the garment of words. . . .'[22] Yeats had also heard tales of the power of Raftery's satiric verses,[23] and in *Poets and Dreamers* (1903) Lady Gregory had given many stories of how his satires had been feared.[24] Appropriately, Standish O'Grady was among those present at a demonstration of the new art in 1902; and Lady Gregory provided Yeats with some material for performance from Irish legendary literature.[25] In one of his lectures on the 1906 tour with Florence Farr he declared that 'laws and education tried to perpetuate a type which their authors thought would be of use to the race, but the poet shaped the type which benefited the race.' Various circumstances prevented Yeats from carrying out this element of his scheme, and thus the primary burden for several years fell upon the theatre.[26]

III

His own creative efforts during the first decade of the century went largely into the writing of plays. Lecturing on the theatre in 1902, he had argued that modern 'problem' plays 'will always stir the heart less nobly than plays which set before the imagination men and women living in a more splendid and passionate world than our eyes have seen, and speaking a loftier language than our ears have heard'. He had then gone on to express his desire to 'have Ireland awaken again the heroic life that has been so long asleep', to 'have her take from her own stern past exalted images of abundant men and illuminate a joy which is not for the loosening of the knees and the softening of the will but the awakening of the hard creative energy'. In March, 1903, thanking John Quinn for a copy of *The Dawn of Day*, he wrote that Nietzsche 'has been of particularly great service to me just now, because I am setting out to try & re-create an heroical ideal in [=of?] manhood – in plays of old Irish life–'[27] Yeats may have found encouragement in Nietzsche in asserting that 'with the heroic poetry comes the sense of form, the dramatic or epic portion of the work of art, the heroic discipline, which, of course, has no relation to morality as generally understood or to service to the State and mankind.'[28] It was Lady Gregory, though, more than Nietzsche, who made such plays possible. Her renderings of saga, tale, and lyric had greater coherence and literary merit than O'Grady's, and despite Yeats's hopes O'Grady had objected that 'the Red Branch ought not to be staged.... That literature ought not to be produced for popular consumption for the edification of the crowd.... You may succeed in degrading Irish ideals and banishing the soul of the land.'[29] So, if it was his work that had 'started us all', it was to hers that Yeats turned for the foundation of the plays that would 'put before the people strong, great types, and so contribute to the evolution in Ireland of a great democracy.'[30] Her versions led him to see the tales anew as 'the energies ... behind all our movement here' (*L* 436; see also *E&I* 513). When Clement Shorter objected to his claim in the Preface to *Cuchulain of Muirthemne* that it was 'the best [book] that has come out of Ireland in my time', Yeats defended his statement in personal terms, saying he had 'found but one thing in Ireland that has stirred me to the roots – a conception of the heroic life come down from the dawn of the world and not even yet utterly extinguished. . . .' The legends were, he went on, 'the chief influence of my youth' (*UP2* 328). Elsewhere he predicted the book would 'take its place between the *Morte d'Arthur* and the *Mabinogion*' (*L* 354) – the two favourite books of the young protagonist of *The Speckled Bird*.[31] In his Preface he had gone on to assert that 'if we will but tell these stories to our children the Land will begin again to be a Holy Land, as it was before men gave their hearts to Greece and Rome and Judea.'[32] In his Preface to *Gods and Fighting Men* two years later Yeats spelled out the process at greater length:

> One cannot say how much that [Gaelic] literature has done for the vigour of the race, for one cannot count the hands its praise of kings and high-hearted queens made hot upon the sword-hilt, or the amorous eyes it made lustful for strength and beauty. One remembers indeed that when the farming people and the labourers of the towns made their last attempt to cast out England by force of arms they named themselves after the companions of Finn. . . . Surely these old stories, whether of Finn or Cuchulain, helped to sing the old Irish and the old Norman-Irish aristocracy to their end. They heard their hereditary poets and story-tellers, and they took to horse and died fighting against Elizabeth or against Cromwell; and when an English-speaking aristocracy had their place, it listened to no poetry indeed, but it felt about it in the popular mind an exacting and ancient tribunal, and began a play that had for spectators men and women that loved the high wasteful virtues. . . . had they understood the people and the game a little better, they might have created an aristocracy in an age that has lost the meaning of the word. (xxi–xxii)

The reference to those 'high-hearted queens' connects this passage to the concerns of *The Old Age of Queen Maeve* and 'Old Memory', recently written. As his historical survey of the process reached the eighteenth century, he revealed a mixture of positive feelings and reservations about what he would later come to identify as that 'one Irish century that escaped from darkness and confusion' (*VPl* 958). He was not yet ready to put 'Hard-riding country gentlemen' with Finn and Cuchulain as 'types'. Turning to the present and future he asserted that 'if we would create a great community – and what other game is so worth the labour? – we must recreate the old foundations of life, not as they existed in that splendid misunderstanding of the eighteenth century, but as they must always exist when the finest minds and Ned the beggar and Seaghan the fool think about the same thing, although they may not think the same thought about it' (xxiii). Irish-speaking peasants will have access to the legends and thus be able to tell them to their children. Until the appearance of Lady Gregory's books, it was 'the owners of the land whose children might never have known what would give them so much happiness.' Now, however,

> they can read this book to their children, and it will make Slieve-na-man, Allen, and Benbulben, the great mountain that showed itself before me every day through all my childhood and was yet unpeopled, and half the country-sides of south and west, as populous with memories as are Dundealgan and Emain Macha and Muirthemne; and after a while somebody may even take them to some famous place and say, 'This land where your fathers lived proudly and finely should be dear and dear and again dear'; and perhaps when many names have grown musical to their ears, a more imaginative love will have taught them a better service. (xxiv; see also *Mem* 124)

Yeats remembered O'Grady, a member of that land-owning class, asserting that 'Slieve-na-mon would yet be more famous than Olympus '(*E&I* 475; also 512). The language of 'a better service' is vague, perhaps protectively: some of the earlier parts of the passage might imply revolution. As Yeats undertook his own share of the task of peopling Ben Bulben by bringing heroic literature onto the stage, he was to find just how powerful such art really could be. Could *excess* of 'love' bewilder men 'till they died', a play send out more men to die fighting at the hands of the English?

Deirdre (begun in 1904) offers a particularly appropriate example of Yeats's efforts in this decade to write plays embodying a heroic ideal, for it dramatises the achievement of what Yeats would increasingly emphasise as one of the greatest of all heroic virtues, 'tragic joy', 'the heroic cry in the midst of despair' (*LDW* 8). Its principal characters are those kings and especially one of those 'high-hearted queens' praise of whom had made hands 'hot upon the sword-hilt' and 'amorous eyes ... lustful for strength and beauty'. Moreover, the play is concerned self-referentially with the process of art shaping life. This concern is developed in the text through allusions to Lugaidh Redstripe and his seamew wife, Devorgill – a legend unconnected before Yeats's play with the Deirdre story (Rohan 50–3) and introduced by him in order to build into the action the same experience for the characters that the play they were in was intended to produce for its audience.

The pair are first referred to early in the play, when Fergus urges the musicians to greet the arrival of Deirdre and Naoise with

> ... a verse
> Of some old time not worth remembering,
> And all the lovelier because a bubble.
> Begin, begin, of some old king and queen,
> Of Lugaidh Redstripe or another; no, not him,
> He and his lady perished wretchedly. (*VPl* 351)

His suggestion is important both because it evokes an image of an *unimportant* past and because he can see in the lovers' deaths only a wretchedness *inappropriate* to the happy circumstances of the present moment. Shortly after the arrival of the lovers, Naoise recognises the chessboard in the guest-house as the very one on which the earlier couple had played 'upon the night they died'. Although the presence of the board seems a *bad* omen, Naoise does recall here a positive image of the lovers:

> If the tale is true,
> When it was plain that they had been betrayed,
> They moved the men, and waited for the end,
> As it were bedtime, and had so quiet minds
> They hardly winked their eyes when the sword flashed.
> (*VPl* 355–6)

Then, when Deirdre hears of the bridal bed Conchubar has prepared, she *contrasts* her fate with Devorgill's:

> Here is worse treachery than the seamew suffered,
> For she but died and mixed into the dust
> Of her dear comrade, but I am to live
> And lie in the one bed with him I hate. (*VPl* 362)

It is only at the point when Conchubar's treachery has been fully revealed that Naoise suggests that he and his beloved should cast their minds on other days and take the earlier lovers' heroic courage in the face of death as a model for their own deaths. 'They knew that there was nothing that could save them' (*VPl* 373) – in Yeats's mind an indispensible prerequisite for tragic joy, for, as he wrote years later, 'the east has its solutions always and therefore knows nothing of tragedy' (*LDW* 8). Their refusal of vain action or emotion showed that they were worthy of their part in the play. Naoise's recognition – 'I never heard a death so out of reach / Of common hearts, a high and comely end' – evokes again the 'high-hearted queens' of the Preface to *Gods and Fighting Men* and Maud's 'lofty' strength. He asks the musicians,

> Had you been here when that man and his queen
> Played at so high a game, could you have found
> An ancient poem for the praise of it?
> It should have set out plainly that those two,
> Because no man and woman have loved better,
> Might sit on there contentedly, and weigh
> The joy comes after. (*VPl* 373)

That 'game', itself dominated by kings and queens, was the very one the Ascendancy gentlemen of the eighteenth century had only partly understood. The musicians here represent the author within his text, juxtaposing a present act with 'an ancient poem'. In Deirdre's next speech she draws further attention to the literary process, urging the 'singing women' to 'set it down in a book' and praise Naoise and herself for their own heroic deaths (*VPl* 374). In one manuscript version of this passage she had even suggested that such deaths so recorded would make them 'seem to *coming times* as they were gods / And had their images ...' (Rohan 48; emphasis added). Thus her concern to ensure that the women can prove they 'have Deirdre's story right' (*VPl* 377). Although she lacks 'the cold blood of the sea in her veins' (*VPl* 375) she wavers only briefly before achieving a similar sang-froid, and when Conchubar sees her response to Naoise's death he asks in bewilderment, 'But why are you so calm? / I thought that you would curse me and cry out, / And fall upon the ground and tear your hair' (*VPl* 383). Even Conchubar's curtain lines contribute to the effect, for he not only acknowledges Deirdre's own merit but is himself (rather sur-prisingly) a figure of strength and dignity:

I have no need of weapons,
There's not a traitor that dare stop my way.
Howl, if you will; but I, being king, did right
In choosing her most fitting to be queen,
And letting no boy lover take the sway. (*VPl* 388)

An audience leaving the theatre would thus find itself at the end of a series beginning in the earliest past of Lugaidh Redstripe and his seamew bride, to which Deirdre and Naoise in the present of the play had turned for ideal models, making themselves in turn part of a past that *would be* 'worth remembering' and that Yeats had brought into the present as a paradigm that would help him 'create a great community'.

Deirdre certainly lived up to the promises of 'ancient idealism' made in the preliminary public announcement back in 1897. It was not, however, the most popular of Yeats's plays from the early years of the theatre movement. That distinction of course belongs to yet another text focused upon a 'queen', *Cathleen ni Houlihan* (written in the fall of 1901, published and performed in 1902).[33] Given its transparent nationalist allegory, that popularity and the widely attested impact of the play upon subsequent history are not surprising.[34] What might at first not be so obvious is that it, too, not only exemplifies Yeats's aesthetic of artistic power but takes the process as one of its own central subjects. In a sense the play is a new version of *The Countess Cathleen*; while the newer play was still in rehearsal Yeats published an interpretation of it as 'the perpetual struggle of the cause of Ireland and every other ideal cause against private hopes and dreams, against all that we mean when we say the world '(*VPl* 234). A choice of public 'idealism' characterises both texts; but what had been so controversial when couched in theological terms was safe from misunderstanding when the question was clearly political. By comparing the plays in the light of Yeats's statement about the newer one, we can in fact see a potential source of offence in *Cathleen ni Houlihan*. 'Private hopes and dreams, could apply equally well to Aleel's romantic passion and immersion in the faeryland world of the Gaelic past and to Michael Gillane's imminent domestic happiness with Delia Cahil. But 'all that we mean when we say the world' could suggest also the prominent concern in the play with economic questions of holdings and dowries, which in its most unpalatable form, in Peter's reluctance to part with a shilling for the Poor Old Woman, anticipates the virulent critique of the graspingly materialistic basis of middle-class Nationalist piety that Yeats would later give such memorable expression in 'To a Wealthy Man . . .' and 'September 1913'. At the time, however, no offence seems to have been taken; 'Crowds have been turned away from the doors every night. . . . There is continual applause', wrote Yeats of the 1902 performances (*L* 368). (There was *Unionist* opposition, but this could only seem to validate the play's unimpeachable nationalist vision.)[35] Within the overall structure of the play, features such as these represent the shortcomings of the present moment, highlighted by contrast with the past and destined to be changed for the better in the future.

Situated within the 'present' of 1798, the Old Woman (like the author) looks both back and ahead in time, enumerating some of those 'that died for love of me':

> There
> Was a red man of the O'Donnells from the north,
> and a man of the O'Sullivans from the south, and
> there was one Brian that lost his life at Clontarf by
> the sea, and there were a great many in the west,
> some that died hundreds of years ago, and there are
> some that will die tomorrow. (*VPl* 224–5)

Her later claim that 'there have been many songs made for me' (*VPl* 228) both implies that there *will be* others and points indirectly to one of them, the play in which she is a character. For the author of that play, 1798 is not the present but the past, and only an intermediate one at that. Beyond it are several earlier pasts. One of those who had written a song for the Old Woman was Yeats's Hanrahan, whose mid-eighteenth century verses Yeats showed spreading among the people and perhaps planting seeds for the year of the French. In one early printing, the play had the following epigraph:

> Young she is, and fair she is, and would be crowned a queen,
> Were the King's son at home here with Kathaleen-Ny-Houlahan!
> (*VPl* 214)

These lines, taken from Mangan's translation of the Irish original by William Dall Heffernan, evoke both Mangan's time, the Young Ireland era, and an earlier, Jacobite, past.[36] The immediately preceding lines in Mangan's version – 'Think her not a ghastly hag, too hideous to be seen, / Call her not unseemly names, our matchless Kathaleen' – point to the far more remote era of early legend. At the very end of the play Yeats alludes to the same legend when Peter asks Patrick 'Did you see an old woman going down the path?' and the latter replies, 'I did not, but I saw a young girl and she had the walk of a queen' (*VPl* 231). Yeats on several occasions claimed that the first conception of the play had come to him in a dream, and that conception was appropriately archetypal. In a sovereignty myth clearly rooted in fertility rituals and well attested in early Irish texts, the future king encounters the Goddess in the form of a 'ghastly hag'; if he embraces rather than spurning her she will become a young, beautiful woman, he will have proven his right to be her consort, and the fertility (literal and, by extension, political) of the land will be restored.[37] The role of bards in the accompanying inaugural ceremonies had been brought to Yeats's attention in the 1880s in Connellan's essay in the *Transactions of the Ossianic Society* (xxiii). In Heffernan's poem, the Stuart is a failed consort, while the bardic speaker recognises the true identity of the Old Woman. Aleel in *The Countess Cathleen* and Hanrahan in Yeats's stories also fail; the latter is tended during his last illness by an old hag who proves to be the embodiment of the Goddess (and who is referred to in the rewritten version, *Stories of Red Hanrahan*, as Winny Byrne of the Cross Roads, perhaps identical with the Winny of the Cross Roads who had served as precursor of the Old Woman in *Cathleen ni Houlihan* [*VPl* 216]. And another Michael, the young protagonist of *The Speckled Bird*, had been called to 'begin the work' by the Goddess figure in her beautiful form. The implication of this matrix of associations, and of the play itself, is to identify its author as the visionary bard who recognises the queen in the hag and presents her in a play that might lead to the restored health of the polity.

In the nineties, as part of a critique of Young Ireland facileness, Yeats had quoted a letter from Thomas Davis to a friend urging him to write a national *play*: 'Have you ever tried dramatic writing? Do you know Taylor's "Philip Van Artevelde" and Griffin's "Gissipus"? I think them the two best serious dramas written in English since Shakespeare's time. A drama equal to either of them with an Irish subject would be useful and popular to an extent you can hardly suppose' (*UP2* 33–4). Young Ireland drama never got off the ground, but now in a sense Yeats might seem to have written the play Davis had called for, and its popular success, although gratifying, made him uncomfortable, for it seemed to validate a mode of national art that could easily become restricting. Thus in October, 1903 he sent to the *United Irishman* a letter in which he attempted to distinguish between propagandist drama and a play like *Cathleen ni Houlihan*. He began with the past:

> When we were all fighting about the selection of books for the New Irish Library some ten years ago we had to discuss the question, 'What is National Poetry?' In those days a patriotic young man would have thought but poorly of himself if he did not believe that 'The Spirit of the *Nation*' was great lyric poetry, and a much finer kind of poetry than Shelley's 'Ode to the West Wind,' or Keats's 'Ode to a Grecian Urn.' When two or three of us denied this we were told that we had effeminate tastes or that we were putting Ireland in a bad light before her enemies. If one said that 'The Spirit of the *Nation*' was but salutary rhetoric England might overhear us and take up the cry. We said it, and who will say that Irish literature has not a greater name in the world to-day than it had ten years ago. One never serves one's cause by putting one's head into a bag.

Then he turned to the immediate issue:

> To-day there is another question that we must make up our minds about, and an even more pressing one, 'What is a National Theatre?' A man may write a book of lyrics if he have but a friend or two that will care for them, but he cannot write a good play if there are not audiences to listen to it. If we think that a national play must be as near as possible a page out of 'The Spirit of the *Nation*' put into dramatic form, and mean to go on thinking it to the end, then we may be sure that this generation will not see the rise in Ireland of a theatre that will reflect the life of Ireland as the Scandinavian theatre reflects the Scandinavian life. The brazen head has an unexpected way of falling to pieces. We have a company of admirable and disinterested players, and the next few months will, in all likelihood, decide whether a great work for this country is to be accomplished. The poetry of Young Ireland, when it was an attempt to change or strengthen opinion, was rhetoric; but it became poetry when patriotism was transformed into a personal emotion by the events of life, as in that lamentation written by Doheny on his keeping among the hills. Literature is always personal, always one man's vision of the

world, one man's experience, and it can only be popular when
men are ready to welcome the visions of others. A community
that is opinion-ridden, even when those opinions are in
themselves noble, is likely to put its creative minds into some
sort of a prison. If creative minds preoccupy themselves with
incidents from the political history of Ireland, so much the better,
but we must not enforce them to select those incidents. If in the
sincere working out of their plot, they alight on a moral that is
obviously and directly serviceable to the National cause, so much
the better, but we must not force that moral upon them.

The personal implication was inevitable:

I am a Nationalist, and certain of my intimate friends have made
Irish politics the business of their lives, and this made certain
thoughts habitual with me, and an accident made these thoughts
take fire in such a way that I could give them dramatic expression. I had a very vivid dream one night, and I made
Cathleen ni Houlihan out of this dream. But if some external
necessity had forced me to write nothing but drama with an
obviously patriotic intention, instead of letting my work shape
itself under the casual impulses of dreams and daily thoughts, I
would have lost, in a short time, the power to write movingly
upon any theme. I could have roused opinion; but I could not
have touched the heart, for I would have been busy at the
oakum-picking that is not the less mere journalism for being in
dramatic form. Above all, we must not say that certain incidents
which have been a part of literature in all other lands are
forbidden to us.[38]

The distinction was essentially a simple one: the impetus must
come from within rather than from without. The role of dreams
here is a variation upon the idea of the bard or artist as visionary.

No Nationalists, in fact, had been objecting to any 'incidents' in
Cathleen ni Houlihan. What was pressing upon Yeats's thought here
was Synge's play *The Shadow of the Glen*, which had just been
attacked in the Nationalist press and which was about to generate a
storm of protest, aimed at, among other things, its suggestion of an
adulterous relationship in the Wicklow glens. Yeats first resorted to
fairly obvious grounds to defend Synge's use of such a situation:

It may be our duty, as it has been the duty of many dramatic movements, to bring new kinds of subjects into the theatre, but it cannot be our duty to make the bounds of drama narrower. For instance, we are told that the English theatre is immoral, because it is pre-occupied with the husband, the wife and the lover. It is, perhaps, too exclusively pre-occupied with that subject, and it is certain it has not shed any new light upon it for a considerable time, but a subject that inspired Homer and about half the great literature of the world will, one doubts not, be a necessity to our National Theatre also.

Then he invoked the concept of art's shaping power (the word 'power' itself again stressed by repetition), but in this context, engaged as he was with work he admired very much but work based upon an aesthetic very different from his own, he momentarily adopted a stance inconsistent with the principles informing *Cathleen ni Houlihan* and most of his oeuvre:

Literature is, to my mind, the great teaching power of the world, the ultimate creator of all values, and it is this, not only in the sacred books whose power everybody acknowledges, but by every movement of imagination in song or story or drama that height of intensity and sincerity has made literature at all. Literature must take the responsibility of its power, and keep all its freedom: it must be like the spirit and like the wind that blows where it listeth, it must claim its right to pierce through the every crevice of human nature, and to describe the relation of the soul and the heart to the facts of life and of law, and to describe that relation as it is, not as we would have it be, and in so far as it fails to do this it fails to give us that foundation of understanding and charity for whose lack our moral sense can be but cruelty. It must be as incapable of telling a lie as nature, and it must sometimes say before all the virtues, 'The greatest of these is charity.' Sometimes the patriot will have to falter and the wife to desert her home, and neither be followed by divine vengeance or man's judgement. At other moments it must be content to judge without remorse, compelled by nothing but its own capricious spirit that has yet its message from the foundation of the world. Aristophanes held up the people of Athens to ridicule, and even prouder of that spirit than of themselves, they invited the foreign ambassadors to the spectacle.

'To describe that relation as it is, not as we would have it be' – both Synge and Yeats would assert that such things *did* happen in Ireland, Irish countrywomen did sometimes take lovers and the people told stories of such things. But Yeats's own primary commitment had been, and would continue to be, to an art that depicted life 'as we would have it be': thus in a lecture delivered in 1907 he spoke of the Celtic legends as 'the most powerful of all things, above all, because they pictured men and women as the poets would have them to be'.The ground he adopted here no doubt reflected the heat of journalistic controversy as well as the natural impulse to harmonise his views with Synge's own (as he perceived them). Yeats had in fact already completed a more impressive 'defence' of Synge, one not only consistent with but an overt celebration of his own position: *The King's Threshold.*[39]

IV

Catheleen ni Houlihan had been a popular success because it had fortuitously struck just the right note in the volatile political atmosphere of 1902, but as events would shortly demonstrate once again, a theatre such as Yeats envisaged was certain to find itself much of the time in conflict with what a large segment of the Nationalist audience *really* wanted. It seems ironic but predictable that a key force behind the popular opposition that developed was Yeats's own Queen Maud. Stephen Gwynn's account of the impact of *Catheleen ni Houlihan* stresses her contribution to it: 'I went home asking myself if such plays should be produced unless one was prepared for people to go out to shoot and be shot. Yeats was not alone responsible; no doubt Lady Gregory had helped him to get the peasant speech so perfect; but above all Miss Gonne's impersonation had stirred the audience as I have never seen another audience stirred.'[40] Political tension in Ireland increased in 1903, in part as a result of Edward VII's visit. Maud, now Mrs John MacBride, began attacking the Theatre. Early in the year she accused Willie Fay of having altered Padraic Colum's *The Saxon Shillin'* in order to weaken its political message. She withdrew from the Irish National Theatre Society and supported rival performances by the Cumann na nGaedheal Irish Theatre Society.[41] When *The Shadow of the Glen* was first read to the Irish National Theatre Society in June, it offended some of the players, including Dudley

Digges and Maire T . Quinn, who resigned from the group and took part in the Cumann na nGaedheal performances; they, along with Maud, were to walk out of the theatre when Synge's play was performed.[42] And William Martin Murphy's *Irish Independent* and Arthur Griffith's *United Irishman* waged a vicious campaign against the play for allegedly damaging Irish national aspirations.

In September 1903 Yeats wrote about the current situation with what now seems unwarranted optimism: 'I think that a political theatre would help us greatly in the end ... by making it easier for us to keep a pure artistic ideal. It will satisfy the propagandist feeling and at the same time make plain the great effectiveness of our work.'[43] In the *Samhain* of the same month he made several references to developing events. In one he mentioned Colum's play and said he had no doubt that there would be a good many more such plays in the next few years and perhaps even a permanent company of political players; in contrast, he went on, his own group 'has no propaganda but that of good art.' 'A pure artistic ideal' and 'good art' sound like Yeats the Rhymer, and in the *Samhain* passages he continued in the same vein, asserting that 'beauty and truth are always justified of themselves, and that their creation is a greater service to our country than writing that compromises either in the seeming service of a cause.' There was a certain caginess in his wording, the one statement implying that 'good art' might *function like* 'propaganda', the other vague about the ways in which beauty and truth might be a 'service to our country' – not just as national cultural treasures, but as agents of change.[44]

In 'The Theatre, the Pulpit, and the Newspapers', which appeared in Griffith's paper the week following the piece in which Yeats had explained the origins of *Cathleen ni Houlihan*, he referred directly to *The King's Threshold*: 'if the priest or the politician should say to the man of letters, "Into how dangerous a state of mind are you not bringing us?" the man of letters can but answer, "It is dangerous, indeed", and say, like my Seanchan, "when did we promise safety?" '(*UI*, 17 October 1903, p.2). At the same time, the Theatre was putting Yeats's principles into action by giving his new play its first performance on the same bill with *The Shadow of the Glen* and a revival of *Catheleen ni Houlihan*. Were they not all, the implication was, legitimately national drama?

The Gaelic text on which Yeats based *The King's Threshold* had been published in the fifth volume of the *Transactions of the Ossianic Society*, a series from which he had drawn a great deal in the mid–1880s. In 1895 he recommended to Katharine Tynan that she read Edwin Ellis's *'Scancan the Bard* . . . a poem on an Irish story out of Lady Wilde & . . . a bit of "The Celtic Revival" which may interest you' (*CL1* 424). In a note to his own play Yeats said it was 'founded on' an 'Old Irish Prose Romance', but that he had also 'borrowed some ideas for the arrangement of my subject . . . from "Sancan the Bard," a play published by Mr. Edwin Ellis some ten years ago' (*VPl* 314–5). Ellis in fact had heard the story originally from Yeats (*VPl* 1284). It is certainly not surprising that Yeats should have kept the tale in mind for so long, for it was obviously relevant to his own concerns about the role of the artist in society. But *The Shadow of the Glen* may have been responsible for heightening his sense of the importance of the story, perhaps even for his choosing to write a play based upon it just when he did. At the very least it must have lent added urgency to the process of composition at some point. There is a reference to *The King's Threshold* in a letter he sent Lady Gregory on 14 January 1903, but it is clear that composition, if begun at all, had not proceeded very far. Yeats heard a reading of *The Shadow of the Glen* by 2 February. He was at work on his own play not long afterwards; the first draft was dictated to Lady Gregory between 31 March and 11 April, and he finished the play in mid-August.[45] In June *The Shadow of the Glen* had already given rise to controversy within the Theatre Society and the potential for more trouble would have been clear as Yeats developed and completed the text.

In 1906 Yeats recalled the moment, saying the play 'was written when our Society was having a hard fight for the recognition of pure art in a community of which one half was buried in the practical affairs of life, and the other half in politics and a propagandist patriotism. I took the plot of it from a Middle Irish story about the demands of the poets at the court of King Guaire, but twisted it about and revised its moral that the poet might have the best of it' (*VPl* 315; also *VP* 843). Although Yeats was working on his play at the time he wrote to John Quinn about his efforts to 're-create an heroical ideal in manhood – in plays of old Irish life', the sources for *The King's Threshold* made them a somewhat improbable choice for use in such a project. Of course much of the legendary material had to be 'purified', unattractive elements purged, so it would serve the needs of modern writers; Cuchulain's grotesque 'distortions' represent an obvious example of troublesome material. But in this case, before the past could be held up as a model for the future, Yeats had to do more than just twist the story about: he had to turn it upside down, changing the swollen pride and absurd demands of the bards satirised in the Gaelic version into a fable about political and religious threats to legitimate poetic power.

The paradigm for this striking metamorphosis was of course Yeats's own aesthetic. At various points in the play, most of the key sources upon which he drew in developing that aesthetic manifest themselves in one way or another. Harold Bloom has gone so far as to claim that 'Shelley is the ultimate model for Seanchan, and *A Defence of Poetry* the deepest quarry for Sanchan's [*sic*] convictions.'[46] Perhaps the most brilliant evocation of the *Defence* comes at the very end of the play, where the King puts the crown on Seanchan's head, *acknowledging* him as 'legislator' because 'he has the greater power' (*VPl* 308). Yeats amplified these lines in an early revision (published in 1906) to give yet greater stress to 'power':

> There is no power but has its root in his –
> I understand it now. There is no power
> But his that can withold the crown or give it,
> Or make it reverent in the eyes of men,
> And therefore I have laid it in his hands, ... (*VPl* 308)

When Seanchan's Oldest Pupil recalls his master's claim that

> ... the poets hung
> Images of the life that was in Eden
> About the childbed of the world, that it,
> Looking upon those images, might bear
> Triumphant children ... (*VPl* 264)

his words combine a virtual paraphrase of a key passage in *The Decay of Lying* with Blake's 'all these things are written in Eden. The artist is an inhabitant of that happy country and if everything goes on as it has begun, the world of vegetation and generation may expect to be opened again to Heaven, through Eden, as it was in the beginning.'[47] In Seanchan's encounter with the Chamberlain, the former's assertion that

> ... none alive
> Would ride among the arrows with high heart

Or scatter with an open hand, had not
Our heady craft commended wasteful virtues ... (*VP1* 290)

is a verse equivalent of the passage from Yeats's contemporary
Preface to *Gods and Fighting Men* in which he had speculated about
how many hands the 'praise of kings and high-hearted queens' in
bardic literature had 'made hot upon the sword-hilt', and described
the Gaelic and Old English aristocracy who, having 'heard their
hereditary poets and story-tellers, ... took to horse and died
fighting', and their successors, the new aristocracy that 'listened to
no poetry indeed, but ... felt about it in the popular mind an
exacting and ancient tribunal, and began a play that had for
spectators men and women that loved the high wasteful virtues....'
Although now largely overshadowed by Lady Gregory's more
polished volumes, the work of O'Grady was still crucial here. And
when Seanchan tells the Chamberlain to

> ... shake your coat
> Where little jewels gleam on it, and say
> A herdsman, sitting where the pigs had trampled
> Made up a song about enchanted kings,
> Who were so finely dressed one fancied them
> All fiery, and women by the churn
> And children by the hearth caught up the song
> And murmured it, until the tailors heard it.... (*VPl* 290)

we can hear an echo of the passage in 'The Symbolism of Poetry' in
which Yeats had alluded to O'Shaughnessy and the world-shaping
power of 'something that a boy piped in Thessaly.' O'Shaughnessy's
lyric, ending with its 'Great hail! we cry to the comers / From the
dazzling unknown shore' would reverberate in Seanchan's call
(uttered as he returns the crown to the King's head) for the
trumpeters to 'cry to the great race that is to come' (*VPl* 311)

   The 'images' that will serve as models for that 'great race' come
from the divine, 'venerable things / God gave to men before he
gave them wheat', and men should guard them 'as the men of
Dea / Guard their four treasures, as the Grail King guards / His
holy cup, or the pale righteous horse / The jewel that is underneath
his horn ...' (*VPl* 265). As in so many of Yeats's earlier texts, the
matrix of associations surrounding those images includes pre-
Christian Celtic religion, fertility rituals, and other strands of occult

tradition. Later in the play Seanchan rejects Fedelm's urgings that they marry before harvest:

> ... it's a certainty,
> Although I never knew it till last night,
> That marriage, because it is the height of life,
> Can only be accomplished to the full
> In the high days of the year. I lay awake,
> There had come a frenzy into the light of the stars
> And they were coming nearer and I knew
> All in a minute they were about to marry
> Clods out upon the plough-lands, to beget
> A mightier race than any that has been. .... (*VPl* 301)

The hierosgamos, the sacred marriage of artist and Goddess or Muse, is here further linked to seasonal rituals. Significantly, Yeats does not depict in the play the actual coming of the new race. Seanchan, resisting Fedelm's temptation, tells her, 'If I had eaten when you bid me, sweetheart, / The kiss of multitudes in times to come had been the poorer' (*VPl* 305–6).The stratified social structure of king, lords, and commons in the play is perhaps intended to suggest the chain of gradual diffusion. *The King's Threshold* differs in this regard from *Cathleen ni Houlihan*, where the final suggestion is one of revolution or *imminent* change.

H.W.Nevinson, an English war correspondent and man of letters who greatly admired Yeats and sympathised with the Irish cause, saw *The King's Threshold* as a Nationalist allegory along the lines of the earlier play:

> The proud starvation of the poet inevitably suggests the proud refusal of Ireland to be satisfied with anything less than her highest claim, and the king, who protests his love, and is only frightened about 'the Crown' and its rights, is inevitably the hesitater, the trimmer, the 'Unionist' and half-hearted friend, who wants to keep on calling himself a Liberal, but is driven bit by bit to coercion and the hangman's rope.[48]

Nearer the mark, perhaps, is S. B. Bushrui's suggestion that the play contains 'a hidden message to Maud Gonne: the poet's treatment of Fedelm shows the resistance she would meet if she were to continue her efforts to involve Yeats in politics at the expense of his art.'[49] Fedelm may indeed owe something to Maud, but as the character's actual plan is to take Seanchan away to a pastoral retreat, it is hard to identify her with pressure to involve Yeats more fully in Nationalist activism: she seems in fact closer to Aleel, trying to draw the Countess away from the public realm of self-sacrifice into a private dream-world. A more accurate away of describing the opposition would be to identify Seanchan with the artist who, though his work *may* serve the cause of state, will not betray his artistic principles for *any* cause (the same point Yeats had made about *Cathleen ni Houlihan*); and all those who tempt him with the forces – external and within their own psyches – tempting modern Irish artists to do precisely that.

In this regard, the later history of the play seems ironic. Bushrui has suggested (119) that after Synge's death in 1909, Yeats began to feel the need to give his play the tragic ending he was later to claim he had always intended (*VPl* 313, 315–6); and making the change would have been consistent with the original identification of Seanchan with the artist at odds with the Nationalist movement over political expedience. but Yeats only changed the final scene after the death on hunger strike of Terence MacSwiney, Republican Lord Mayor of Cork, in 1920. Insofar as this new association is felt, the original vision of the play threatens to blur into an allegory of divisions between 'Die-hard' Republicans and all those, from more moderate Nationalists to the English monarch, who would accept something less than total independence. On the other hand, the new ending introduced some lines that link the play verbally with Yeats's programmatic texts about art and life from the 'Apologia . . .' to 'Under Ben Bulben'; while Seanchan's body is being borne away, the Youngest Pupil calls for 'triumphant music; . . . / For coming times will bless what he has blessed / And curse what he has cursed' (*VPl* 311).

V

Despite these lines, the final version of the play has a somberness that gives a misleading sense of Yeats's mood at the time of its composition and original production. At that point he was still able to adopt a generally optimistic attitude towards the prospects for success of his principles of national art. During the next three years he worked at strengthening his practical position. Early in 1904 he informed Lady Gregory of a plan for 'challenging Griffith to debate with me in public our two policies – his that literature should be subordinate to nationalism, and mine that it must have its own ideal.... He will refuse, of course, but the tactical advantage will be mine' (*L* 421–2). Yeats's unwillingness to sacrifice art to propaganda was a crucial factor in winning the support of Miss Horniman and thus in obtaining the Abbey Theatre and the annual subsidy. At the same time he was in his own eyes 'just as strenuous a Nationalist as ever' (*L* 432; *UP2* 257) and he had Fenian support.[50] But Maud Gonne and the patriotic clubs considered him lost to the movement (*L* 427, 445), and he devoted much of *Samhain* for 1904 to answering their criticisms and confidently reasserting his own principles. In doing so he returned to the implications of *The King's Threshold:* 'If literature is but praise of life, if our writers are not to plead the National Cause, nor insist upon the Ten Commandments, nor upon the glory of their country, what part remains for it, in the common life of the country. It will influence the life of the country immeasurably more, though seemingly less, than have our propagandist poems and stories.' And, defiantly, he asserted that 'Mr. Synge ... is truly a National writer.'[51]

1905 began with renewed attacks on *The Shadow of the Glen*, which had been revived as part of the Abbey's inaugural programme.[52] At the same time Yeats was involved in a new journalistic controversy with Griffith, he had written to Gilbert Murray, from whom he wanted a translation of *Oedipus Rex* for the Theatre, that 'nothing has any effect in England, but here one never knows when one may affect the mind of a whole generation. The country is in its first plastic state, and takes the mark of every strong finger.'[53] We can see his own strong fingers at work during 1905 in the reorganisation of the Theatre company so that he, Synge, and Lady Gregory had essential control.[54] Their principle was to refuse to add anyone to the group 'unless we were quite sure they would leave us independent as to politics and religion.'[55] In that November's *Samhain* Yeats defended the directors' position:

All fine literature is the disinterested contemplation or expression of life, but hardly any Irish writer can liberate his mind sufficiently from questions of practical reform for this contemplation. Art for art's sake, as he understands it, ... seems to him a neglect of public duty. It is as though the telegraph boys botanized among the hedges with the undelivered envelopes in

their pockets.... Till [these principles] are accepted by writers
and readers in this country it will never have a literature, it will
never escape from the election ryhme and the pamphlet. So long
as I have any control over the National Theatre Society it will be
carried on in this spirit, call it art for art's sake if you will; and no
plays will be produced at it which were written, not for the sake
of a good story or fine verses or some revelation of character, but
to please those friends of ours who are ever urging us to attack
the priests or the English, or wanting us to put our imagination
into handcuffs that we may be sure of never seeming to do one or
the other.[56]

Again in this passage his terminology reflects the need to assimilate
Synge, 'the pure artist' (*CA* 166) basically unsympathetic with the
supernatural element in Yeats's own art and perhaps without
Yeats's desire to use his art to shape the future of the nation.
Shortly after this, writing in the context of his own work, he
asserted more characteristically that 'all art is in the last analysis an
endeavour to condense as out of the flying vapour of the world an
image of human perfection, and for its own, and not for the art's
sake' (*VP* 849). That image, 'a new species of man' embodying
Unity of Being (*Au* 273), would in turn serve as a model for the
'Profane perfection of mankind'.

In October, Yeats wrote to Florence Farr that he was 'now
entirely certain that we will make a great Theatre and get an
audience for it' (*L* 463) The reorganisation of the company caused
the secession of Padraic Colum and several of the players, who
formed the rival Theatre of Ireland, dominated by individuals who
put nationalism before all else; the loss of talent was offset by the
increase in freedom and power for those who remainded.[57] Yeats's
optimism carried on through 1906, manifesting itself among other
ways in his plan to send out trained minstrels to reach rural
audiences inaccessible through books or from the Abbey stage.
That plan, as described in 'Literature and the Living Voice', was
presented as part of an effort to bring back the oral culture of
Ireland, largely submerged since the days of Raftery. Yeats had
recently attended a memorial ceremony in his honour and described
it at the beginning of the essay. He went on then to explore familiar
territory:

How the old is to come again, how the other side of the penny is
to come up, how the spit is to turn the other side of the meat to

the fire, I do not know, but that the time will come I am certain; when one kind of desire has been satisfied for a long time it becomes sleepy, and other kinds, long quiet, after making a noise begin to order life. Of the many things, desires or powers or instruments, that are to change the world, the artist is fitted to understand but two or three, and the less he troubles himself about the complexity that is outside his craft, the more will he find it all within his craft, and the more dexterous will his hand and his thought become. I am trying to see nothing in the world but the arts, and nothing in this change – which one cannot prove but only foretell – but the share my own art will have in it.

One thing is entirely certain. Wherever the old imaginative life lingers it must be stirred into life, and kept alive, and in Ireland this is the work, it may be, of the Gaelic movement. But the nineteenth century, with its moral zeal, its insistence upon irrelevant interests, having passed over, the artist can admit that he cares about nothing that does not give him a new subject or a new technique. Propaganda would be for him a dissipation, but he may compare his art, if he has a mind to, with the arts that belonged to a whole people, and discover, not how to imitate the external form of an epic or a folk song, but how to express in some equivalent form whatever in the thoughts of his own age seem, as it were, to press into the future.[58]

The homely metaphors of penny and cooking spit represent 'Apollonic' equivalents of the apocalyptic imagery typical of his work in the nineties, but they reveal the same concern with the difficult question of the relationship between Yeats's aesthetic and his commitment to a cyclical theory of history. This issue would concern him regularly and would underline such major late poems as 'The Statues' and 'Under Ben Bulben'. Most generally, the question was how much influence art could have, if the basic patterns of human experience were already fixed. A passage from *On the Boiler* epitomises the uncertainty: '. . . We may, if we choose, not now or soon but at the next turn of the wheel, push ourselves up . . . beyond [Classical Greek civilisation]. But no, these things are fated; we may be pushed up' (*OB* 29). More specifically, were some eras more propitious than others? The historical process itself being dominated by an unchanging pattern involving the alternation of antithetical eras and burgeoning and decline within each era, presumably some eras, and portions of every era, would by

their nature be less receptive than others; consequently the strength
of the artist's influence and the time required for it to be felt must
vary with the whirling of the gyres.[59] First the *fin de siècle* and the
dawn of the new century were natural points at which to expect
change, and at the present moment Yeats was inclined to feel
hopeful. The ambiguity of 'At Galway Races', a poem written in
1908, points towards an underlying ambivalence that may reflect a
darkening mood. In a present dominated by merchants and clerks,
the artists, who 'had good attendance once', have lost their
audience; but things *will* get better:

> Sing on: sometime, and at some new moon
> We'll learn that sleeping is not death,
> Hearing the whole earth change its tune,
> Its flesh being wild, and it again
> Crying aloud as the race course is,
> And we find hearteners among men
> That ride upon horses. (*VP* 266, 1910 version)

The first published version of the first line quoted read 'But some
day and at some new moon'; the added clause 'Sing on' *might* have
been intended to suggest that the artists' 'singing will *cause* the
change, and this suggestion would be reinforced by the extension
of the musical metaphor in 'change its tune'. But 'Hearing' indicates a passive role and even the revised text could mean no more
than that the artists must keep working through the dark times till
the beginning of a new, more congenial cycle. During the years
from 1907 on, events would sometimes lead to fears of impotence –
fears epitomised in a passage from the final version of *The King's
Threshold* (1921–2)

> . . . nor song nor trumpet-blast
> Can call up races from the worsening world
> To mend the wrong and mar the solitude
> Of the great shade we follow to the tomb. (*VPl* 312)

But there would be, too, other periods in which the more confident
voice would make itself heard again.

VI

The two major events that made 1907 a year of discouragement
were the controversy over *The Playboy of the Western World* in

January, and the death of John O'Leary in March. In Yeats's mind, these events were symbolically interconnected. F.S.L.Lyons noted that from 1900 on, with the end of the nine-year split in the Parliamentary Party, conservative, middle-class nationalism was in the ascendant in Ireland and 'romantic nationalism was at a discount'[60] – though there was of course still a common tendency to romaticise Irish life and history, sacrificing one's self or one's life for the cause seemed anachronistic. During the *Playboy* riots Yeats had commented on those developments: 'When I was a lad, Irishmen obeyed a few leaders; but during the last ten years a change has taken place. For leaders we have now societies, clubs, and leagues. Organised opinion of sections and coteries has been put in place of these leaders, one or two of whom were men of genius. Instead of a Parnell, a Stephens, or a Butt, we must obey the demands of commonplace and ignorant people, who try to take on an appearance of strength by imposing some crude shibboleth on their own and others' necks.'[61] These groups organised much of the opposition to *The Playboy*; and although Yeats thought he discerned a younger generation already wearying of the 'tyranny' of the clubs and leagues (*UP2* 352, Ex 228), that generation in fact failed to become a significant counter-force; and with O'Leary's death it seemed that Ireland had lost perhaps the last of the old leaders.

O'Leary died on March 16, 1907, and in 'Poetry and Tradition', finished in August of the same year, Yeats treated his death as the watershed between the era of the leaders and the era of the clubs. In this essay, which might be considered a scenario for 'September 1913', O'Leary served as epitome of the old 'romantic conception of Irish Nationality' – on which, as Yeats noted, his own art had been largely founded. He and the other figures of the early years of the modern literary movement, drawing upon 'heroic legend' (*CA* 120) and a spiritualist philosophy 'so mixed into the common scenery of the world, that it would set the whole man on fire' (yet another echo of the first Ferguson essay of 1886), 'were to forge in Ireland a new sword on our old traditional anvil for that great battle that must in the end re-establish the old, confident, joyous world' (121). They did not foresee that 'as belief in the possibility of armed insurrection withered, the old romantic nationalism would wither too' and that 'a new class, which had begun to rise into power under the shadow of Parnell, would change the nature of the Irish movement, which, needing no longer great sacrifices, nor bringing any great risk to individuals, could do without exceptional men, and those activities of the mind that are founded on the exceptional moment.... Power passed to small shop-keepers, to clerks, to that very class who had seemed to John O'Leary so ready to bend to the power of others, to men who had risen above the traditions of the countryman, without learning those of cultivated life...' (136–8). As the reverberation of the word through these sentences suggests, the issue of power was once again very much in Yeats's mind, and the essay ends on an elegiac note: 'We artists, who are the servants not of any cause but of mere naked life, and above all of that life in its nobler forms, where joy and sorrow are one, Artificers of the Great Moment, became as elsewhere in Europe protesting individual voices. Ireland's great moment had passed...' (138). But if he was being forced to consider that 'that ideal Ireland' in whose service he would continue to labour might be 'perhaps from this out an imaginary Ireland' (116), he was also even in this essay turning to new myths that would prove vitally empowering for his efforts to realise that ideal Ireland in the years to come. The aristocrat has joined the peasant at opposite poles of the social spectrum, highlighting the deficiencies of the Paudeens in between. The eighteenth century, a 'splendid misunderstanding' in the Preface to *Gods and Fighting Men*, now emerged more positively as Yeats asserted that his opponents represented 'a type of mind which had been without influence in the generation of Grattan, and almost without it in that of Davis...' (122). The positive associations of Grattan's era were heightened by being linked with Castiglione, reflecting Yeats's recent reading of *The Book of the Courtier* and his visit to Italy in the spring of 1907[62]:

> If we would find a company of our own way of thinking, we must go backward to turreted walls, to courts, to high rocky places, to little walled towns, ... to the Duke Guidobaldo in his sickness, ... to all those who understood that life is not lived, if not lived for contemplation or excitement. (125–6)

The backward glance *here* seems largely nostalgic; at other times Yeats would recall that poets who had built Babylon and Nineveh might also make an Irish Urbino.

In the present, he continued to be subjected to conflicting pressures, fellow Nationalists wanting him to be more 'political' and Unionist supporters of his artistic projects questioning his national activities. His father, writing to console him about some recent attacks and disappointments, offered what must have been encouraging words by asserting that 'artists are the real leaders of mankind.... The ecclesiastics and moralists would build the palace for man to live in and leave the artist some side chapel, making it as small and noisome as possible. But no, it is we who must build and who do build man's dwelling' (*LTWBY* 217). Yeats's own journal entries of 1909 and 1910 reveal a predictable preoccupation with the problem of national literature. A series of entries for March 1909 began with the premise that 'there is a sinking away of national feeling ...' because Ireland lacked 'models' for the development of its identity (*Mem* 183–5). The Young Ireland movement had provided some simple images – 'Wolfe Tone, King Brian, Emmet, Owen Roe, Sarsfield, the Fisherman of Kinsale' – and Yeats's own movement 'began by trying to do the same thing in a more profound and enduring way.' But the advent of Synge made Yeats realise that the 'Irish people were not educated enough to accept as an image of Ireland anything more profound, more true of human nature as a whole, than the schoolboy thought of Young Ireland.' Consequently the modern Irish writers would 'have to give up the deliberate creation of a kind of Holy City in the imagination, a Holy Sepulchre, as it were, or Holy Grail for the Irish mind, and ... be content to express the individual.' This did not mean they could exert no shaping influence. 'You can only create a model of a race which will inspire the action of the race as a whole, as apart from exceptional individuals, if you share with it some simple moral understanding of life'; failing that shared understanding, the artists might still 'inspire the active life' of their nation, as Shakespeare and Milton did theirs, 'through exceptional individuals whose influence on the rest is indirect.' Meanwhile, from his own work and that of Lady Gregory, Synge, O'Grady, Katharine Tynan and Lionel Johnson, a school of journalists could cull models upon which they could 'build up an historical and literary nationalism as powerful as the old and nobler.'

In a subsequent entry he stressed once more the negative view, that 'in our age it is impossible to create, as I had dreamed, an heroic and passionate conception of life ... and to make that conception the special dream of the Irish people.' There was a time when he had thought of a profound union of opposites, 'a noble body for all eyes, a soul for subtle understandings, and, to unite these two, Eleusinian rites.' But for the present, it now seemed, there could only be short-term expedients and 'the Irish people till

they are better educated must dream impermanent dreams ...'
(*Mem* 185). Only two days later he was speculating more optimistically that 'the success of the Saturday *Daily Express* under Gill
proved that the ideas of cultivated life could at this moment be
made most powerful in *Ireland*' and the right individuals could found
'a new *Nation*' that 'could change the future of Ireland' (*Mem* 186–7).

A short time later Synge was dead. This event seemed to Yeats
even more symbolic than O'Leary's death; it provoked him to great
personal bitterness towards Synge's enemies (*Mem* 200–4), but also
to renewed efforts to satisfy himself about the issues raised once
more by the work of his friend. In May of 1910, he and Maud
Gonne revived their old argument about the attacks on Synge, and
there was still passion on both sides (*Mem* 247). He determined to
include in his essay 'J. M. Synge and the Ireland of his Time' (dated
14 September 1910) a statement about national literature.[63] Entries
in the journal offer a glimpse of that statement in the process of
formulation.

He began with the observation that work such as Synge's (or his
own), 'created for its own sake or for some eternal spiritual need
can be used by politicians ... but it seldom can be used at once.' At
the period he and Maud had disputed about, he 'did not know this'
– in fact, it would be more accurate to say that the controversies
about Synge had reinforced a lesson already painfully learned but
to that point still partly resisted. He then went on to define quite
explicitly the nature of the art-life dynamic as he now saw it: 'A
nation can only be created in the deepest thought of its deepest
minds ... who have first made themselves fundamental and profound and then realized themselves in art. In this way they rouse
into national action the governing minds of their [time] – few at any
one time – by an awakening of their desire towards a certain mood
and thought which is unconscious to these governing minds themselves. They create national character' (*Mem* 247–8). In describing
the process of transmission he referred back specifically to *The
King's Threshold*:

> The more unconscious the creation, the more powerful. A great
> statesman, let us say, should keep his conscious purpose for
> practical things. But he should have grown into and find about
> him always, most perhaps in the minds of women, the nobleness
> of emotion created and associated with his country by its great
> poets. If a man is not born into this, he cannot acquire it if he is to

do anything else, for it will fill all his life. This is the golden cradle which in my *King's Threshold* Seanchan would prepare for his future children. It is this culture that makes the birth of heroes possible. . . . (*Mem* 248–9)

When the play is thus translated into contemporary terms, the significance of the dearth of leaders in twentieth-century Ireland becomes clear. We can see here also the seeds of the hopes Yeats would later rest upon a figure such as Kevin O'Higgins.

During this period, a visit with Maud to Mont-Saint-Michel precipitated further thoughts about the relationship between history and the power of art. The Unity of Culture that the abbey seemed to represent was not currently possible – 'Thought old enough to be a habit cannot face modern life and shape educated men. . . .' Yet the urge to try was irrepressible:

When I try to create a national literature, for all that, do I not really mean an attempt to create this impossible thing after all, for the very reason that I always rouse myself to work by imagining an Ireland as much a unity in thought and feeling as ancient Greece and Rome and Egypt. . .? Am I not therefore un-national in any sense the common man can understand? . . . I must . . . be content to be but artist, one [of] a group, Synge, Lady Gregory – no, there is no other than these – who express something which has no direct relation to action. We three have conceived an Ireland that will remain imaginary more power-fully than we have conceived ourselves. The individual victory was but a separation from casual men as a necessary thing before we could become naturalized in that imaginary land which is, as it were, the tradition-bound people of the West made independent from America or from London, and living under its own princes. (*Mem* 250–1)

Decades later these meditations would re-emerge in 'The Statues' and in 'The Municipal Gallery Re-visited' (not only in the lines about Synge, Lady Gregory and himself but also in the earlier passage in which the poet sees that the works around him depict '"not . . . / The dead Ireland of my youth, but an Ireland / The poets have imagined, terrible and gay"').

In 'J. M. Synge and the Ireland of his Time' Yeats drew heavily upon the meditations in the journals, and further explored the issues involved. He made it clear that he could sympathise with the *efforts* of the Young Irelanders, who had rightly 'understood that a country which has no national institutions must show its young men images for the affections . . .' (CA 148–9). Their error lay in the attempt to influence the masses directly, for 'ideas and images which have to be understood and loved by large numbers of people, must appeal to no rich personal experience, no patience of study, no delicacy of sense. . . .' In other contexts he might have said that they were, in fact, not *visionary* artists, had no contact with the Moods, their work embodied not the Divine Ideas but rather abstract moral conceptions; the terms of this essay clearly reflect his 'Apollonic' emphasis during these years and also the pressure to accommodate Synge's art and values to his own. Later in the essay he would make a similar effort by way of the image of the mirror. Synge's plays had seemed strange to audiences because of an apparent distortion:

> The imaginative writer shows us the world as a painter does his picture, reversed in a looking-glass that we may see it, not as it seems to eyes habit has made dull, but as we were Adam and this the first morning; and when the new image becomes as little strange as the old we shall stay with him, because he has, besides, the strangeness, not strange to him, that made us share his vision, sincerity that makes us share his feeling. (191)

Thus Synge's plays, like Seanchan's verse, place 'Images of the life that was in Eden' about the childbeds of the Irish nation. A related act of accommodation is discernible in a passage in which Yeats suggests that 'it was . . . to seek that old Ireland which took its mould from the duellists and scholars of the eighteenth century and from generations older still, that Synge returned again and again to Aran, to Kerry, and to the wild Blaskets' (167). Years later in a draft of 'The Tower' Yeats would link himself to 'John Synge and those people of Grattan'; later still, in 'The Statues,' Cuchulain and Bishop Berkeley, the old Gaelic world and the Anglo-Irish tradition, are connected harmoniously as forces contributing to the character of the Ireland that will emerge with the next reversal of the gyres.

In the final paragraphs of the essay Yeats drew a distinction between 'popular and picturesque' writers such as Burns and Scott, who 'can but create a province', and Homer, Dante, Shakespeare, and Goethe, whose more profound work helped forge the conscience of their races; in this second group he placed Synge, who, 'like all the great kin, sought for the race, not through the eyes or in history, or even in the future, but where those monks found God, in the depths of the mind.' (Here 'Dionysiac' terminology has reappeared.) At the moment it might seem that Synge had failed, but 'in all art like his, although it does not command – indeed because it does not – may lie the roots of far-branching events.' Only that art 'which does not teach, which does not cry out, which does not persuade, which does not condescend, which does not explain, is irresistible. It is made by men who expressed themselves to the full, and it works through the best minds. . . .' The final lines return to the idea of the men of action who will do their work better if they are surrounded by 'the nobleness of emotion associated with the scenery and events of their country by those great poets who have dreamed it in solitude, and who to this day in Europe are creating indestructible spiritual races' (193–5).

Yeats's own plays, themselves dramatisations of 'the deeps of the mind' (*E&I* 224; also *IGE* 29), were intended to carry on the same work.[66] In 1910, however, the theatre that had been founded to show that Ireland was 'the home of an ancient idealism' was dominated by Padraic Colum's sordid *Thomas Muskerry* and the emergence of the 'Cork Realists', Lennox Robinson, T. C. Murray, and R. J. Ray.[65] Robinson himself defined the new emphasis as a conscious reaction against the Yeatsian vision of Ireland:

> We young men, a generation later than Yeats ... didn't see [Ireland] as a queen, didn't see her all fair in purple and gold, we loved her as truly as Yeats ... and the rest – maybe we loved her more deeply, but just because we loved her so deeply her faults were clear to us. Perhaps we realists saw her faults too clearly, perhaps we saw her too often as a grasping, middle-aged hag. She was avaricious, she was mean, for family pride she would force a son into the Church against his will, she would commit arson, she would lie, she would cheat, she would murder and yet we would write all our terrible words about her out of our love.[66]

It is obvious that such a response reflects a fundamental misunderstanding of Yeats's art. He was at this very time just as well aware of the reality of old Paudeen fumbling 'in a greasy till'. Where he and the Realists differed was in their conceptions of how

art might change things for the better, they imagining an art that
would effect change by revolting the Paudeens themselves with
their own images in the mirror (as Joyce had once told a recalcitrant
publisher dragging his feet about *Dubliners* that he would 'retard
the course of civilisation in Ireland by preventing the Irish people
from having one good look at themselves in my nicely polished
looking- glass'[67]); whereas Yeats, as we know, thought no change
possible without positive models for the people to emulate. In
addition, the merely mimetic conventions of realistic drama
worked against his efforts to bring the supernatural and 'an ideal of
beauty' onto the stage.[68] In the modern theatre, realism was 'the
delight ... of all those whose minds, educated alone by schoolmasters and newspapers, are without the memory of beauty and
emotional subtlety' (*E&I* 227). Herein lay one source of his fear that
such an audience, the very audience most needing to be reached,
could not be changed *directly* by *any* art.

The early versions of *The Player Queen*, written during the years
1908–1910, reflect such concerns. In one passage the Player Queen
declares she 'must be Herodias, or Maeve, or the Queen of Sheba
...' but her rival in the acting troupe says 'That is no use. He will
never let you play any of those parts because the people don't like
them any more. They want somebody like themselves. What do
they care about great people?'[69] In another version of the same
passage the audience is said to prefer 'people like themselves,
pettish, troublesome, ordinary people like Noah'wife ...' (82).
However, some of these early versions, unlike the play in its
finished form, derive their central dramatic structure from Yeats's
own paradigm of a life-moulding art. In those versions the poet
Yellow Martin (the Septimus of the published texts) has written a
play called *The Queen of Babylon* that has inspired the Player Queen
to emulate a real queen. The Player Queen herself particularly
admired 'one great scene in the fourth act where she outfaces the
mob who'd stormed the palace' (83). In the final act of Yeats's play
she, too, outfaces the mob, and when she tells the people 'I seek my
death because I think it well, instead of a few more years of
lessened royalty, to choose a death that shall be a life forever and,
as it were, mock at you with a sweet laughter' (238), Yellow Martin
reveals that 'those very words are not her own, but from a play I
once thought to write' (239). There is a definite connection here
between Yeats's aesthetic and his developing concept of the Mask
or Antithetical Self (*VPl* 761), the idea that 'all happiness depends

on the energy to assume the mask of some other life, on a re-birth as something not one's self, something created in a moment and perpetually renewed' (*Myth* 334). This concept convinced him that 'every passionate man ... is, as it were, linked with another age, historical or imaginary, where alone he finds images that rouse his energy' (*Au* 152). Significantly, Yeats's poem 'The Mask' is supposed to have been part of yellow Martin's play (214) and is linked throughout the drafts with the Player Queen. In one version the Chancellor tells the real Queen that 'Queens that have laughed to set the world at ease / ... but stir our wonder / That they may stir their own, and grow at length / Almost alike to that unlikely strength' (208) – a link between the play and 'Old Memory'. It is tempting to speculate that the autobiographical matrix of this aspect of the play lay in Yeats's feeling that his 'old play' about a 'queen", and presumably various of his other works such as *The Countess Cathleen* as well, had inspired Maud (who had literally played the role in *Cathleen ni Houlihan*) to behave like a queen facing down threatening enemies.

In a different version of the speech in which the Player Queen defies the mob, she had taunted them: 'Your father's [*sic*] lives and the lives of their fathers before them were but twigs woven into the nest that gave the eagle birth. Who amongst you dares to face this eagle?' (94–5). The 'eagle' image, too, was supposed to have been in Yellow Martin's play: the Queen there 'speaks of her fathers as the true eagles – here she feels their eyes looking to her, and at the end she goes to death so firmly and sure' (252–3). The Player Queen offers her similar self-possession as proof of her royal blood, asking 'do you think that you will make them believe that anyone could speak with so much calm as I am speaking, with such quiet breath, death being so near, and have no royalty in her?' (239) Such a description evokes the learned self-possession in the face of death of the heroine of Yeats's own *Deirdre*, at the end of which the 'eagle' image appears: 'Eagles have gone into their cloudy bed' (*VPl* 387).[70] In one version of the passage in which the Player Queen speaks of her desire to play a queen's part, she says 'I must grow greater and make all those that look upon me grow greater' (202), replicating the pattern found in both 'Old Memory' and *Deirdre* in which the heroine imitates ancient queens and, having come to embody similar strength, becomes a model for yet others. At the end of this version, the Player Queen crowns the Chancellor as King (243–4); as Yellow Martin's art has made her queen, here as in *The King's*

Threshold with its climactic 'crowning' scene, royal power ultimately derives from the artist. The 'eagle' image has a proleptic connection with yet another of Yeats's works about noble behaviour and the power of art, 'To a Wealthy Man ...', which contains a reference to the Lane pictures as 'the right twigs for an eagle's nest'.

Yeats had immense difficulties in writing *The Player Queen*, and was so dissatisfied with the early versions that he laid them aside and did little or no work on the play between 1910 and 1915. In the new version that finally emerged Septimus appears as 'a con- servator of traditional values and as a prophet who knows what is wrong with the world and would like to change it' but fails to do so (454). Lying drunk on the stage and raving while various characters mock him, he seems a parody of Seanchan. Moreover, the device of his 'old play' disappears and the art-life aesthetic is no longer formative, possibly because it did not seem compatible with the 'farce' into which he converted the play (*VPl* 761). Perhaps, as Yeats suggested, the change to farce was essential to the nature of his material; but had the play in its earlier form been completed and performed in 1910 it would certainly have provided fare un- palatable to the audiences that appreciated the Cork Realists.[71]

Concerns similar to those pervading the early drafts of *The Player Queen* may also at least partly define the context of his obscure little lyric 'The Realists', first published in December, 1912:

> Hope that you may understand!
> What can books of men that wive
> In a dragon-guarded land,
> Paintings of the dolphin-drawn
> Sea-nymphs in their pearly waggons
> Do, but awake a hope to live
> That had gone
> With the dragons? (*VP* 309; 1914 version)

Yeats's brilliant use of syntax and word placement, enjambment and caesura, alerts the reader to the most important word in the poem, 'Do'. The question is precisely one of efficacy. To a realist, art devoted to heroic and romantic visions seems remote from contemporary life, irrelevant. Anyone with such an attitude would have found it difficult indeed to 'understand' the letter in which Yeats had told the Duchess of Sutherland that 'our Celtic books mean to me not in the end books but in the end a most passionate kind of life – a present revery, "calling up a new age, calling to mind the queens that were imagined long ago" as I say in the poem of a fair woman.' The foundation of the poem, therefore, and the answer to its question, is the same paradox Yeats had formulated in regard to Synge's work – 'It will influence the life of the country immeasurably more, though seemingly less,' than realistic art. Yeats later wrote two poems on the subject of men wiving in a dragon-guarded land, 'Michael Robartes and the Dancer' and 'Her Triumph'.[72]

VII

Both the period at which Yeats wrote 'The Realists' and the reference to 'paintings' link the poem also to a contemporary affair that at first seemed to offer 'hope' for Ireland's future but in its collapse compounded the discouragements following O'Leary's death, the loss of Synge, and the dominance of the Realists at the Abbey. The controversy over Hugh Lane's plan to give Dublin a valuable collection of modern paintings once again brought to the fore the issue of art's power to affect the life of a nation; this was especially true of Sir Edward Lutyens's spectacular design for a bridge gallery, which would have facilitated the transaction by bringing Dubliners into contact with the pictures not on rare special occasions but, presumably, as part of daily routine.[73] 'Shocked Montreal' had hidden the Discobolus in a cellar, but 'Dublin is the capital of a nation, and an ancient race has nowhere else to look for an education' (*VP* 818). The project fell through, largely, in Yeats's eyes, as the result of opposition from the same class that had opposed *The Playboy*: 'our new middle class which showed as its first public event, during the nine years of the Parnellite split, how base at moments of excitement are minds without culture ' (*VP* 820). Yeats would return to that 'baseness' in 'Under Ben Bulben'. The opposition also included Maud Gonne, who disliked Lane for reasons that had nothing to do with art and in one hate-filled letter revealed a passionate desire to 'show him up' in *Sinn Fein*. Opposition from such a quarter was disappointing not only for the obvious personal reasons but also because, as Yeats had speculated in his journal, it might be 'in the minds of women' that an Irish statesman would find 'the nobleness of emotion created and associated with his country by its great poets' (*Mem* 248–9). And Lord Ardilaun's lack of enthusiasm was a further disappointment. In 'Poetry and Tradition' Yeats had claimed that aristocracies had helped make 'all beautiful things', for 'being without fear, they have held to whatever pleased them' (*CA* 124) instead of asking 'the people' what to do. Yeats's corrrespondence shows that 'To a Wealthy Man . . .' was received positively by at least one aristocrat, Lady Alix Egerton, as well as provoking a hostile response from William Martin Murphy. In writing a poem on a topical subject Yeats was taking a considerable artistic risk; as he said in a contemporary interview, 'the poet is always looking for the things that do not change from generation to generation. But if he deals with politics, he must think of his audience, and that is entirely destructive. The moment he begins to think of his audience, he begins to think not of what is true and beautiful, but of what will appear true and beautiful to the people he is addressing. I feel this all the more strongly because in Ireland there is a great temptation to write about politics and patriotism'. Apparently he was willing to take the chance in this instance because so much was at stake: 'Ireland is now plastic', but 'If Sir Hugh Lane is defeated, hundreds of young men and women all over the country will be discouraged – will choose a poorer ideal, it might be'.[74] Again in 'To a Wealthy Man . . .' we see Yeats exemplifying the process about which he is writing. The images from Castiglione lauded in 'Poetry and Tradition' are evoked in the poem as models from the past upon which the Irish aristocrat might cast his mind – evoked in vain. The description of the Renaissance 'sucking at the dugs of Greece' drives ultimately from 'The Decay of Lying'; and the final lines,

> Look up in the sun's eye and give
> What the exultant heart calls good
> That some new day may breed the best
> Because you gave, not what they would
> But the right twigs for an eagle's nest! (*VP* 288; 1913 version)

employing an avian version of Wilde's statues in bridal chambers, represent a further anticipation of the 'coming days' of 'Under Ben Bulben'.

In March, 1913, Yeats wrote to the *Irish Times* urging Dubliners to support the gallery so that 'our children's children will love their town the better, and have a better chance of that intellectual happiness which sets the soul free from the vicissitudes of fortune' (*L* 579–80). 'To a Shade', written after the plan had clearly failed, links Parnell's opponents to those of Lane, 'who had brought / In his full hands what, had they only known, / Had given their children's children loftier thought, / Sweeter emotion, working in their veins / Like gentle blood ...' (*VP* 292–3). The letter stressed art's power to bring men's souls to God, and a few years later Yeats the new father would write of his hopes for his own child's future happiness in similar terms in 'A Prayer for my Daughter'; 'To a Shade' emphasised the profane strengthening of racial fibre. Yeats's discouragement about the Lane Gallery plan affected also 'September 1913'; although it was a more general indictment of the new Nationalists, its original subtitle was 'On reading much of the correspondence against the Art Gallery' (*VP* 289) and in it Yeats once again interprets the current controversy in the terms of 'Poetry and Tradition'. The impact of the affair can even be seen in the poem 'Peace', written in May, 1910, apparently just before the re-newed arguments with Maud about Synge. The drafts, echoing the lines in 'Old Memory' about the beloved's 'strength ... call[ing] up a new age', had referred to the artists painting her noble form 'Till they had roused us to that strength' (*Mem* 245–6). This line did not appear in the poem the first two times it was published; it was restored, slightly altered, in a 1912 printing, then deleted sometime between 1913 and 1917 (*VP* 258–9). The changes may reflect Maud's opposition and the collapse of the Lane scheme. In December, 1916, as part of Yeats's energetic campaign for the return of the pictures, he argued that Dublin *needed* the pictures more than London; he had based his 'whole life' on the conviction 'that it is more important to give fine examples of high art to a country that is still plastic, still growing, than to an old country where national character has been formed for centuries' (*UP2* 418).

'The Grey Rock' (published in April, 1913), another poem from the era of the Gallery controversy, shows Yeats reaffirming in verse his assertion in the *Samhain* of November, 1905 that 'so long as I have any control over the National Theatre Society it will be carried on in this spirit, call it art for art's sake if you will; and no plays will be produced at it which were written, not for the sake of a good story or fine verses or some revelation of character, but to please those friends of ours who are ever urging us to attack the priests or the English, or wanting us to put our imagination into handcuffs that we may be sure of never seeming to do one or the other.' Yeats addressed the poem to his fellow Rhymers, whose association with 'art for art's sake' would enable them to appreciate its 'moral'. In praising them for having

> *. . . never made a poorer song*
> *That you might have a heavier purse,*
> *Nor gave loud service to a cause*
> *That you might have a troop of friends . . .* (VP 270–6)

Yeats was obviously identifying himself with them; they and he alike had *'kept the Muses' sterner laws'*. Presicely what that meant in *Yeats's* case requires some consideration of the Irish legend he adapted as the vehicle for his parable. In incidents supposedly concerned with the Battle of Clontarf (1014), the goddess Aoibhell appeared to Brian Boru and warned him in vain that he would be killed in the battle; she also gave to her favourite, Dunlaing O'Hartigan, the gift of invisibility, but he cast it off to be equal with his friend Murrough and they too were killed. In other circumstances Yeats might have treated such a refusal as a positive act, an example of heroic recklessness, but here he made it a betrayal of principle. Aoibhell (Aoife in the poem), like Hanrahan's Cleena, is a Muse figure, the Grey Rock her Parnassus; and, being a goddess, she suggests *supernatural* inspiration (*VP* 802; see also *Ex* 283). Dunlaing, claiming 'his country's need was most', was untrue to her; Yeats, in contrast, had kept *his* faith, *'though faith was tried, | To that rock-born, rock-wandering foot.'*

Although it was *'the loud host before the sea, | That think sword strokes were better meant | Than lover's music'* who had pressed Yeats to put the needs of country before all, the poem also reveals a subtle tension with Lady Gregory's play *Kincora*, finished in July 1904 and almost at once put into rehearsal for the Abbey.[75] In a contemporary letter Synge revealed that several of the players preferred it to plays by Yeats and himself and speculated that this preference might be a sign of the continuing influence of the 'Neo-patriotic-Catholic clique' in the Theatre.[76] The source of the play's appeal to that group is easy to see. It opened with a scene in which Aoibhell appeared to Brian (one of the Young Irelanders' 'simple images') and sought to tempt him: 'I am come to bid you give up the sweetheart you have chosen, that hard sweetheart, Ireland. Come to me in place of her and I will bring you into the hidden houses of the hills. . . .' Brian's refusal was couched in explicity patriotic terms: 'I will not go with you; I will not give up Ireland. For it is a habit of my race to fight and to die, but it never was their habit to see shame or oppression put on their country by any man on earth. . . . *I will never break my faith with the sweetheart I have chosen* nor turn from her service till she can lift up her head in the sight of the whole world!' Later in the play she appeared to Murrough in a virtually identical scene. He, too, rejected her, comdemning her as a 'demon'.[77]

Yeats frequently expressed positive opinions of the play, which was first performed on March 25, 1905, but one serious reservation appeared in his responses.[78] On April 26, Joseph Holloway recorded in his diary the opinion that 'the "Murrough" and "Aoibhell" incident, though full of noble patriotic sentiment, ought to go.' He 'had a chat with W. B. Yeats and Lady Gregory after the play on this matter, and they agreed that something was required to be done with those scenes, but what it was they had not as yet settled upon. . . .'[79] Lady Gregory eventually rewrote the entire play; in the new version both the 'Aoibhell' scenes were deleted and she was only referred to in passing. Yeats's opinion of the change is suggested by an entry he made in his journal in 1909. W. A. Henderson had expressed a preference for the earlier version, to which Yeats had replied, 'The old version pleased the half-educated because of its rhetoric; the new displeases because of its literature' (*Mem* 167). 'Rhetoric', the word so often used by Yeats for low-quality, propagandistic art, here must mean the 'noble patriotic sentiment' Holloway had praised. The germ from which 'The Grey Rock' grew appeared in the same journal a year later, at a period between the death of Synge and the thoughts about national literature that were carried over into 'J. M. Synge and the Ireland of his Time': 'I would write a poem I had long thought of about the man who left Aoibhinn of Craiglea to die at Clontarf and put in it all the bitter feeling one has sometimes about Ireland. The life of faery would be my lyric life' (*Mem* 241). From these facts we can reasonably conclude that at one level 'The Grey Rock' was Yeats's own rewriting of *Kincora*, a rewriting in which the offending portions were not omitted but rather preserved and given a totally opposite significance – signalled in the inverted echo of Brian's 'I will never break my faith. . . .' But although 'The Grey Rock' shows Yeats continuing to stand firm in the face of ongoing widespread opposition and multiple discouragements, it also reflects one of those moods in which he apparently found no comfort in the concept of artistic power bridging the gap between being faithful to the Muse and serving the needs of his country.

Although 'The Dolls' was written in September, 1913, after the collapse of the Lane Gallery scheme and coeval with the poetic lament for O'Leary and romantic Ireland, it does not at first glance seem to be connected with such issues; but Yeats's own note to the poem draws attention to its origin in the contemporary Irish matrix of controversy concerning art and patriotism. He revealed that 'the fable for this poem came into my head while I was giving some lectures in Dublin. I had noticed once again how all thought among us is frozen into "something other than human life"'(*VP* 820). Ten years earlier, in a 1903 essay concerning the controversy over *The Shadow of the Glen*, he had characterised the opposition to Synge as an opposition to 'life' by the 'enemies of life' (*Ex* 119–21). For life these enemies substituted generalisations, 'partisan fictions'. The task of the artists was to shatter these 'wooden images': 'The man of letters looks at those kneeling worshippers who had given up life for a posture, whose nerves have dried up in the contemplation of lifeless wood. He swings his silver hammer and the keepers of the temple cry out, prophesying evil, but he must not mind their cries and their prophecies, but break the wooden necks in two and throw down the wooden bodies. Life will put living bodies in their place till new image-brokers have set up their benches.' A decade later, the opposition of life and the artists on the one hand and repressive patriotic and religious forces and wooden images on the other, reappeared in Yeats's poem.

In his journal for March 6, 1909, Yeats recorded a meeting with the Nationalist poet Thomas MacDonagh in which he was discouraged to find that MacDonagh's political activities were affecting him adversely: 'He is being crushed by the mechanical logic and commonplace eloquence which gives the most power to the most empty mind because, being "something other than human life" it has no use for distinguished feeling or individual thought' (*Mem* 177–8). The use of Blake's phrase here to describe the current atmosphere is another anticipation of 'The Dolls'.[80] Shortly after this Yeats wrote 'On those that hated "The Playboy of the Western World", 1907' (April 5, 1909), in which the Nationalist groups are depicted as eunuchs staring upon the virile power of the artist. At the same period, he reflected in his journal upon Maud's recent efforts to learn Gaelic: 'I fear for her any renewed devotion to an opinion. Women, because the main event of their lives has been a giving of themselves, give themselves to an opinion as if [it]were some terrible stone doll. . . . They grow cruel, as if [in] defense of lover or child, and all this is done for something other than human life. At last the opinion becomes so much a part of them that it is as though a part of their flesh becomes, as it were, stone, and much of their being passes out of life. . . . Women should have their play with dolls finished in childish happiness, for if they play with them again it is amid hatred and malice' (*Mem* 191–2).

With this background in mind, we can see that certain elements in 'The Dolls' reflect early twentieth-century disputes over national art. The 'baby' corresponds to the vital depiction of experience in the work of Synge, Yeats, and the other true artists. The 'dolls' suggest their opponents among their fellow Nationalists, trumpeting Irish virtues ('. . . There's not a man can report / Evil of this place') and asserting that the offensive art they are being offered is not genuinely Irish at all, but imported 'hither' from France, decadent Greece, or England. Mother and infant together link this poem, too, to the image of artistic power in 'The Decay of Lying', but at this point any precise allegorical interpretation becomes problematical. Instead of statues of Greek gods we have the clearly negative dolls. Their 'parents' would seem to have to play a double role: leaders of Nationalist public opinion on one hand, the artists themselves on the other. Perhaps a distinction is implied between the influence of the artist when putting art before all and when immersed in partisan quarrels. Yeats did suggest such a distinction in a journal entry contrasting his own response to Synge's enemies with his father's: 'I fought them, he was nobler – he forgot them' (*Mem* 161); and in his famous maxim that out of the quarrels with others we make rhetoric, of the quarrels with ourselves, poetry (*Myth* 331). It seems most likely, however , that what began as a poem grounded in parochial Irish concerns moved increasingly during the process of composition towards an exploration of ontological questions involving Neoplatonism and 'incarnation'[81]. The political level would then represent a sort of palimpsest. Its web of associations with nationalism, MacDonagh, Maud Gonne, and opinion hardening 'as though a part of their flesh becomes . . . stone, and much of their being passes out of life' would resurface dramatically in 'Easter, 1916'.

'The Fisherman' was not published until 1916, but it originated in a 'subject for a poem' recorded in May, 1913, and was completed by

June 4, 1914. Not surprisingly, therofore, the prose 'subject' reveals a preoccupation with artistic power:

> Who is this by the edge of the stream
> That walks in a good homespun coat
> And carries a fishing [rod] in his hand
> We singers have nothing of our own.
> All our hopes, our loves, our dreams
> Are for the young, for those whom
> We stir into life. But [there is] one
> That I can see always though he is not yet born
> He walks by the edge of the stream
> In a good homespun coat
> And carries a fishing rod in his hand.[82]

The poem itself sketches in the grim present 'reality' behind that preoccupation: the controversies involving Synge, Lane, and the entire artistic movement Yeats had worked so hard for so long to nurture and develop. The harshness of the language – 'hate', 'craven', 'insolent', 'knave' – suggests a mood close to despair, as does the image of the poet brooding 'All day'; but the response provoked is rather one of defiance:

> Maybe a twelvemonth since
> Suddenly I began,
> In scorn of this audience,
> Imagining a man ... (*VP* 347–8)

The stance he was adopting here was one he would repeat nearly twenty-five years later in *The Death of Cuchulain*:

> No body like his body
> Has modern woman borne,
> But an old man looking back on life
> Imagines it in scorn ...[83]

The choice of Cuchulain as an ideal figure was quite predictable; the prose sketch for the earlier text suggests that Yeats was initially unsure of the symbolic identity of the fisherman. He himself, of course, had climbed Ben Bulben's back with 'rod and fly' and was fond of pursuing pike and perch on the lake at Coole. In 'The Song of 'Wandering Aengus' the fisherman had been pre-Christian Celtic deity and lover, the fish a metamorphosis of the beloved; and in 'Three Movements' fish would correspond to literary epochs. Although Christian fish symbolism would not be irrelevant, we can be sure that Yeats would have seen it within larger mythic patterns involving fertility and the contents of the unconscious. (Eliot's Fisher King in *The Waste Land* and the trout-fishing idyll of Jake Barnes in *The Sun Also Rises* would draw upon similar patterns). The reference to 'the beating down of the wise' and to the figure himself as being 'wise' may be intended to evoke associations with Finn MacCool. When Finn was a young man, he went

to learn poetry from Finegas, a poet that was living at the Boinn, for the poets thought it was always on the brink of water poetry was revealed to them. And he did not give him his own name, but he took the name of Deimne. Seven years, now, Finegas had stopped at the Boinn, watching the salmon, for it was in the prophecy that he would eat the salmon of knowledge that would come there, and that he would have all knowledge after. And when at the last the salmon of knowledge came, he brought it to where Finn was, and bade him to roast it, but he bade him not to eat any of it. And when Finn brought him the salmon after a while he said: 'Did you eat any of it at all, boy?' 'I did not,' said Finn; 'but I burned my thumb putting down a blister that rose on the skin, and after doing that, I put my thumb in my mouth.' 'What is your name, boy?' said Finegas. 'Deimne,' said he. 'It is not, but it is Finn your name is, and it is to you and not to myself the salmon was given in the prophecy.' With that he gave Finn the whole of the salmon, and from that time Finn had the knowledge that came from the nuts of the nine hazels of wisdom that grow beside the well that is below the sea. (*GFM* 162)

That Finn's identity as 'a seer and a poet; a Druid and a knowledgeable man' (168) was balanced by his Apollonic affirmation of 'the music of what happens' enhances his appropriateness. In 'The Phases of the Moon' Yeats's visionary personae Robartes and Aherne wear 'Connemara cloth' (*VP* 372).[84]

At about the time Yeats wrote the poem, he went to Mirabeau, France 'to investigate a miracle.'[85] Kneeling in the Catholic chapel, he realised that, like the devout believers around him, 'I too had my conception of the Divine Man, and a few days before had schemed out a poem, praying that somewhere upon some seashore or upon some mountain I should meet face to face with that divine image of myself. I tried to understand what it would be if the heart of that image lived completely within my heart, and the poetry full of instinct[,] full of tenderness for all life it would enable me to write and then I wondered what it would be if the head awoke within my head, and here my understanding was less clear. . . .' If, as seems likely, Yeats was referring to 'The Fisherman', 'head' and 'heart' here would correspond to the 'cold' and 'passionate' qualities of the poem the figure would inspire.[86]

The 'fisherman' figure has a primal, archetypal identity which is reflected in the fallen world not only in the poet but also in the poet's audience. In the 1930s, recalling the genesis of the poem, Yeats was to emphasise this aspect of it:

> I had founded Irish literary societies, an Irish Theatre, I had become associated with the projects of others, I had met much unreasonable opposition. To overcome it I had to make my thoughts modern. Modern thought is not simple; I became argumentative, passionate, bitter; when I was very bitter I used to say to myself, 'I do not write for these people who attack everything that I value, not for those others who are lukewarm friends, I am writing for a man I have never seen.' I built up in my mind the picture of a man who lived in the country where I had lived, who fished in mountain streams where I had fished; I said to myself, 'I do not know whether he is born yet, but born or unborn it is for him I write.' I made this poem about him. . . . (Torchiana 294)

As an image of the audience, the fisherman himself yokes antinomies: his homespuns and flyrod, pointing to opposite ends of the social scale, suggest a synthesis of the countrymen and gentry whom Yeats set up against the middle classes in 'Poetry and Tradition' and who would reappear in 'Under Ben Bulben' as 'the peasantry' and 'Hard-riding country gentlemen'. He is 'A man who does not exist, / A man who is but a dream' – and, in the draft 'subject', one 'not yet born' – in two different senses. Although he does not exist in the 'reality' of contemporary Ireland ('No body like his body / Has modern woman borne'), he has the higher reality of the images in the ideal realm with which the poet's visionary imagination is in contact. Yeats's act of composition corresponds to Seanchan 'labouring / For some that shall be born in the nick o' time' (*VPl* 266); the fisherman's 'birth' will be his incarnation in this poem. There, in turn, he will condition this world until in future generations there are actual audiences with virtues like his, capable of appreciating 'great art' with its strenuous synthesis of opposites. The "dawn' atmosphere points back to his Edenic origins, ahead to the new era he would help usher in. By the time Yeats wrote 'The Tower' he would name as his heirs 'up-standing men / That climb the streams until / The fountain leap, and at dawn / Drop their cast at the side / Of dripping stone ...' (*VP* 414).

VIII

But the note of quiet confidence on which 'The Fisherman' ends should not be mistaken for any easy short-term optimism. It is highly unlikely that Yeats in 1914 expected an *imminent* 'dawn'. The Easter Rising, less than two years later, surprised him: 'I did not foresee 1916' (*VP* 820). The event was troubling not only for the obvious reasons of the death and destruction that accompanied it, the turmoil that threatened the substantial cultural advances he had played so central a role in bringing about (*L* 614), but because it raised dramatically the question of Yeats's own relation to it as man and as artist; and because many of its leaders were from the very class *not* suggested by the ideal image of the fisherman and had seemed in his eyes to wear not 'grey Connemara clothes' but only the motley of the clown.

Yeats's harsh vision of Ireland at this time was shared by AE. In *The National Being*, written before the Rising and focussing upon the era of the recently passed and suspended Home Rule Bill of 1914, he described the country as 'an intellectual desert where people read nothing and think nothing' and wrote scathingly of 'Our mean and disordered little country towns in Ireland, with their drink-shops, their disregard of cleanliness or beauty. . . .'[88] His assertion that 'we were more Irish truly in the heroic ages. We would not then have taken, as we do to-day, the huckster or the publican and make them our representative men, and allow them to corrupt the national soul' (125) sounded very much like Yeats (who in 'Pardon, Old Fathers . . .,' dated January, 1914, boasted of having blood *'That has not passed through any huckster's loin ...'* (*VP* 269). According to AE, 'the image of Kathleen ni Houlihan anciently was beauty in the hearts of poets and dreamers. We often thought her unwise, but never did we find her ignoble; never was she without a flame of idealism in her eyes . . .' (128). Although he was particularly critical of Ireland, he saw the situation there as typical, finding that 'none of our modern States create in us such an impression of being spiritually oversouled by an ideal as the great States of the ancient world' (13). Again like Yeats he discerned a lack of leadership: 'The leaders of nations too have lost that divine air that many leaders of men wore in the past . . .' (13). But in assessing the responsibility for decline he pointed his finger neither at politicians nor at publicans:

> Perhaps the artists who create ideals are to blame. In ancient Ireland, in Greece, and in India, the poets wrote about great kings and heroes, enlarging on their fortitude of spirit, their chivalry and generosity, creating in the popular mind an ideal of what a great man was like; and men were influenced by the ideal created, and strove to win the praise of the bards and to be recrowned by them a second time in great poetry. . . . It is the great defect of our modern literature that it creates few such types. How hardly could one of our modern public men be made the hero of an epic. It would be difficult to find one who could be the subject of a genuine lyric. . . . The poets have dropped out of the divine procession, and sing a solitary song. They inspire nobody to be great. . . . (13–14)

Yeats, of course, had never stopped trying to provide the inspiration, and though neither he nor AE saw evidence of present success, events were soon to prove that there *were* men who had been influenced by the ideal created or embodied; and if there is no reason to think that winning the praise of the bards for themselves provided important motivation, they would nevertheless be 'recrowned . . . a second time in great poetry' – by Yeats himself.

Yeats's most extreme formulation of his relationship to the Rising – 'Did that play of mine send out / Certain men the English shot?' – has to be seen in the context of 'The Man and the Echo', as part of a personal struggle with remorse rather than as a claim of sole responsibility. We know far too little about the human mind itself and its relation to external forces to justify confident assertions about motivation. Unconscious drives, the effects of heredity, family, religion, national tradition, the course of contemporary political events, the personal influence of others, and of course other aspects of cultural nationalism such as the Gaelic League all contributed to making a figure such as Patrick Pearse commit himself to revolution. For example, Pearse's disappointment with the human failings of others predisposed him to accept an idealised vision of ancient Ireland; he *'wanted* to believe in the great heroes of the past. He needed great symbols of nobility, courage and selflessness to compensate for the many self-seeking, weak and timid people who surrounded him.'[89] This need, in turn, made him particularly susceptible to the impact of *Yeats's* art. Pearse himself was to acknowledge that 'it was through his writings many of us made our first acquaintance with our early traditions and literature' (93); and although he did not accept all of Yeats's theories about literature he praised him as a 'great artist' and 'the poet who has most finely voiced Irish nationalism in our time.'[90] His own poem 'The Mother', though rooted in the facts of his own life, gave those facts a national perspective by replicating the situation of *Cathleen ni Houlihan*, with Pearse's mother directly echoing the Poor Old Woman: 'They shall be spoken of among their people, / The generations shall remember them, / And call them blessed. . . .'[91]

Whether Pearse was aware of Yeats's views about the relationship of art to life is unclear. He does not seem to have regarded his own literary productions as forces for change.[92] But St. Enda's, the school he founded in 1908, *was* clearly designed to serve such a purpose. One of his models for it was the boy troop at Emain Macha in the Ulster sagas (119). The school's literary magazine was intended to be 'a rallying-point for the thought and aspirations of all those who would bring back again in Ireland that Heroic Age which reserved the highest honour for the hero who had the most childlike heart, for the king who had the largest pity, and for the poet who visioned the truest image of beauty' (130). This goal corresponds quite closely to Yeats's desire to 're-create an heroical ideal in manhood – in plays of old Irish life'; and, as with Yeats, the idea was not nostalgia for the past but its recovery. Even the works of art decorating the school were intended to contribute to the process. The artist Beatrice Elvery recounted that she had 'painted an allegorical picture of a seated, hooded figure of Cathleen ni Houlihan, with a child on her knee, presumably Young Ireland, stretching out his arm to the future, and behind her a ghostly crowd of martyrs, patriots, saints and scholars'; Maud Gonne bought the picture and presented it to St. Enda's. Later Elvery met one of the boys from the school 'and he told me that this picture had inspired him "to die for Ireland!" I was shocked at the thought that my rather banal and sentimental picture might, like Helen's face, launch ships and burn towers' (117). Among the other works, by such artists as Sarah Purser, Jack Yeats, and AE, there was a painting by Edwin Morrow showing Cuchulain as a boy taking arms, 'framed in his most famous words: "I care not though I were to live but one day and one night provided my fame and my deeds live after me"' (117). Among the literary figures who visited the school were Douglas Hyde, Edward Martyn, and Padraic Colum, as well as O'Grady and Yeats himself. At one of the school's dramatic productions (O'Grady's *The Coming of Fionn*), O'Grady and Yeats chatted together and the former, reversing his earlier opposition, made a speech in which he expressed the hope 'that Yeats and other great literary folk around him would bring the heroes of our ancient literature more before the people of today' (121–3). Even the crusty Joseph Holloway was moved to the lyrical assertion that 'each and all felt as they left the hall that they had just witnessed a unique and inspiring show and one that promises great hope for the Ireland of the near future' (123).

And yet Yeats apparently did not see the cause for hope the others felt. Although one would never guess it from the vagueness of 'kept a school' in 'Easter, 1916', he clearly recognised the merit of what Pearse was doing, for in 1913 Pearse asked him to stage a benefit at the Abbey on behalf of the financially troubled school and Yeats agreed with alacrity – '"Of course I shall help you and your boys at St Enda's"' – but though Pearse saw in Yeats's act the great generosity of a great artist (171), Yeats could not see in him, or in MacDonagh (whose intelligence we know he respected [*Mem* 177–8]) or in any other extreme Nationalist leader at this period the potential for heroic action. And thus the lyric in which he was to celebrate that action began with a frank confession of his misjudgement.

The reference to 'close of day' in the first line of 'Easter, 1916' and the later reference to 'nightfall' (l. 65) represent a significant link with and contrast to the 'dawn' imagery in 'The Fisherman'. And instead of the poet producing that promised poem 'cold / And passionate as the dawn' he merely offers 'polite meaningless words' and transforms meetings with the unsuspected rebels into tales or jibes to please 'a companion / Around the fire at the club ...' (*VP* 391–4). His role is that of an Anglo-Irish gentleman, heir of the class whose hegemony was achieved at the expense of the Gaelic Catholic Irish of the 'hidden Ireland' and whose destruction of the indigenous social order severed the nexus of patron and poet upon which the bardic tradition had for centuries depended. In constrast to the famous lines from 'The Man and the Echo', there is nothing in this poem to suggest the poet's *responsibility* for the events of Easter Week. It must come as a surprise, therefore, to find Yeats thirty-five lines into the poem adopting once more a 'bardic' stance in 'Yet I number him in the song'. The mixed nature of Yeats's feelings about the Rising in undeniable;[93] but as he wrote in a note to the poem, 'the late Dublin Rebellion, whatever one can say of its wisdom, will long be remembered for its heroism' (*VP* 820). Yeats's doubts struggle for much of the poem with his impulse to perform the traditional bardic function of celebrating battles and com-memorating heroes. The last few lines not only come to rest in affirmation (though the beauty is still 'terrible') but also show Yeats doing what AE in *The National Being* had lamented the un-commonness of: making 'modern public men' the heroes of poetry that would, in its turn, shape life. Not only are the executed leaders permanently 'changed utterly' *because* of the poet's act of commemorating them – 'I write it out in a verse' – but the poem in which he does so will affect *future* events. It is significant, as Roy Foster has noted, that Yeats chose to republish the poem in 1920, during the War of Independence. The line 'Wherever green is worn' may astonish by its use of the traditional Nationalist rhetoric ('I have always denounced green', he later wrote [*L* 812], but it represents a crescendo comparable to the equally Young-Irelandish 'indomitable Irishry' of 'Under Ben Bulben'.

Despite that ringing conclusion, Yeats remainded ambivalent about the Rising, as *The Dreaming of the Bones* reveals. In a letter written while at work on the play, Yeats said that it was 'I am afraid only too powerful politically' (*L* 626); and in 1918 he was to ascribe to it controversial Nationalist implications for the question of Ireland's relation to World War I: 'England once, the point of view is, treated Ireland as Germany treated Belgium' (*L* 654). The rebel's repeated 'O, never, never / Shall Diarmuid and Dervorgilla be forgiven' embodies Yeats's observation (in 'A General Introduction for my Work') that 'no people hate as we do in whom that past is always alive' (*E&I* 519) and might at first appear to be an instance of casting one's mind on other days for images that would strengthen the patriotic determination of future Irish rebels. (The play was written between the Rising and the War of Independence.) That the rebel is, or is disguised as, an 'Aran fisher' provides a link with Pearse, who shared Synge's idealised vision of Aran life and named his school St. Enda's after the patron saint of the Islands. There is, however, substantial evidence to discourage us from reading the play with any easy assumption that the rebel's intransigence has Yeats's full sympathy.

Helen Vendler surely erred in suggesting that contemporary political events 'are, if not irrelevant to the unravelling of the meaning of the play, at least not its central concern';[95] but she rightly called attention to the roots of the play in the early story 'The Vision of Hanrahan the Red', where there is no Rising and no rebel. It is Hanrahan the bard who has a vision of the tormented lovers, and, unable to endure it, shrieks in terror till the figures fade. The vision had been precipitated by his own meditations, after reading 'certain ancient poems that told of sinful lovers', about whether his spirit and that of his beloved Maive Lavelle would wander like theirs in a state of purgatorial punishment (*VSR* 217). Although Hanrahan is told by Diarmuid and Dervorgilla that their 'sin brought the Norman into Ireland', *he* neither condemns them for the deed nor is asked to forgive them. When Yeats transformed the story into a play, he replaced the bard with the soldier, who does not have comparable personal reasons for *identifying with* the lovers , and thus sharpened the potential conflict and placed the political level in the foreground. A crucial clue for interpreting the play at that level appears in the lines in 'The Grey Rock' about the poet being '*in no good repute / With the loud host before the sea, / That think sword-strokes were better meant / Than lover's music.*' In that poem the fidelity of the poet to his Muse was counterpointed against service of the national cause, and it is possible to detect a similar concern manifested in the play in Diarmuid (who in a sense incorporates fellow-lover Hanrahan's identity) and Dervorgilla on the one hand and the rebel on the other, with the Rising corresponding to the Battle of Clontarf in 'The Grey Rock'. In his journal Yeats had identified the world of the lovers in the poem with 'my lyric life' (*Mem* 241). It is also significant that, as David Clark has pointed out, Yeats apparently put the finishing touches on his play while staying with Maud Gonne in France, and shortly afterwards described her in a letter as being 'in a joyous and self forgetting condition of political hate the like of which I have not yet encountered'.[96] In the light of these considerations, it seems plausible that the rebel's intransigence shadows Maud's and that his refusal to forgive the lovers corresponds to her persistent criticisms of Yeats for not, as she saw it, putting his art in the service of the cause of independence. (Some connections with the centrally opposed impulses of the Countess and Aleel in *The Countess Cathleen* will be apparent here.) The rebel's forgiveness of Diarmuid and Dervorgilla would not affect the success of the contemporary revolutionary movement, but in 1917 the need for a patriotic, even propagandistic art must have seemed greater than ever, and although 'Easter, 1916' might seem to fall into that category, and would have its successors, Yeats would not and could not produce such work *on demand*.

The Young Man's final speech, in which he reveals that he 'had almost yielded and forgiven it all – / Terrible the temptation and the place' (*VPl* 775) points towards a deeper level of meaning in the play at which the opposition is not between Maud and Yeats but between two sides of the poet himself. 'Easter, 1916' demonstrates that Yeats's own patriotic impulses were powerfully stirred by the Rising, and his comments about the political implications of the play make clear that he saw it, too, as having a Nationalist thrust. Although troubled by Maud's joyous political hatred, he must also have envied the active heroism of the rebels (as in 'Meditations in Time of Civil War', V), questioned whether his allegiance to the demands of art was escapist. *The Dreaming of the Bones*, like the lyric, makes no suggestion that it was art – Yeats's or another's – that *caused* the Rising; but the play first appeared in print in January, 1919, the same month as the beginning of the War of Independence, and Yeats may well have seen in it another opportunity to shape future events. It is surely significant that the play ends with the rebel, like Yeats's fisherman, on a rocky summit in the breaking dawn. 'Dawn' has a more ambiguous significance here, banishing the spirits of the lovers as well as heralding a new era. During the troubling and chaotic time of the revolution, Yeats's own feelings about the relationship of art and life were subjected to intense pressures and not always brought into perfect harmony.

Soon enough, with the establishment of the Free State, the expectation of 'dawn' seemed to have been realised, and the new nation offered the artist the most daunting challenge yet, the most exciting opportunity. Already in 1921 he had suggested that AE write an essay on Unity of Culture, offering to send him the final chapter of *Four Years* 'on the subject' and encouraging him with the thought that 'if we can present this one idea from many sides we might affect the future of Ireland!'[97] The goal would remain his own for the rest of his life.

4

The Twenties and Thirties

In a second letter to AE, dated 29 March 1921, Yeats continued to urge his friend to write an essay on Unity of Culture that would reinforce his own exposition of it. 'We writers are not politicians, the present is not in our charge but some part of the future is', he suggested (*L* 666–7). At the moment, the Irish situation was discouraging and Yeats had 'little hope'; before long, however, the Free State was established and promised (as even the *Freeman's Journal* noticed) to be the realisation of Seanchan's dream: the poet as acknowledged legislator in the Senate, the poet as respected adviser of princes (Krimm 60). As the new nation gradually assumed a profoundly disillusioning shape, Yeats was to know new periods of discouragement, but he never permanently lost hope and was able to recover the confidence that his art might yet help realise a greater Ireland. These concerns played a crucial role in many of his most important writings of the 1920s and 1930s.

I. 'THE TOWER' (1925)

The lines

> Does the imagination dwell the most
> Upon a woman won or woman lost? (*VP* 413)

from Part II of 'The Tower' subtly link the poem with the origins of *A Vision*. As we now know, Yeats on his honeymoon was 'in great gloom' (*L* 633), saying to himself 'I have betrayed three people.' He felt he might have done the wrong thing in marrying George rather than Iseult Gonne; though he believed George to be unconscious of his brooding, she was well aware of it and of its causes, and it was in 'Casting about for some means of distraction' that 'she thought of attempting automatic writing.'[1] The rest, as they say, is history. And occult philosophy. But surprisingly, at least at first, the text (the evolution of which from its inception in 1917 to its completion

128

in 1925 spans most of the interval between the composition of *The Dreaming of the Bones* and the composition of 'The Tower') contains virtually nothing about artistic power. (See *AV A* 203 for one rather vague reference.) Even the 'Dove or Swan' section treats works of art primarily as illustrative rather than formative of various phases and eras. The question of the degree to which the artist could affect life was naturally raised by the deterministic implications of a cyclical paradigm of history, but Yeats had been grappling with that problem for many years before his marriage and the concept of artistic power had retained it central place in his thought. That it occupies no such place in *A Vision* seems best explained by the fact that the automatic writing and the 'sleeps' that eventually replaced it were from first to last a conscious or unconscious fabrication of George's, and although she carried over into the 'spirit' communications most of Yeast's abiding literary and occult preoccupations she did not give that of artistic power any significant place, perhaps because she did not recognise its importance but possibly rather because the act of collaboration between her and her husband was in fact an expression of her own creativity and thus in a sense a covert act of artistic power that competed with his own. At one point during the communications Yeats was informed that 'script depends on the love of medium for you – all intensity comes from that' (II: 294).

If George engaged in deception it was of course not, as with many professional mediums, for material gain, self-aggrandisement, or the pleasure of baffling the experts. As a young bride who had grown up before the social watershed of the Great War, she must often at first have found it daunting to speak for herself with a man so renowned for his words. (Years later in 1937, Dorothy Wellesley, already a published poet, still found getting to know Yeats left her 'impotent of language' [*LDW* 125].) The fiction of the Script enabled George to communicate with him on even the most intimate subjects and to share an imagined world of which they were in fact co-creators.

If, as many feminist critics have argued, ordinary language reflects phallocentric values, then the burden under which women and especially women authors labour is to find a way of modifying language to fit it for their own use. The fiction of automatic writing seems, of course, to absolve the writer of responsibility for its content. Additionally, it posits a volition outside the normal range of human experience, and offers by that very feature a first step towards a women's writing, for 'normal' implies the phallocentric status quo.

The earliest preserved page of the Script shows that George extensively modified the vehicle for those ostensibly supernatural revelations; the hand she used was not her ordinary one (present at the top of the page in the date), the words are run together without breaks or punctuation (anticipating Molly Bloom's monologue in *Ulysses*, itself arguably an early paradigm of women's writing), and words themselves are supplemented by astrological symbolism – astrology being one area of the occult with which George was more deeply involved than Yeats (I:9). Common in the Script whenever particularly delicate matters are touched upon is mirror writing, which by reversing the normal order of words again symbolically suggests escape from the phallocentric, while its superficial unintelligibility promises the revelation of 'occult' experience (the feminine realm, as much hidden as that of the spirits). That these features were essential to George for enabling her to find her own voice for both communication and creation is paradoxically underscored by the fact that in the later stages of the experiment she abandoned most of the distinctive features of automatic writing, using her normal hand, using regular punctuation and capitalisation, and leaving breaks between words (I:xiii). Once the barriers between her and her husband were down, her place as a collaborator fully recognised, her own voice, represented by her own handwriting, could exist in a symbolic union with 'his' language.

The 'communicators' told Yeats that they had come to give him 'metaphors for poetry' (*AV B* 8); but an art that would 'affect the future of Ireland' was not one of their – or her – priorities. The Script of 31 October 1918 provides another link between George and 'The Tower'; 'tower renew renew – alone in it – yes through your wife' (II: 163). But in June 1919, with the guerilla war between Ireland and England now under way, Yeats was warned in the Script 'not to be drawn into anything – possible trouble in Ireland . . . you may be tempted to join in political schemes if there is trouble – & you must not. . . . Some are brewing rebellion.' That 'some' unsurprisingly included Maud Gonne: 'Nothing must be said *unless* she speaks of it – then simply say you are destroying the souls of hundreds of young men / That method is most wicked in this country wholesale slaughter because a few are cruel' (II:292). Consistently George urged her husband away from political activism and public involvement in general, towards personal closeness and creativity. She carefully nurtured awareness that the collaborative process was essential. In January 1918, when Yeats suggested that he had 'collaborated with

Lady G (24) both intellectually & practically. So intellectual work is presumably possible with 12 & 24', he was informed that his relationship with Lady Gregory was 'imbalanced – you created she transferred not real collaboration' (I:112). He then queried 'Present of M[edium] & self only condition of true collaboration?' Another passage explained that daemonic communication occurred 'when *both* individuals are creative' (II:369).

George definitely came to think to herself as creator as well as medium. In January 1919, for example, she sketched in the Script a symbolic drawing that became the basis for at least three poems: 'Another Song of a Fool', The Double Vision of Michael Robartes', and 'Towards Break of Day' (II:198ff). It depicted 'Cormac's Chapel' at Cashel, surrounded by key images including hand, eye, book, butterfly, bird, circle and cross. The associated Script warned Yeats that he was 'empty – drained dry' (another anticipation of the concerns of 'The Tower') and urged him to 'go to the past – A historical & spiritual past' for a new inspiration. (When he wrote 'The Tower' he would do precisely that.) George went on to describe 'complementary dreams' that encapsulated the central image pattern of 'Towards Break of Day', so that, as George Harper has observed, 'George must be given credit for the basic organization if not the idea of the poem' (II:202). A passage in the Script for 22 July 1919 identifies the Initiatory and Critical Moments that loom so large in the documents as 'a deliberate work of art' (II:298).

There is no reason to believe that Yeats *resented* George's crucial role; on the contrary, he seems to have been proud of it, for an unpublished draft shows that he thought of dedicating the first version of *A Vision* itself 'to my wife who created this system which bores her.'[2] George did in fact sometimes become bored with the mechanical aspects of the years of recording the communications, but Yeats perhaps never fully realised the satisfaction her role gave her, for he once suggested that they work out a format in which he would do all or most of the writing, only to be told in the Script, 'no, ... because we cant use you alone – must have you & medium *equally*' (II:192). What does seem likely is that the power-sharing process and George's own lack of interest in directing his creative efforts towards the definition of the new Irish nation then emerging were responsible for the absence in *A Vision* of any significant concern with the process of art shaping life and contributed also to the need to reaffirm that process discernible at the heart of 'The Tower' – the composition of which took place in 1925, probably not long after the final portions of his and George's book had been written.[3] Thus the shadow of the 'woman won' left its mark upon the poem as surely as that of the 'woman lost'.

The lines about 'The people of Burke and of Grattan / That gave, though free to refuse' (*VP* 414) echo Yeats's famous speech on divorce on 11 June 1925 and remind us that if work on 'the system' drew him somewhat away from Irish concerns, involvement with the Senate provided a counterbalancing experience, one in which the question of artistic power did figure prominently, even though the Free State was to become something very different from anything that Yeats had desired. The new nation's Minister for External Affairs, Desmond FitzGerald, who 'ascribed his national feelings and convictions to the influence of Yeats's poetry', was determined that Yeats should be named to the Senate.[4] At the time his appointment was being considered, Oliver Gogarty is supposed to have retorted to a doubter on the nominating committee that 'if it had not been for W. B. Yeats there would be no Irish Free State!' (*SS* 15). Similarly, when Yeats won the Nobel Prize Stephen Gwynn praised him, along with Synge and Lady Gregory, for having 'done more to make Ireland really a nation in Europe than all the organised gunmen' (Krimm 63–4). Yeats himself made similar claims in a speech in 1923 in which he referred to 'the old days in Ireland when we began our imaginative movement which, for good or evil, had a little share in bringing about recent events ...' (*SS* 42; see also *Au* 559). The qualifying phrase undoubtedly reflected his continuing ambivalence about artistic power when it led to violence, a feeling heightened by the concurrent spectre of Irishmen killing Irishmen. As Bernard Krimm has noted, the new senator was almost at once thrown into what seemed like a real-life version of *The King's Threshold* when he interceded with Kevin O'Higgins on behalf of Republican hunger-striker Mary MacSwiney, the death of whose brother Terrence had led him to give his play a tragic ending (59–62). He seems also to have undertaken negotiations with British officials and with the Cosgrave Government about removal of the oath called for in the Treaty – an effort to close the gap between Free Staters and diehard Republicans (Krimm 66–9). One of his earliest official projects in the Senate was chairing a committee concerned with the editing and publishing of Irish manuscripts, and he saw this work, too, as an effort to repair some of the damage the Civil War had caused. 'Already', he asserted, 'the traditional imagination in these old books has had a powerful effect upon the life, and I may say upon the politics, of Ireland. People forget that the twenties, forties and fifties of the last century was the forming period of Irish nationality, and that the work was begun by O'Donovan, Petrie and men steeped in this old literature' (*SS* 75–6). At the present moment such literature could help 'build up again the idealism of Ireland ... wasted ... in a year of civil war' (*SS* 44–5). In June 1924 the Senate accepted the report his committee had prepared, but the Government did not implement it (*SS* 77n). Early in that year Yeats had written optimistically that 'Dublin is reviving after the Civil War. ... People are trying to found a new society. Politicians want to be artistic, and artistic people to meet politicians ...' (*L* 702). Characteristically, it seemed to him 'the very moment for a form of drama to be played in a drawing–room' and he set about arranging performances; his lighthearted remark to Edmund Dulac that it would be hard to find appropriately *Irish* hostesses masks a genuine concern for continuing to affect 'the few' (*L* 702).

But troubling developments accumulated. As early as 1921 a conference on education had argued that education in the new nation should be structured so as 'to revive the ancient life of Ireland as a Gaelic state, Gaelic in language, and Gaelic and Christian in its ideals.'[5] The general principle of a future modelled upon the past was Yeatsian, but during the summer and fall of 1924 he organised a concerted campaign against compulsory Gaelic, which he saw as a barrier to reunification of North and South (Krimm 114–5). By July of that year he was expecting an anti–divorce bill, which he felt to be not only an insult to the people of Burke and of Grattan but also another exacerbation of the Ulster problem (Krimm 115). In a revision of the 'Apologia ...' made in 1924 or 1925 for *Early Poems and Stories*, Yeats changed the lines 'And still the thoughts of Ireland brood / Upon her holy quietude' to 'And may the thoughts of Ireland brood / Upon a measured quietude' (*VP* 138). The change may well represent a response to the increased Catholic political power manifested in the anti-divorce legislation against which he spoke so passionately; it also shifts the focus to the future and to the impact of art, suggested by the word 'measured', which would reappear with the same associations in 'The Statues' and 'Under Ben Bulben'. The echo in 'The Tower' of the speech on divorce suggests that, like his work on *A Vision*, the experience of being a sixty-year-old smiling public man led him to incorporate into the poem a quest for the reaffirmation of artistic power. In June 1925, speaking on the preservation of ancient monuments, he jested with irony and perhaps some bitterness about the process of art shaping life, suggesting that T. W. Rolleston's 'Clonmacnoise' was so beautiful 'that it will in all probability bring many tourists into that district if you can protect the ruins', adding that he was 'the first person who has quoted a poem in the Seanad' and only did so 'because I am sure the poem will be, to use the appropriate words, "a definite asset"' (*SS* 88–9). Writing his own poem at this time was a way of 'preparing his peace' with 'the proud stones of Greece' – including Wilde's statues – and those of his own country as well.

In July 1924 he had sent Olivia Shakespear a copy of *The Cat and the Moon and Certain Poems* with the apology that it contained some of his 'best work' but was 'very slim' because 'the philosophy absorbs me. But that once finished I think I shall do deeper and more passionate work than ever before. My head is full of things I want to write' (*L* 707). But in October a speech about the North triggered problems with high blood pressure and his doctor ordered him to refrain from 'public work' and 'every kind of excitement' (Krimm 114–5; *LTSM* 55). The letter to Mrs. Shakespear is echoed in the opening section of 'The Tower':

> Never had I more
> Excited, passionate, fantastical
> Imagination.... (*VP* 409)

and undoubtedly the illness contributed to the sense of 'bodily de-crepitude' counterpointed in the same section of the poem against those creative impulses. A number of the best interpreters of Yeats's work have shown how the poem as a whole explores and finally asserts the creative power of the imagination.[6] What needs greater stress than it has been given is the degree to which the poem emphasises the expression of that creative power in an art that draws upon the past to shape the future.

Although Red Hanrahan himself does not appear until Part II of 'The Tower' the speaker's fear that he must 'bid the Muse go pack' recalls the situation and the tone of the moment in the original first story about Hanrahan, 'The Book of the Great Dhoul and Hanrahan the Red', when Hanrahan cries to Cleena, his fairy-mistress and Muse, 'Woman, begone out of this' (*VSR* 192). In the story, the Muse figure is the source of the poet's visionary power, and the 'woman lost' proves after all impossible to escape. The speaker in

Part I of the poem not only treats art and metaphysics as incompatible but ominously chooses as one of his 'friends' the philosopher about whom Yeats had written in *A Vision* that 'even the truth into which Plato dies is a form of death, for when he separates the Eternal Ideas from Nature and shows them self-sustained he prepares the Christian desert and the Stoic suicide' (*AV A* 183). In the year of his own death Yeats would declare that 'the abstract is not life . . .' (*L* 922); and if 'Meditations in Time of Civil War' had *ended* with the 'ambitious heart' being offered a dubious comfort –

> The abstract joy,
> The half-read wisdom of daemonic images,
> Suffice the ageing man as once the growing boy. (*VP* 427)

– the comparable prospect in 'The Tower' represents only a starting point, and an inability or refusal to acquiesce in such a separation is what leads the poet to the exploration and discovery of what *will* 'suffice' that constitute the remainder of the poem.

In Part II the poet casts his mind on other days, hoping his imagination can find in 'Images and memories' brought to bear upon the present an affirmation of artistic power compatible with his current state. The form chosen for this section itself exemplifies the process of drawing upon the past for strength, being, as George Bornstein has demonstrated, a Yeatsian adaptation of the traditional 'greater Romantic lyric'[7]. The figures conjured up by the imagination all attest to the continued imaginative energy of the speaker,[8] and those of Raftery and Hanrahan focus specifically upon art imitated by life.

Yeats had been writing of Raftery and Mary Hynes as early as 1899, but in the account he gives in *The Celtic Twilight* it was poteen, not poetry, that had led to the death of one of her admirers: ' "There was a lot of men up beyond Kilbecanty one night sitting together drinking, and talking of her, and one of them got up and set out to go to Ballylee and see her; but Cloon Bog was open then, and when he came to it he fell into the water, and they found him dead there in the morning." '[9] 'The Tower' gestures towards this version of events in the lines 'And certain men, being maddened by those rhymes, / Or else by toasting her a score of times . . .'; but 'So great a glory did the song confer' before this passage and 'Music had driven their wits astray' after it really eliminate all uncertainty and make Raftery's verses responsible for the man's death. Yeats may have introduced this explanation into the story as the result of a Senate debate about film censorship in June 1923. The question of the possibly harmful effects of art led Yeats to recall a pertinent instance from his own experience:

> I remember John Synge and myself both being considerably troubled when a man, who had drowned himself in the Liffey, was taken from the river. He had in his pocket a copy of Synge's play, 'Riders to the Sea,' which ... dealt with a drowned man. We know, of course, that Goethe was greatly troubled when a man was taken from the river, having drowned himself. The man had in his pocket a copy of 'Werther,' which is also about a man who had drowned himself. It has again and again cropped up in the world that the arts do appeal to our imitative faculties. We comfort ourselves in the way Goethe comforted himself, that there must have been other men saved from suicide by having read 'Werther.' We see only the evil effect, greatly exaggerated in the papers, of these rather inferior forms of art which we are now discussing, but we have no means of reducing to statistics their other effects. I think you can leave the arts, superior or inferior, to the general conscience of mankind. (*SS* 51–2)

Yeats once more had in mind the concept he had invoked in the controversy of 1901 about art and censorship, 'a masterpiece is a portion of the conscience of the world' (*UP2* 262–4). His most personal reason to be troubled in this regard was hinted at in the succeeding lines of Part II:

> ... the tragedy began
> With Homer that was a blind man,
> And Helen has all living hearts betrayed. (*VP* 411)

The parallels are easy enough to discern. As Homer started the Trojan War through his aggrandisement of Helen, so Yeats's beautiful Irish queen Maud, as Cathleen ni Houlihan, had inspired men to transform their living hearts into hearts of stone so they might initiate the tragedy of Easter 1916. Although forced once again to confront the potentially dangerous aspects of artistic power, the poet is undeterred, and even prays fervently for an art in which 'the moon and sunlight seem / One inextricable beam'; though the resultant intermixture may lead to confusion and death by water, 'a marriage of the sun and moon' was characteristic of the art Yeats took most pleasure in, 'supreme art' (*GFM* xix–xxi).

At this point the poem turns naturally towards Hanrahan, another peasant poet, whom the poet himself 'created'. The specific story upon which Yeats focuses here in fact provides a parallel to the Raftery material. As Raftery's songs had driven a man deceived by 'the brightness of the moon' to drown in a bog's mire on his way to see the 'country wench' chosen by 'mocking Muses', so the old man in the story (and by implication the 'old man' who had written that story 'twenty years ago') sent Hanrahan 'drunk or sober' off on a wild chase under a 'full moon' during which, when the moon clouded over, he nearly fell into a boghole on his way to an encounter with the mysterious Echtge (*VSR* 89–93). The story incorporates a fertility rite, a sort of Grail quest, Echtge replacing Cleena as the White Goddess-Muse-Wisdom figure. That she is surrounded by old women bearing the four traditional talismans of the Tuatha Dé Danann is significant, as is the identification of two of those symbols with 'Power' and Knowledge' (*VSR* 91–2).

Yeats provided a clue to the labyrinth of significance here in a passage in the unpublished version of his autobiography concerning his efforts in the 1890s to found an 'Irish Eleusis or Samothrace' on an island in Lough Key. The rituals were to 'unite the radical truths of Christianity to those of a more ancient world', and his writings were to have 'a secret symbolical relation to these mysteries', giving his work 'doctrine without exhortation and rhetoric'. The rituals would be founded on visions seen by Maud and himself: 'There would be, as it were, a spiritual birth from the soul of a man and a woman'. The symbols in the visions would be drawn 'from the memory of the race itself'. The symbolic fabric that began to emerge 'had for its centre the four talismans of the Tuatha de Danaan, the sword, the stone, the spear and the cauldron, which related themselves in my mind with the suits of the Tarot' (*Mem* 123–5; also *Au* 253–4). The Tarot cards correspond to the ordinary playing cards in the story, which is set on Samhain Eve, one of the crucial points in the seasonal cycle and a time for the manifestation of supernatural beings (*VSR* 83). Hanrahan fails in the encounter with Echtge, but nevertheless knows the symbolic pattern of which she is an essential part. In 'The Twisting of the Rope' (the second story in the Hanrahan group) Hanrahan tells the maiden whom he is trying to seduce that 'the sun and the moon are the man and the girl, they are my life and your life . . .' (*VSR* 98). The early version of this story takes place on

May Eve and places the 'sun and moon' imagery explicitly in the context of seasonal rituals (*VSR* 200–1). We have already noted Graves's argument that such patterns are connected with the creative process. Hanrahan's quest, then, would be that of the visionary artist, a quest for hidden wisdom – drawn, perhaps, from the 'Great Memory' (*VP* 822) of the race – and for the ability to articulate that wisdom. Success would evidence an imaginative vitality comparable to the fertility that was the goal of the traditional seasonal rituals. The supposed participation of early Irish bards in inauguration ceremonies in which the new monarch wed the Mother Goddess, the land itself, seems relevant here. Hanrahan may have failed, but contemplating that failure helps his creator achieve what the character did not. At the beginning of 'The Tower' the role the poet adopts is that of the apparently superannuated priest-monarch, an aged and impotent Fisher King recalling nostalgically boyhood days when he had been successful 'with rod and fly'; as the poem progresses, he discovers that his fertile creativity survives. Symbols associated with the rituals pervade the poem. Mrs French, 'Gifted with so fine an ear', is a sort of Ascendancy Salome or Dectire. The drowned man, like Eliot's Phlebas the Phoenician, evokes a common ritual of death and rebirth. The poet himself longs to achieve the regenerate state of Unity of Being emblematised by the inextricable union of sun and moon.[10] The culmination of the series of references occurs in Part III, with the symbols of fishermen, the 'fabulous horn', the 'sudden shower / When all streams are dry', and the nesting birds; Part III is also where the poet explores the remaining dimension of artistic power, impact on an audience and thus on the future.

Yeats's 'heirs' in fact 'receive' their inheritance by way of the process of life imitating art: the poem itself is meant to move them to emulation of the poet's 'pride' and 'faith'. In the manuscripts of Part III, Yeats cancelled a passage reading 'And choose once more for an heir / Young men . . .'; the 'once more' would have made explicit the return to the concerns of 'The Fisherman' (*YW* 82). Yeats also considered describing the men as wearing 'grey Connemara cloth' (*YW* 88), and in the published text as well as the drafts does have them fishing at 'dawn' – further links with the earlier poem. The young men correspond to the younger, more virile priest-king who becomes the new consort of the Goddess-Muse. Epithets for them in the manuscripts include 'vigourous healthy' and 'young vigourous' (*YW* 90–1). In the prose kernel for

'The Fisherman' Yeats had written that the singer's 'dreams / Are for the young, for those whom / We stir into life. . . .' The 'heirs' also represent the poet's ideal audience, and his own poem will help make the ideal a reality, bring that audience into existence. As models for them to emulate he offers not only himself but also 'types' from the eighteenth-century heyday of the Ascendancy. Figures who gave though free to refuse, 'The people of Burke and of Grattan' evoke by contrast the negative model of Lord Ardilaun, whose *conditional* giving in 'To a Wealthy Man . . .' had frustrated art's life-shaping force. A draft referred also to 'young men / That ride upon horses . . .' (*YW* 88). Such a reference would have implied a contrast with the 'half-mounted' victim of Mrs French's servant and recalled 'At Galway Races', where 'horsemen' also represented the artist's desired audience, 'Hearers and hearteners of the work. . . .' Late poems such as 'The Gyres' and 'Under Ben Bulben' image the coming era partly through 'Lovers of horses' and 'Hard-riding country gentlemen'.

Earlier in the poem the Muses had mockingly chosen a country wench to play the part of Helen; in Part III, with the poet now confident about his own artistic power, his voice *merges* with theirs in mocking the common enemy, the abstract philosophers. The lines following his defiant humanist declaration of 'faith' further extent the exploration of the relationship of art and life. In manuscript versions this concern is clearer. The crucial lines of the published text are

> And further add to that
> That, being dead, we rise,
> Dream and so create
> Translunar Paradise.
> I have prepared my peace. . . . (*VP* 415)

One manuscript passage included the lines

> No further I add to that
> This mockery of the tomb
> That living men create
> Their own eternal home

and

And mine[?] is almost ready
The forms come crowding fast. . . .

Another passage read 'When I go to my final rest / I shall . . .', which makes the process take place after death rather than during life. Yet another passage reversed that change:

I build my eternal peace,
With stories of dead kings
~~The~~ In Ireland ~~Italy or~~ or in Greece
Out of Italian Art
Out of the sculpture of Greece. . . .

Below this passage he wrote 'The dead create', then cancelled it and wrote instead 'Man makes a superhuman / Mirror resembling dream'.[11] Apparently there was uncertainty in his mind as to whether there was one process involved or two and when, in relation to death, it or they took place. But what seems constant is the thought that the state the soul will finally inhabit is itself formed upon models provided by art. Thus 'I have prepared my peace . . .' would mean roughly 'My final state will be modelled upon . . .'. (Yeats may have welcomed the new ambiguity whereby 'prepared my peace with' *could* also mean 'reached accommodation, come to terms with.')

The lines also offer examples of the paradigmatic images. The rejected 'stories of dead kings / In Ireland' might have referred to the epics of Cuchulain and Finn, with their images of heroic behavior. The lines about 'Poet's imaginings / And memories of love, / Memories of the words of women' are glossed by that journal passage in which Yeats had written of a statesman being formed unconsciously by growing into and finding about himself, 'most perhaps in the minds of women, the nobleness of emotion created and associated with his country by its great poets. . . . It is this culture that makes the birth of heroes possible' (*Mem* 248–9). The final lines of the passage recall Yeats's claim in an essay of 1910 that 'the imaginative writer shows us the world as a painter does his picture, reversed in a looking-glass that we may see it, not as it seems to eyes habit has made dull, but as we were Adam and this the first morning . . .' (*CA* 191). At the same period he had expressed his fear that 'in our age it is impossible to create . . . an heroic and passionate conception of life . . . and to make that conception the special dream of the Irish people' (*Mem* 185). Pessimism about the prospect would reappear, but the mood reached at this point in 'The Tower' was a positive one and he would echo the passage in the lines in 'The Statues' describing the development of Greek culture 'when Phidias / Gave women dreams and dreams their looking glass.' (The draft reference to 'the sculpture of Greece' had been more precise.) The metaphor of the bird and her nest refers back to the entire process. The creation of the nest corresponds to the act of 'preparing one's peace', and the 'twigs' are the things one has used to contruct that world, the models or paradigms. They will provide 'a rest for the people of God' – 'God' being defined in 'The Tower' as man's soul itself. The twigs are also, as in 'To a Wealthy Man . . .', the 'right twigs for an eagle's nest'. The baby birds would be future generations, Wilde's Apollonic children. So things above are as the things below, one's 'Translunar Paradise' being modelled upon ideal images just the way the fallen world is.

Lord Ardilaun may have failed to appreciate the 'learned Italian things' enumerated in the poem addressed to him, but here the poet himself has shown the way and when he makes his soul does so by compelling it once more 'to study / In a learned school'. Yeats's aesthetic was unquestionably a central source of the optimistic thrust that develops during the course of 'The Tower'. That optimism appeared also in a lecture Yeats gave to the Irish Literary Society on 30 November 1925, in which he declared that 'Ireland has been put into our hands that we may shape it, and I find all about me in Ireland to-day a new overflowing life' (*UP2* 455); and it carried over into the first two sections of 'Blood and the Moon', a poem that constitutes a sort of sequel to 'The Tower'. Meanwhile, the revolution Yeats felt his art had helped to inspire had led to a Free State engaged in the process of marginalising the class designated in 'The Tower' as the poet's 'heirs' to the point that it seemed highly unlikely they would ever be able to translate his 'faith and pride' into the realities of Irish life.

II. 'BLOOD AND THE MOON' (1926–7)

Yeats himself referred to 'Blood and the Moon' as 'a new Tower series' (*L* 726–7), and in some ways the new poem definitely does develop from the earlier one. In addition to using the central image of the tower itself, it returns to and expands Yeats's concern with the Anglo-Irish eighteenth century and its (and his) heirs in the modern world. The positive, assertive tone of the passage in Part III of 'The Tower' beginning 'And I declare my faith ...' is echoed in the line 'I declare this tower is my symbol; I declare ...' in 'Blood and the Moon'; confident mockery is also present in both instances. The poet's ability to sustain the positive vision through Parts I and II of the new poem may reflect gratifying involvement beginning in June 1926 with the process of designing a new Irish coinage – in itself an opportunity to bring art to bear upon life, as the designs were to be submitted by notable sculptors and medallists and would make their way into the pockets – and consciousness – of every Paudeen.[12] The manuscripts of Part III of 'The Tower' show Yeats describing 'Translunar Paradise' with the line 'The blessed life / dream of the dead' (*YW* 86); 'Blood and the Moon' dramatises an attempt to apply the same adjective to the fallen world.

The word 'blessed' has other significant contexts. One of them may by Joyce's *Ulysses* (1922), on the first page of which Buck Mulligan 'blessed gravely thrice the tower, the surrounding country and the awaking mountains' (1.10–11, 1922 version). The passage pre-dated the publication of Yeats's 'A Prayer on going into my House', which begins 'God grant a blessing on this tower and cottage / And on my heirs ...' (*VP* 371); Joyce's chapter in fact appeared in *The Little Review* in March 1918, Yeats's poem in the same journal in October of that year. Were the similarities independent, or did Yeats intentionally echo Joyce? Yeats had read at least one instalment there, for in a letter of 23 July 1918 he wrote that Joyce's 'new story in the *Little Review* looks like becoming the best work he has done', but his description of it – 'neither what the eye sees nor the ear hears, but what the rambling mind thinks and imagines from moment to moment' – would seem to refer to 'Proteus', which had appeared in the May issue (*L* 651). If he did not see the passage in the periodical version he might well have thought, as he opened the novel a few years later, that Joyce was commenting wryly upon his poem. This suspicion would have been heightened by the satiric references, a few pages farther into the first chapter, to the Dun Emer Press (1.365–7); though he praised the 'beauty' of 'the Martello Tower' pages (which incorporated his lyric 'Who Goes with Fergus?') he also characterised Joyce's mind as a 'cruel playful' one (*L* 679). Suspicion would have become certainty if Yeats read far enough to reach the devastating parody of 'Baile and Aillinn' in 'Scylla and Charybdis'.[13]

A decade after the publication of *Ulysses* the tower and the allusions were still vivid in Yeats's mind, for he began one section of a lecture by recalling that 'in 1904 the Abbey Theatre gave its first performance, [and] a friend of mine was entertaining in the Martello Tower at Sandycove James Joyce. . . . He has never returned to Ireland except for a few weeks once, but in books written twenty years after that life in the tower he records the jokes, the casual allusions of the time, often writing sentences that need a memory like his own to make them intelligible' (*IR* 19–20). Still, Yeats had found himself defending *Ulysses* against charges of indecency and anti-Irishness in Senate debates about copyright protection in March and May 1927, shortly before he began actual composition of 'Blood and the Moon' (*SS* 142, 145–8); and though admitting to being unsure of whether it was 'a great work of literature', he declared it 'the work of an heroic mind'. In fact, his feelings about the novel as a whole were mixed and complex, and in beginning his new poem

> Blessed be this place,
> More blessed still this tower . . . (*VP* 480)

with a repetitive stressing of 'this', he may have been signalling further engagement with it. The symbolic locations of the two structures, one facing the Continent, the other rooted in the strongly Gaelic West, suggested a difference of values; but Yeats's tower had its Anglo-French associations, too. In both texts the juxtaposition of past and present cultures is central; and if there is no reason to think that Joyce had any interest in the Ascendancy, he at least shared Yeats's sense of alienation from the pervasive forces of Catholicism in the modern Irish state. Mulligan's subtly blasphemous act of 'blessing' and Yeats's vigorously affirmative one have in common a rejection of the dominant orthodoxy. Yeats may also have felt that Joyce reinforced his own sense of the central importance of art and its right to be free from the pressures of moral and political expediency, if not, perhaps, sharing his belief in its potentially central role in defining the national future. He feared, though, as 'Coole Park and Ballylee, 1931' would make clear, that the Modernist movement of which *Ulysses* was a central text had helped undo all that he and his own literary associates had tried to build up.

In 1925, D. H. Lawrence published his essay 'Blessed Are the Powerful'. There is no external evidence that Yeats had read this piece, but if he did he would certainly have found it congruent with his own contemporary concerns. Lawrence, too, saw modern culture at the end of a historical cycle, with the same corresponding political trends: 'The reign of love is passing, and the reign of power is coming again. ¶ The day of popular democracy is nearly done. Already we are entering the twilight, towards the night that is at hand.'[14] Declaring that 'the communion of power will always be a communion in inequality' (440), Lawrence would have been easily alignable with the Burkean political philosophy that 'Cast but dead leaves to mathematical equality.' The problem, as Lawrence defined it, was *where* to get 'Power, or Might, or Glory, or Honour, or Wisdom' (439). His survey of contemporary dictators found all wanting, but he affirmed nevertheless the concept of submitting oneself to whatever leader might genuinely have greater power – 'Is it not better to serve a man in whom power lives, than to clamour for equality with Mr. Motor-car Ford, or Mr. Shady Stinnes?' (441) In Yeats's poem, by contrast, men 'clamour in drunken frenzy for the moon', reaching for a perhaps unobtainable ideal. 'Blood and the Moon' extends considerations comparable to Lawrence's to the contemporary Irish scene; his poem might have offered Kevin O'Higgins as a legitimate contemporary power figure of the sort Lawrence had been unable to find, but with the collapse of that possibility the final vision of the poem would darken in a way that contrasts sharply with Lawrence's rather hopeful tone.

A definite context within Yeats's own oeuvre was the new ending of *The King's Threshold* that he had first published in 1922, in which at the moment of Seanchan's death the Youngest Pupil predicts that 'coming times will bless what he has blessed / And curse what he has cursed' (*VPl* 311). Although the play in its revised form ended with the much more sombre note sounded by the Oldest Pupil, 'Blood and the Moon' begins with 'Blessed' as if to support the more positive prediction and in fact actually to *realise* what the Youngest Pupil had foreseen. The passive petition to a divine being that opens 'A Prayer on going into my House' gives way to the action of the poet himself, verbally embodying a vision designed to change the values of his world. The echo of *The King's Threshold* helps establish the speaker's voice and stance in 'Blood and the Moon' as bardic, and suggests that the poem, like the play, will focus upon the claims of art to shape life. Furthermore, the self-conscious reference to the poetic act in 'sing it rhyme upon rhyme' corresponds to the lines 'Yet I number him in the song' and 'I write it out in

a verse –' that point to the bardic element in 'Easter, 1916', a text overtly concerned, like *The King's Threshold*, with shaping the future.

The bold adoption of the bardic voice in 'Blood and the Moon'
may reflect familiarity with the exploration of the bardic tradition
in Daniel Corkery's *The Hidden Ireland*, published in 1925. In Corkery's
Introduction he criticises Lecky, the greatness of whose *History of
Ireland in the Eighteenth Century* he acknowledges, for having omitted
all concern with the *Gaelic* culture of the era, a side 'which to him
and his authorities was dark'.[15] As a young man, Yeats shared a
similar sense of Lecky's limitations (*UP1* 356, 385) and would have
been enthusiastic about a study such as *The Hidden Ireland*, an entire
chapter of which is devoted to that O'Sullivan the Red upon whom
Yeats had modelled Hanrahan. By this point in his life, though,
Yeats had of course come increasingly to share Lecky's interest in the
Ascendancy side of eighteenth-century Ireland, which, with the
same sort of error of omission for which Corkery criticised Lecky,
he was before long to call 'that one Irish century that escaped from
darkness and confusion' (*VPl* 958). In 'The Tower', though, he had
linked both strands of the tradition, the world of Barrington's
Recollections and that of Gaelic bards Hanrahan and Raftery.
Corkery's own most polemically exclusionist definition of Irish
culture, in *Synge and Anglo-Irish Literature*, was yet to come (see
Torchiana 107–9), but in his discussion in *The Hidden Ireland* of the
Protestant poet Mícheál Coimín, who had (as Yeats in a less literal
sense was attempting to do) shared 'in the recklessness of the
Anglo-Irishman and in the traditions of the Gael' (292), he asserted
that 'his work enables us to understand a great deal of literary
work done in Ireland since his day by very worthy men who have
stood, perhaps, just a little too far off from the *storms* that in their
time have harried and worsted their people' (298; emphasis added).
In contrast, Yeats's tower, associated with the Anglo-Irish tradition,
rises '*from*' the 'Storm-beaten cottages' representing the Gaelic world
in decline. Corkery saw in the tradition of which the eighteenth
century bards were a late and generally inferior phase, models on
which a truly national 'modern literature' could be based (xiii, xix).
Whether or not Yeats had read *The Hidden Ireland*, he was deeply
engaged with the political and cultural trends in contemporary Ireland
of which Corkery's book was a manifestation, and in Part I of 'Blood
and the Moon' he extends that engagement by incorporating a
passage from Lecky's *History* – 'A Protestant gentry grew up,
generation after generation, regarding ascendancy as their inalien-

able birthright; ostentatiously and arrogantly indifferent to the interests of the great masses of their nation . . .'[16] – but articulating it in a 'bardic' voice.

'Blood and the Moon' is about the possibility of reconciling or combining wisdom and power; and the bardic poet, whose muse is the figure of Wisdom, the White Goddess of the moon, who is in touch thereby with the archetypal realm of the Moods, who brings the past to bear upon the present and embodies his vision in verse of such power that monarchs seek his counsel and fear incurring his displeasure, seemed the persona most likely to be able to achieve that goal – to both 'utter' and 'master'. And this would be especially so if that poet would draw upon the eighteenth-century Ascendancy culture that had destroyed his own hegemony. The poem contains a number of echoes of earlier passages in Yeats's work that underscore by contrast the value that merging a bardic voice with Anglo-Irish values could have. Writing in his journal in 1909, Yeats had considered with a sense of impotence that 'to oppose the new ill-breeding of Ireland, which may in a few years destroy all that has given Ireland a distinguished name in the world . . . I can only *set up* a secondary or interior personality created by me out of the tradition of myself, and this personality (alas, to me only possible in my writings) must be always gracious and simple' (*Mem* 142; emphasis added). As modern-day bard he had an external tradition behind him, a 'powerful emblem' to set up, and could adopt a bolder, sometimes mocking voice. In 'J. M. Synge and the Ireland of his Time' he recalled how in his youth 'Young Ireland had taught a study of our history with the glory of Ireland for event, and this . . . wrecked the historical instinct. . . . There was no literature, for literature is a child of experience always, of knowledge never; and the nation itself, instead of being a dumb struggling thought seeking a mouth to *utter* it or hand to show it, a teeming delight that would *re-create the world*, had become, at best, a subject of knowledge (*CA* 154–6; emphasis added).

Similar limitations upon the free exploration of truth were becoming a hallmark of Ireland after the Revolution; by 1925 Lady Gregory had written of 'the general intolerance that is afoot' (*J*, II, 11). Thus there was a similar need for a voice that *could* genuinely '*utter*' it. In journal passages related to the Synge essay Yeats had meditated upon the image of Unity of Culture offered by Mont-Saint-Michel, 'a marvellous *powerful* living thing created by a community working for hundreds of year and allowing only a very little place for the individual. Are there not groups which obtain, through *powerful*

emotion, organic vitality?' On the other hand, 'one cannot have a
national art in the Young Ireland sense, that is to say an art recognized
at once by all as national because obviously an expression of what
all believe and feel, . . . because *no modern nation* is an organism like
a monastery by rule and discipline, by a definite table of values
understood by all, or even, as the Western peasants are, by habit of
feeling and thought. Am I not right; is there not an organism of
habit – a race held together by folk tradition, let us say? And this is
now impossible because thought old enough to be a habit cannot
face modern life and shape educated men, and an organism of
discipline has hitherto proved impossible *in the modern world* because
no nation can seclude itself' (*Mem* 250–1; emphasis added). As we
have already noted, Yeats was not then daunted by the impossibility,
and went on to ask himself, 'when I try to create a national literature,
for all that, do I not really mean an attempt to create this impossible
thing after all, for the very reason that I always rouse myself to
work by imagining an Ireland as much a unity in thought and feeling
as ancient Greece and Rome and Egypt . . .?' At the time it seemed
that Synge, Lady Gregory and he himself had 'conceived an Ireland
that will remain imaginary more powerfully than we have conceived
ourselves' (*Mem* 251). In 1910 Yeats had of course already long
considered the bardic role legitimately his to play, but had not yet
acquired his tower or developed a clear sense of the intellectual and
cultural heritage of the Prostestant eighteenth century. Thoor Ballylee
represented a sort of Irish Mont-Saint-Michel: 'The Normans had
form', he would say to Gogarty concerning the latter's own tower
at Kinvara (Torchiana 100); and in refurbishing the property his
conscious plan was 'to keep the contrast between the mediaeval
castle and the peasant's cottage' (*L* 625). Berkeley, Swift, Burke and
Goldsmith seemed to offer an indigenous body of thought that
could 'face modern life and shape educated men'. Ireland in the
twenties had not yet begun in earnest the attempt to seclude itself
that de Valera would carry to such lengths, but the reaction against
the chaos of war and civil war seemed to demand the discipline to
which the Cosgrave Government was committed. In 1925 Yeats had
detected 'a greater desire than ever before for expression, I think I
may also say for discipline' (*UP2* 455). In 'Blood and the Moon',
then, the bardic poet looked back, not to the ancient past which lay
closest to the Edenic state, but to a more recent period in which
wisdom seemed to have incarnated itself in the concrete form of the
Protestant Nation. (Years later he would repeat the same gesture, in

similar language but with a turn to the earlier world, in *The Death of Cuchulain*, where the Old Man 'imagines' Cuchulain's body 'in scorn' of those bodies borne by 'modern woman'.)

Even before the Free State era Yeats had asserted that 'daimon-possessed' men such as Swift 'had created nations' (*Mem* 84). In 1930 he was to write that 'the thought of Swift, enlarged and enriched by Burke, saddled and bitted reality and that materialism was hamstrung by Berkeley, and ancient wisdom brought back; that modern Europe has known no men more powerful' (*D* 10–11); and it was precisely for this *combination* of wisdom and power that Yeats celebrated the Anglo-Irish tradition in Part II of 'Blood and the Moon'. The tower, rooted in the earth but rising into the heavens towards the moon, emblematised the link between those antinomies. Addressing the Irish Literary Society in November 1925 on 'The Child and the State', Yeats had argued that the Irish had 'in Berkeley and Burke a philosophy on which it is possible to base the whole life of a nation' and advocated the study of their thought in Irish colleges, especially the teacher-training schools: 'Feed the immature imagination upon that old folk life, and the mature intellect upon Berkeley and the great modern idealist philosophy created by his influence[,] upon Burke who restored to political thought its sense of history, and Ireland is reborn, *potent*, armed and *wise*' (*UP2* 458–9; emphasis added). His poem visualised a figure such as O'Higgins – 'the one strong intellect in Irish public life' – as a contemporary model of yoked power and wisdom and as the sort of individual who could play a major role in the practical implementation of such values (*L* 727; also *VP* 831). Appropriately, O'Higgins was active in efforts to recover the Lane pictures and like Yeats 'most anxious for Lutyens' as architect (*J*, II, 142). As Bernard Krimm has demonstrated, Yeats the Senator was not afraid to disagree with O'Higgins on certain matters, such as legislation that seemed to threaten artistic freedom or potential reunification of North and South (Krimm 71ff); but in the mythic pattern underlying the poem the Vice–President of the Executive Council was the rightful sovereign wedding the Goddess (who had associations both with the moon and with the land) in ceremonies sanctified by the bards.

O'Higgins had seemed to Yeats 'the next best thing to Burke reborn' (Torchiana 180), and in different circumstances might have been celebrated as such in the poem. In 'Death' Yeats was to praise his bravery: 'Many times he died, / Many times rose again' (*VP* 476). But he could not see in the assassination itself the redeeming sacrifice of the priest-king whose death brings about the regeneration of the polity. As in some of Yeats's early poetry, the Wisdom figure proved inaccessible. Blood had been shed in vain. In 'Under Ben Bulben' the poets of the next generation would be urged to 'Sing the lords and ladies gay / That were beaten into the clay / Through seven heroic centuries', but at present those same 'seven centuries' seemed more an unheroic history of violence. Yeats wrote to Mrs O'Higgins that 'the country has lost the man it most needed, its great builder of a nation', equating him implicitly with the 'Immortal Moods which are the true builders of nations', but finding none of the hope that might have come from an efficacious sacrificial ritual (Torchiana 183; *UP1* 361). In another letter he even blamed himself because he had had strange experiences that seemed (with the benefit of hindsight) to be premonitions of the event:

Had we seen more he might have been saved, for recent evidence seems to show that those things are fate unless foreseen by clairvoyance and so brought within the range of free-will.... Are we, that foreknow, the actual or potential traitors of the race-process? Do we, as it were, forbid the banns when the event is struggling to be born? Is this why – even if what we foresee is not some trivial thing – we foresee too little to understand? (*L* 727)

He went on to say that he was working on 'Blood and the Moon', 'partly driven to it by this murder'. The self-condemnation here seems to manifest itself in the poem in the lines describing how 'we that have shed none must gather there / And clamour in drunken frenzy for the moon' and would reappear in the image of the self-condemning bard in 'Parnell's Funeral'.

The final stanza of the poem is a meditation upon the *failure* of art to shape life. For the present, at least, the concept of the poet as mediator between the realm of wisdom and the realm of power fails to sustain conviction. Similar doubts can be traced as far back in Yeats's oeuvre as 'Fergus and the Druid', where the king's quest for Druidic wisdom leads to psychically crippling self-knowledge. In 'The Wisdom of the King' the divine protagonist causes disaster in the world of mundane affairs; his final realisation that 'wisdom the gods have made, and no man shall live by its light' (*VSR* 33) re-echoes in Part IV of 'Blood and the Moon':

> Is every modern nation like the tower,
> Half dead at the top? No matter what I said,
> For wisdom is the property of the dead,
> A something incompatible with life; and power,
> Like everything that has the stain of blood,
> A property of the living; . . . . (*VP* 482)

The poem thus returns once more to the journal passage of 1910 in which Yeats had expressed the fear that 'no modern nation' possessed the proper conditions for the achievement of Unity of Culture. One explanation is ontological, the other historical; in either case the poem, having begun with arrogant assertion and the confidence that change was possible, ends with a discouraged acquiescence in the thought that the ideal Ireland the poet has imagined *must* 'remain imaginary'.[17] The moon is free from stain but beyond human reach, and it can be obscured. The poet can now use language only descriptively, but perhaps it is the demonstration of that strength in the vivid final tableau that saves the poem from ending in despair. 'A Dialogue of Self and Soul', on which Yeats was at work soon after finishing 'Blood and the Moon', again set up the tower as an emblem; it ended where the other poem had begun, with the condition in which the artist can bless. But if it is in this sense more positive than 'Blood and the Moon' it achieves that state only by moving away from the specifics of the Irish political situation to the generalised realm of Self and Soul; and though art itself is reaffirmed, the poetic act of presenting models to shape life does not come into play, for the phrase 'When such as I' colours the ensuing plural pronouns so that they have the effect of the singular and the poet's exultation seems solipsistic, far from the genuinely inclusive 'we' he will be able to utter at the end of Part V of 'Under Ben Bulben' in referring to the blessed Irish nation of the future.

III. 'COOLE PARK AND BALLYLEE, 1931' (1931)

In the same journal passage that lay behind so much of 'Blood and the Moon', Yeats had reluctantly tried to convince himself to 'be content to be but artist, one [of] a group, Synge, Lady Gregory – no, there is no other than these – who express something which has no direct relation to action' (*Mem* 251). When he wrote these words Synge was already dead; and in 1931, as Lady Gregory's death approached and his own must at times have seemed not far off, he renewed his earlier meditations; the result was one of his bleakest works, 'Coole Park and Ballylee, 1931', a poem 'suffused by an omnipresent doom' (Harris 231).

Yeats's contemporary essay 'Ireland, 1921–1931' shows that he was still able to see some developments to approve of during the era of the Free State (*UP2* 486–90). But all of these must have seemed insignificant in the face of the personal loss of so close a friend, even more so because he saw it as the end also of a cultural era and of 'a great Irish social order'.[18] To reinforce the sense of decline he linked the poem with 'The Tower' and 'Blood and the Moon' through the presence of the tower itself and the ongoing concern with the Anglo-Irish tradition as well as through key images such as the swan, allusions to Raftery and Homer, and verbal echoes ('glittering', 'emblem', 'arrogantly', 'ancestral', 'bless'). Looking still further back he echoed also 'Easter, 1916', but there although Pearse, who 'rode our wingèd horse', was dead, and 'All changed', Yeats could find some good in the tragedy and see the text in which he explored it as itself instrumental in making a better future. In 'Coole Park and Ballylee, 1931', art offers *no* hope. On the contrary, however noble its inspiration it represents at best a futile, at worst a destructive act. The poem dramatises the situation of one who, confronted with the prospect of death and an end to earthly satisfactions, looks beyond life for comfort. But is there any comfort to be found? All around himself the poet discovers images of the soul and its 'history' (*AV A* xi), the water its birth, the swan its departure from the phenomenal world. The latter image lacks the affirmative value of the swan song in 'The Tower', recalling instead the atmosphere of 'Nineteen Hundred and Nineteen', where it leaps 'into the desolate heaven'. The context there suggests one source of the grimness of the later poem:

> A man in his own secret meditation
> Is lost amid the labyrinth that he has made
> In art or politics;
> Some Platonist affirms that in the station
> Where we should cast off body and trade
> The ancient habit sticks,
> And that if our works could
> But vanish with our breath
> That were a lucky death,
> For triumph can but mar our solitude. (*VP* 431)

The meditation in both poems moves towards recognition that art, however great, cannot be permanent, while creating it actually has a harmful effect upon the soul of its creator. Requiring immersion in the fallen realm it remains, even when it might bring the souls of others to God, a source of 'attachment' for the artist, retarding the process of spiritual purification and ultimate escape. Thus in 'Nineteen Hundred and Nineteen' seeing the swan's departure brings 'a rage / To end all things, to end / What my laborious life imagined, even / The half-imagined, the half-written page' – that is, the page on which the poet was even then writing that poem and thereby perpetuating the destructive effects of practising his trade. The idea of art shaping life is similarly rejected:

> O but we dreamed to mend
> Whatever mischief seemed
> To afflict mankind, but now
> That winds of winter blow
> Learn that we were crack-pated when we dreamed.

'Coole Park and Ballylee, 1931' recalls the earlier text not only in the use of the 'swan' image but also in its allusions to the Platonic tradition: 'What's water but the generated soul?' The 'dry sticks' of the woods in winter and the sound of 'a stick upon the floor' may be fortuitous, but 'The Choice', originally present as penultimate stanza of the poem, contained unmistakeable echoes:

> The intellect of man is forced to choose
> Perfection of the life, or of the work,
> And if it take the second must refuse
> A heavenly mansion, raging in the dark,
> And when the story's finished, what's the news?
> In luck or out the toil has left its mark:
> That old perplexity an empty purse,
> Or the day's vanity, the night's remorse. (*VP* 495)

The toil has left its mark – the ancient habit sticks. Choosing perfection of the work, Lady Gregory and Yeats dreamed they could create a new Ireland; now the Galway mansion had been sold to the Government, 'all that great glory spent', and they had lost their chance of a 'heavenly mansion', their souls ('murdered with a spot of ink') condemned to the agonies of extended purgatorial suffering. It is significant that *The Words Upon the Window Pane*, written in 1930, was dedicated to 'Lady Gregory[,] in whose house it was written' (*VPl* 937),[19] for the play deals with the Anglo-Irish tradition at its high-point and depicts the greatest artist of that era still trapped in the agonies of 'the night's remorse'; Swift's experience was premonitory of the fates of his modern successors.

The appearance of Homer in the final stanza of 'Coole Park and Ballylee, 1931' is connected with the same dark theme. In 'The Tower' he had served as a prime example of the powerful artist, but here he too evokes Neoplatonic thought. Plotinus had reconciled Homer with Plato:

"Let us flee then to the beloved Fatherland" [Iliad, 11, 140]: this is the soundest counsel. But what is this flight? How are we to gain the open sea? For Odysseus is surely a parable to us when he commands the flight from the sorceries of Circe or Calypso – not content to linger for all the pleasure offered to his eyes and all the delight of sense filling his days. ¶The Fatherland to us is There whence we have come, and There is the Father.[20]

From this point of view, Homer's art leads away from art, his Muse a sorceress or femme fatale, but not the holy Wisdom figure. Porphyry, following Plotinus's lead, argued that 'when we consider the great wisdom of antiquity, and how much Homer excelled in prudence and in every kind of virtue, we ought not to doubt but that he has secretly represented the images of divine things under the concealments of fable.' Thus Odysseus 'represented to us a man who passes in a regular manner over the dark and stormy sea of generation. ... [He] deprived [the Cyclops] of sight that he might by this means while sailing over the stormy ocean be reminded of his sins, till he was safely landed in his native country.'[21] Allegorising Homer was a neat way of saving the bard for theological orthodoxy. Yeats made use of this tradition in 'Vacillation', another 'choice' poem. When Soul urges the poet to 'Seek out reality, leave things that seem' it echoes the argument of Plotinus, and 'What theme had Homer but original sin?' is not a rejection of the soul itself but rather of the flight beyond mortal experience (the sea over which the hero travels) to the transcendent realm of the Divine (*VP* 502). The choice, in other words, is for the Apollonic rather than the Dionysiac phase of the Homeric fables, the soul incarnating rather than transcending forms. In 'Vacillation', which, like 'A Dialogue of

Self and Soul', deals with experience in generalised terms, the choice of Homer can be an affirmation of art and even bring 'blessings' on the head of a spokesman for the Soul. In the highly specified Irish world of 'Coole Park and Ballylee, 1931', however, being Homer's modern counterparts offers no consolation. Even as the impermanence of their cultural achievements manifests itself all around them, the image of the swan drifting upon a darkening flood (combining the two dominant 'emblems' from earlier stanzas) offers an ominous foretaste of what lies in store for their souls. Plotinus, mocked in 'The Tower', has here the last word:

> He that has the strength, let him arise and withdraw into himself, foregoing all that is known by the eyes, turning away for ever from the material beauty that once made his joy. When he perceives those shapes of grace that show in body, let him not pursue: he must know them for copies, vestiges, shadows, and hasten away towards That they tell of. For if anyone follow what is like a beautiful shape playing over water – is there not a myth telling in symbol of such a dupe, how he sank into the depths of the current and was swept away to nothingness? So too, one that is held by material beauty and will not break free shall be precipitated, not in body but in Soul, down to the dark depths loathed of the Intellective-Being, where, blind even in the Lower-World, he shall have commerce only with shadows, there as here. (I.6.8, p. 87)

Turning away from 'material beauty' is precisely what the artist *cannot* do: 'What, be a singer born and lack a theme?' As a result he or she can only expect to sink into the depths of the current and be swept away, 'blind' (like Homer and the other 'man who made the song', Raftery), and plunged in 'dark depths' of separation from the 'Intellective-Being', the 'intellect' that made the wrong choice enduring agonies of remorseful suffering in the shadow state between incarnations.

Even the artists' place on the gyre of literary history exacerbated their plight. In his Introduction to *Fighting the Waves* (1934), Yeats would describe how during the nineteenth century art that embodied shaping ideals began to fade as literature gradually conformed to Stendhal's Realist definition of a masterpiece as a '"mirror dawdling down a lane"': 'Balzac became old-fashioned; romanticism grew theatrical in its strain to hold the public'; till in the major texts of the Naturalists 'the principal characters ... were the passive analysts of events, or had been brutalised into the likeness of mechanical objects.' *Their* successors, the Modernists, revealed yet another stage: 'Certain typical books – *Ulysses*, Mrs. Virginia Woolf's *Waves*, Mr. Ezra Pound's *Draft of XXX Cantos* – suggest a philosophy like that of the *Samkara* school of ancient India, mental and physical objects alike material, a deluge of experience breaking over us and within us, melting limits whether of line or tint; man no hard bright mirror dawdling by the *dry sticks* of a hedge, but a swimmer, or rather the waves themselves. In this new literature . . ., as in that which it superseded, man in himself is nothing' (*WB* 72–3; emphasis added; also *E&I* 405). The 'last romantics', committed to 'The book of the people' and to blessing 'The mind of man', survived anachronistically through the bleak season of the Realists and the Naturalists ('Now all dry sticks under a wintry sun . . . all the rant's a mirror of my mood') to be finally overwhelmed by the waves of Modernism, the 'deluge' of chaotic experience, the 'darkening flood'. The new title of Yeats's Cuchulain play suggests the artists' hopeless struggle against such waves. It can scarcely be coincidental that of the three Modernist texts Yeats specifically mentions, two had co-opted Homer.

In October 1931 Yeats was at Coole, working on the section of *A Vision* dealing with 'the future'.[22] The idea of historical cycles offers the potential for hope in even the worst of times: what has gone will return – if not the same civilisation, at least one embodying comparable values. The reincarnate souls of the artists, their purgatorial experiences behind them (for the time being) could reappear in better times. Yeats could and sometimes did find comfort in such hopes, 'The Gyres' and 'The Statues' being memorable instances. In each case, a positive sense of artistic power plays a central role in the text. As we have seen, it did not do so in 'Coole Park and Ballylee, 1931' – again like 'Nineteen Hundred and Nineteen' in this regard. While the image of the 'darkening flood' implies (as in 'The Second Coming') the end of a cycle, and therefore the *possibility* of a better time ahead, there is here no reference to such a time, 'sometime, and at some new moon', when all things will run once more on the currently unfashionable gyre and Athenian ideals embody themselves in Dublin – the very absence of reference an index of Yeats's current mood. Still later in his life he would write that 'the east has its solutions always and therefore knows nothing of tragedy. It is we, not the east, that must raise the heroic cry' (*LDW* 8; also *LTSM* 154). In 'Coole Park and Ballylee, 1931' he knew tragedy; for his raising of the heroic cry we must look elsewhere. [23]

IV. 'PARNELL'S FUNERAL' (1932–34)

In 1890, the same year in which Parnell lost control of the Irish Parliamentary Party and began the defiant struggle that led to his death, Sir James Frazer published the first edition of *The Golden Bough* – the book from which Yeats learned how to interpret Parnell's fall and even to see it as a fortunate one.[24] Ireland's 'uncrowned king' was easily assimilated into the ubiquitous pattern of priest-kings sacrificed in order to restore the health of the land. Thus in the opening stanzas of 'Parnell's Funeral' the burial at Glasnevin evokes 'the Cretan barb that pierced a star' and ancient and modern events merge into the archetypal pattern. When the poem was published as part of *A Full Moon in March* (1935) the archetypal level was further underscored, for the volume title gestured toward one of the points in the calendar at which such rituals were most frequently performed. According to the scenario provided by 'the old ritual of the year: the mother goddess and the slain god' (*VPl* 1010), the Irish equivalent of the Great Mother could be Cathleen ni Houlihan, for love of whom so many men had already died. In Yeats's own 'Commentary' on the poem he makes it clear that the fall of a star during the funeral indicated 'an accepted sacrifice' (*VP* 834). During his trip to America from October 1932 to January 1933, Yeats gave a lecture called 'Modern Ireland'; he later revealed that in an effort to escape the poetic barrenness he had experienced after 'Coole Park and Ballylee, 1931' he had decided to force himself to write, and to do so had 'rhymed passages from a lecture I had given in America' into Part I of 'Parnell's Funeral' (*VP* 855). In the lecture he had asserted that 'from that national humiliation, from the resolution to destroy all that made the humiliation possible, from that sacrificial victim I derive almost all that is living in the imagination of Ireland today' (*IR* 15). That is, the rebirth crucial to the Frazerian paradigm was what has come to be known as the 'Irish Renaissance', the movement the imminent end of which Yeats had foreseen in 'Coole Park and Ballylee, 1931'. Following Parnell's death, 'we began to value truth' (*VP* 835). Yeats was once more drawing a contrast with the Young Ireland movement, which had 'degraded literature with rhetoric and insincerity' and 'founded or fostered a distortion we have not yet escaped' (*VP* 834). Given the original title of Part I, 'A Parnellite at Parnell's Funeral', the speaker's assertion that 'All that was sung, / All that was said in Ireland is a lie' would seem to illustrate the reaction that Yeats describes beginning in 1891, even as the sacrifice took place. His extended reference in the lecture to the Christmas dinner scene in *A Portrait of the Artist* reinforces this possibility (*IR* 15). But it is clear, too, that there is a sort of doubleness in the chronology of Part I: a level that describes the 1890s and a level contemporary with the writing of the poem in the 1930s. Between those two periods, Parnell's sacrifice had been followed by those of the leaders of the Rising, an event appropriately linked with the fertility rites by its coincidence with Easter. As Yeats recalled in 'Modern Ireland', someone had warned him that '"there is going to be trouble – Pearse is going through Ireland preaching the blood sacrifice – he says blood must be shed in every generation"'[25] This portion of the lecture is clearly related to the emerging poem:

> Something new and terrible had come in Ireland, the mood of the mystic victim. For a generation speeches, commemorations led before men's minds the martyrs for the national cause, all the more popular national songs were in their praise; not one of them, not Lord Edward, not Wolfe Tone, was the victim. They had served their cause and met their deaths, but they had not deliberately sought suffering. The man who dedicates his suffering is more powerful than any orator, because we measure his love by his suffering. We say he could not [have] endured all this if [he] had not loved that country or that cause with a passion so great nothing else could weigh against it; and then, that we may be completely alive, we want to share his love. Parnell had been the victim, the nation the priest, but now men were both priest and victim – they offered the nation a terrible way out [of] humiliation and self-detraction. Since then the substitution of the hunger strike for [the] silence of the imprisoned Fenians has helped to make deliberate suffering a chief instrument in our public life. A few weeks ago I asked an important government official about an obscure revolutionary leader, and he replied as if he was saying the most natural thing in the world, 'He has a passion for suffering; he is always compelling people to persecute him.' I do not say that this instinct is wholesome or that it is unwholesome; I may say that it is not wholesome for a people to think much of exceptional acts of faith or sacrifice, least of all to make them the sole test of [a] man's worth. (*IR* 23)

This passage itself carries the sacrificial paradigm up to Yeats's own day. In a contemporary letter Yeats added specifics, writing Olivia

Shakespear that 'this country is exciting. I am told that De Valera
has said in private that within three years he will be torn in pieces.
It reminds me of a saying by O'Higgins to his wife "Nobody can
expect to live who has done what I have." No sooner does a politician
get into power than he begins to seek unpopularity. It is the cult of
sacrifice planted in the nation by the executions of 1916. . . . I asked
a high government officer once if he could describe the head of the
I.R.A. He began "That is so and so who has [the] cult of suffering
and is always putting himself in positions where he will be
persecuted"' (*L* 809). Implicit but crucial in both speech and letter
were the destructiveness of the Civil War and the violence and
increasing restrictiveness of the first decade of the Free State's
existence. Mythically, such developments were signs that the land
was again faced with blight, dearth, sterility. Although in early
1933 Yeats was actively involved in formulating an authoritarian
'social theory' as a basis for political opposition to de Valera, his
own historical vision warned that political machinations might
prove insufficient, that as both Pearse and the archetypal patterns
of *The Golden Bough* suggested, blood would have to be shed in
every generation (*L* 808, 811–2).

  Although 'Modern Ireland' shows Yeats's uneasiness about the
idea of 'the victim', the martyr who 'deliberately sought suffering',
a letter he wrote some months after composing Part I of the poem
reveals a continued fascination with the idea and links it,
approvingly, with Swift: 'When a [man] of Swift's sort is born into
such dryness, is he not in the Catholic sense of the word its *victim*?
A French Catholic priest once told me of certain holy women. One
was victim for a whole country, another for such and such a village.
Is not Swift the human soul in that dryness, is not that his tragedy
and his genius? Perhaps every historical phase may have its victims
– its poisoned rat in a hole' (*L* 818–9). The 'dryness' Yeats writes of
here referred to Swift's eighteenth-century milieu, but also corresponds to the 'waste land' condition that signals the need for
another sacrifice. Who, then, would be the *next* victim? As
Torchiana has pointed out (331–2), a few years later Yeats would
quote with approval Swift's scathing witticism '"When I am told
that somebody is my brother Protestant . . . I remember that the rat
is a fellow creature"' (*L* 876). The voice of the speaker in Part I
becomes not only Swiftian but bardic as well.[26] Swift knew Sidney's
reference to the bards' power. In its most ludicrous form, the bardic
voice utters 'the rhyme rats hear before they die'. Through their

links with Druidism the bards may have been associated in ancient times with sacrificial rites.[27]

In modern Ireland, Yeats the poet had perhaps nourished the cult of sacrifice that underlay the Rising and Pearse's death, the power of art leading in this case to remorse as well as pride. The assassination of O'Higgins had deprived him of the chance to exert such power less violently by bringing Swiftian values to bear upon the Free State; the guilt Yeats felt about O'Higgins's death may also lie behind 'I thirst for accusation' (*L* 727). And Lady Gregory's death had forced him to face up to the impermanence of the renaissance that had followed Parnell's sacrifice. Part I of 'Parnell's Funeral' was in fact the first poem he had written since she died (*L* 808, 814). Now in April 1933, even as he set about developing practical measures for opposing de Valera, he seems also to have imagined *himself* becoming the victim that contemporary events might necessitate. In the fourth stanza the speaker identifies himself with Lear, like Parnell 'more sinned against than sinning', a figure of potentially redemptive suffering. In the 'Commentary' to the poem Yeats had compared the Irish experience after Parnell's fall to 'an initiation like that of the Tibetan ascetic, who staggers half dead from a trance, where he has seen himself eaten alive and has not yet learned that the eater was himself' (*VP* 835). Whitaker has cited this passage in support of the suggestion that 'the speaker is both Irish satirist and Irish rat being rhymed to death. He is both slayer and slain in the ritual sacrifice' (249).[28] In the Introduction to *Fighting the Waves*, a few paragraphs after the lines that became the third stanza of 'Parnell's Funeral', Yeats returned to the subject of victimage, noting that 'here in Ireland we have come to think of self-sacrifice, when worthy of public honour, as the act of some man at the moment when he is least himself, most completely the crowd. The heroic act, as it descends through tradition, is an act done because a man is himself, because, being himself, he can ask nothing of other men but room amid remembered tragedies; a sacrifice of himself to himself, almost, so little may he bargain, of the moment to the moment' (*WB* 75). In the same Introduction he had already described how 'in the eighties of the last century Standish O'Grady, his mind full of Homer, retold the story of Cuchulain that he might bring back an heroic ideal' (*WB* 70), revealing once again his own contemporary preoccupation with an art that could shape life. The reference to 'the crowd', chiming with the O'Connellite era in 'Parnell's Funeral', suggests a distinction between *objective* and *subjective* self-sacrifice; in the former one loses one's identity, while in the later one preserves it (see *Au* 330–1). The latter type could inspire, as Yeats felt Parnell's had, a new renaissance in Ireland. Yeats's own movement might be moribund, but by depicting himself 'dying' heroically, a sacrifice of himself to himself, facing unflinchingly the end foreseen in 'Coole Park and Ballylee, 1931', he could stimulate future cultural emulation of 'the heroic ideal'. For reasons that will emerge below, this plan was not realised in the poem actually written, but he would return to the thought at the very end of his life in *The Death of Cuchulain*.

The tone of the fourth stanza is grim, recalling the heath scenes in *Lear*. The Shakespearian context, the 'remembered tragedy', shows us reduced to the essential form of 'unaccommodated man' and raises the question of whether we *are* human – animal or man. It recalls what Yeats said in the Introduction to *Fighting the Waves* of the Modernist movement that had eventually supplanted his own: in its representative texts, 'man in himself is nothing'. The sacrifice contemplated at this point in 'Parnell's Funeral', an act done because a man is himself', would have an affirmative force: 'Whatever flames upon the night / Man's own resinous heart has fed' (*VPl* 931)

So after the despair of 'Coole Park and Ballylee, 1931' Yeats seems to have briefly recovered faith in some of his most cherished values; but events would soon threaten that recovery. Between the completion of Part I of 'Parnell's Funeral' (by April 1933) and the composition of Part II he even sought to affect public opinion directly with his 'Three Songs to the Same Tune',[29] but after the fiasco involving the Blueshirts and General O'Duffy he was disillusioned again, and Part II (written possibly as late as August 1934) represents a dis-couraged reconsideration of the situation.[30]

'The rest I pass, one sentence I unsay'; that sentence, presumably, was 'None shared our guilt; nor did we play a part / Upon a painted stage when we devoured his heart.' What the poet has had to take back is not the blame and the self-condemnation but the suggestion that *anyone* of the Free State era had been Parnell's legitimate successor, had assimilated his vital essence and assumed his role as priest-king (see *WG* 126–7). Although Yeats had diligently supported Cosgrave's Government and saw de Valera as a threat to the civic order restored at so great a cost since the Civil War, from the perspective adopted in this poem he could make no real distinction between the two leaders. Both looked only slightly better than the ultimately ludicrous O'Duffy. O'Higgins, if anyone, would have been the man, but in 'Blood and the Moon' Yeats had already explored and had had to reject the applicability of that scenario to his life and death. Part II of 'Parnell's Funeral' does return to the meditations about wisdom and power that had been central in the earlier poem. Borrowing his imagery from the first chapter of *The Golden Bough* Yeats depicted Swift as the aged priest-king guarding the sacred grove and Parnell as the younger man who was required to pluck a bough from the sacred tree before he could challenge the incumbent and, if victorious, reign as his successor. Yeats, allowing here what in 'Blood and the Moon' he had come to deny was possible, suggests that Parnell did find 'there' (the Neoplatonic term for the divine state in which all antinomies are reconciled or transcended) both wisdom and power. The consolation was no greater, though, for *he* had had no successor and consequently the land now lay barren. (In 'The Black Tower' Yeats would suggest that the 'king' himself was eventually to return.)

The suggestion in Part I that the poet himself might assume the sacrificial role has disappeared. It has been argued that 'the speaker himself, in dancing a *measure* on that grave, has eaten [Parnell's] heart. He now has the bitter wisdom of the heart in Swift's "blood-sodden breast": the knowledge of his own participation in that evil of which he is victim' (Whitaker 250); but even if the ultimate truth of this be granted, the poet, as his reiterated past perfect constructions emphasise, experiences no saving *recognition* of it in Part II. And in a letter of February 1935 he wrote negatively of 'the vertigo of self-sacrifice' as 'one of the means whereby we escape from thought.'[31] The alternative possibility, central to 'Blood and the Moon', that he might bring past ideals to bear upon the present and so inspire one of the public men of his own time to play the sacrificial role appears here not ultimately to have been *possible*. The barrier this time seems to have been one of phase: 'Their school a crowd, his master solitude.' The word 'solitude' reverberates through the final lines, tolling Yeats back to his own 'sole self'. Already in 1930 he had recognised in Augustus John's portrait of him 'Anglo-Irish solitude, a solitude I have made for myself, an outlawed solitude' (*D* 22; see also *VP* 431, *E&I* 400). Now, with the defeat, as it seemed, of all his hopes for Ireland and the corresponding sense of the impotence of his art, he felt more isolated than ever. (His Steinach operation in April 1934 seems ironic in this light.) As Krimm has emphasised, the act of publishing the full poem, in October 1934, was a public act of dissociation from all Irish political parties (Krimm 163–5; see also *VP* 837). It is no wonder that the following year he wrote to

Ethel Mannin 'I want to plunge myself into impersonal poetry, to get rid of the bitterness, irritation and hatred my work in Ireland has brought into my soul' (*L* 835–6). But this was far easier said than done, and his sense of 'outlawed solitude' continued to gnaw at him, like the fox in the fable, until it found expression in 'The Curse of Cromwell'.

V. 'THE CURSE OF CROMWELL' (1937)

In the Introduction to *The Oxford Book of Modern Verse* Yeats included a discussion of the Irish writers who had remembered 'the Gaelic poets of the seventeenth and early eighteenth centuries wandering, after the flight of the Catholic nobility, among the boorish and the ignorant, singing their loneliness and their rage; James Stephens, Frank O'Connor made them symbols of our pride. . . . I showed Lady Gregory a few weeks before her death a book by Day Lewis. "I prefer", she said, "those poems translated by Frank O'Connor because they come out of original sin"' (xiv–xv). This passage was the nucleus from which 'The Curse of Cromwell' developed. There are obvious verbal echoes of it in 'there is an old beggar wandering in his pride'. ('Pride' also links the poem to 'The Tower', with the significant difference that in the later poem the 'pride' has associations with the Gaels of the hidden Ireland.) The poets' 'loneliness' could serve to express that 'outlawed solitude' Yeats himself had been feeling. The 'boorish' and 'ignorant' who remain after the patrons have gone suggest a central concern of the new poem, the problem of *audience*. The reference to Lady Gregory's death recalls 'Coole Park and Ballylee, 1931', itself pervaded by a profound sense of loss and containing a reference (in the later-excised stanza) to the artist's soul 'raging in the dark'. Homer, whose conspicuous absence is noted at the end of that poem, had been linked in 'Vacillation' with the artist's necessary if painful choice of 'original sin'. And Day Lewis and the other young English writers of the Left were to become a primary target of the satiric thrust of 'The Curse of Cromwell'. Shortly after writing the poem Yeats told a correspondent that his poetry was 'generally written out of despair' and that he had 'just come out of a particularly black attack', the immediate stimulus for which was largely a book alleging that the infamous 'black diaries' of Roger Casement had been forged (*L* 886; *LDW* 107–16, 122–3). In typical fashion he sought to balance his subjective emotion with the objective vehicle of tradition. The example of this process that he offered in 'A General Introduction for my Work' clearly refers to 'The Curse of Cromwell':

> Our mythology, our legends, differ from those of other European countries because down to the end of the seventeenth century they had the attention, perhaps the unquestioned belief, of peasant and noble alike; Homer belongs to sedentary men, even to-day our ancient queens, our mediaeval soldiers and lovers, can make a pedlar shudder. I can put my own thought, despair perhaps from the study of present circumstance in the light of ancient philosophy, into the mouth of rambling poets of the seventeenth century, or even of some imagined ballad singer of to-day, and the deeper my thought the more credible, the more peasant-like, are ballad singer and rambling poet. Some modern poets contend that jazz and music-hall songs are the folk art of our time, that we should mould our art upon them; we Irish poets, modern men also, reject every folk art that does not go back to Olympus. (*E&I* 516; see also *LDW* 126–7, *L* 892)

Thus the use of a bardic persona could connect Yeats's own time with the Homeric world as well as the intervening Irish era. The 'end of the seventeenth century' was a crucial watershed in Irish history, for the Williamite triumphs of 1690–91 meant the virtually total eclipse of the traditional Gaelic way of life, including the death, banishment, flight, or economic ruin of the last of the Gaelic and Old English patrons upon whom the bards had for centuries depended. In the Introduction to the Oxford anthology Yeats had suggested a second, related set of negative associations with that era, developments in philosophy and science with destructive literary concomitants: 'The mischief began at the end of the seventeenth century when man became passive before a mechanized nature; that lasted to our own day with the exception of a brief period between Smart's *Song to David* and the death of Byron, wherein imprisoned man beat upon the door. Or I may dismiss all that ancient history and say it began when Stendhal described a masterpiece as a "mirror dawdling down a lane"' (xxvii). Except for the years of the Romantic Movement, the period had been one in which man had dwindled in importance and the view that art must copy nature had dominated over the view that nature might copy art. The phrase 'we Irish poets' connects the passage from the 'General Introduction' with Yeats's argument that when Berkeley rejected the tenets of British materialist philosophy with 'we Irish do not hold with this' he had won 'the Irish Salamis' (an argument to which he would return in 'The Statues') and with the exhortation to 'Irish poets' in Part V of 'Under Ben Bulben' (*D* 51; see also 49–55). The rejection of 'jazz and music-hall songs' as the basis for modern art suggests that formally, too, 'The Curse of Cromwell' was part of yet another Battle of Salamis, between Yeats and antagonistic forces among the writers whom he had been surveying in the course of his preparation of the anthology.

Although Yeats's persona was undoubtedly a composite figure, he was modelled primarily upon Aogán O'Rathaille (c1675–1729), whose dates span the period Yeats had singled out as crucial and whose work constitutes a poetic chronicle of the descent of growing darkness upon the tradition with which he had identified his fortunes. At the source of that tradition were the McCarthys, Gaelic patrons of family predecessors. His family's immediate source of maintainance were the Brownes, of Elizabethan planter stock, Catholic, Jacobite, and favourable to the native Irish. They had supplanted and there-after often supported the McCarthys (*AD* 138–9). After the Battle of the Boyne their estates were confiscated for the lifetime of the current head of the family, Sir Nicholas Browne; as a result of this confiscation O'Rathaille had to leave his native district. The poet became particularly known for his satires, and was supposed to have killed a man by the venom of one of them (*DUR* xxix–xxx). During the years 1708 to 1715 and 1719–20 there were frequent expectations of a landing in Ireland by the Stuart Pretender, and Sir Nicholas Browne was jailed for refusing to take an oath renouncing him. O'Rathaille wrote of the hoped-for return, using the Gaelic convention of the *aisling* in which the poet has a dream vision of Ireland, personified as a woman – the Goddess, the 'ancient queen' – reunited with her rightful husband, the Stuart monarch. All such expectations were disappointed, of course, but in 1720, O'Rathaille felt new hope when Sir Nicholas died and his English-educated son Sir Valentine inherited his estates (*AD* 161). The bard anticipated 'a resumption of the pre-1690 order of things' but Sir Valentine did not share his father's values and the faithful retainer died as an im-poverished tenant, despairing of Stuart intervention or the restoration of his own status.

Yeats had referred positively to O'Rathaille in *The Trembling of the Veil* (1922), suggesting that at least in some parts of Ireland the peasants of his own youth 'had not lost the habit of Gaelic criticism, picked up, perhaps, from the poets who took refuge among them after the ruin of the great Catholic families, from men like that O'Rahilly, who cries in a translation from the Gaelic that is itself a masterpiece of concentrated passion: – The periwinkle and the tough dog-fish / Towards evening time have got into my dish' (*Au* 217). The poem he quoted from was a bitter lamentation over O'Rathaille's dispossession subsequent to the confiscation of the estates of Sir Nicholas Browne. The translation, by James Stephens, was also quoted by Yeats in the passage in the Introduction to the anthology. But Yeats's main source of information about O'Rathaille was O'Connor, with whom he worked closely on the translations published by the Cuala Press in 1932 as *The Wild Bird's Nest*. That volume contained 'A Sleepless Night', O'Connor's version of the lyric about the bard's dispossession; 'Reverie at Dawn', an *aisling* in which 'The tall queen, Eevul, so bright of countenance' tells the poet of 'the king that will come to us over the sea, / And make us happy and reign in a fortunate land' (*WBN* 19); 'A Grey Eye Weeping', included by Yeats in the anthology, in which the poet, lamenting that 'foreign devils have made our land a tomb', 'royal Cashel is bare of house and guest', and 'great verse . . . lacks renown' (20–1) makes his unsuccessful petition to Sir Valentine; and finally 'Last Lines', in which '*The poet on his deathbed writes to a friend, having fallen into despair about certain matters*' (22–3). That 'despair' over the prospects for a Stuart restoration or any further patronage makes this poem the bleakest of them all. It was also Yeats's primary source for 'The Curse of Cromwell', providing him not only with language and images, especially 'His fathers served their fathers before Christ was crucified', but also with the basic situation of the patronless poet at the lowest ebb of his fortunes, his world crumbling around him, recognising 'the time to die':

I shall not cry for help, not till death strike me dumb.
And what if I should cry? Help is no longer here
Since that great prince who would have heard me call and come
Can come no more, since all is lost that once was dear.

Mind shudders like a wave, the dearest hope is dead,
Bowels and heart alike are pierced and filled with pain –
Our lands, our hills, our fields, our gentle neighbourhood
A plot where any English upstart stakes his claim!

The Shannon and the Liffey and the tuneful Lee,
The Boyne and the Blackwater a sad music sing,

The waters of the west run red into the sea,
No matter what be trumps, your knave will beat our king.

I shout my loss and still I weep, eternal tears,
I am a man oppressed, afflicted and undone
Who where he wanders weeping no companion hears
But some grave waterfall that has no cause to mourn.

For all the rout that came upon the blood of kings
Tears in a voiceful torrent plough my wintry face
And add their mournful tribute to the stream that springs
Into the sea at Youghal and passes by this place.

Henceforth I cease. Death comes and will have no delay
By Laune and Lane and Lee diminished of their pride.
I shall go after the heroes, ay, into the clay!
My fathers followed theirs before Christ was crucified.

Yeats's debt to this poem was great enough for him to boast wryly
to O'Connor that he had 'stolen' it.[32] He compounded the theft by
drawing also upon O'Connor's translation of the folk poem 'Kilcash',
printed immediately after 'Last Lines' in *The Wild Bird's Nest* and
chosen by Yeats for his anthology. Kilcash had been the 'big house'
of one branch of the Butler family; O'Connor later recorded that he
did not think Yeats knew this, but 'it was one of his favorite poems,
and there is a good deal of his work in it.'[33] The poem had a
connection also with O'Rathaille, for a woman of this Butler family
was married to Sir Valentine Browne at the time of O'Rathaille's
disagreement with him (*AD* 328–9). Yeats may not have been aware
of these associations, but he surely saw in the poem an analogue for
Lady Gregory's death and the end of Coole Park:

> What shall we do for timber?
> The last of the woods is down,
> Kilcash and the house of its glory
> And the bell of the house are gone;
> The spot where her lady waited
> That shamed all women for grace
> When earls came sailing to greet her
> And Mass was said in that place.

My cross and my affliction
Your gates are taken away,
Your avenue needs attention,
Goats in the garden stray;
Your courtyard's filled with water

And the great earls where are they?
The earls, the lady, the people
Beaten into the clay.

Nor sound of duck or of geese there
Hawk's cry or eagle's call,
Nor humming of the bees there
That brought honey and wax for all,
Nor the sweet gentle song of the birds there
When the sun has gone down to the West
Nor a cuckoo atop of the boughs there
Singing the world to rest.

There's a mist there tumbling from branches
Unstirred by night and by day,
And a darkness falling from heaven,
And our fortunes have ebbed away;
There's no holly nor hazel nor ash there
But pastures of rock and stone,
The crown of the forest is withered
And the last of its game is gone.

I beseech of Mary and Jesus
That the great come home again
With long dances danced in the garden
Fiddle music and mirth among men,
That Kilcash the home of our fathers
Be lifted on high again
And from that to the deluge of waters
In bounty and peace remain. (*WBN* 23–5)

'The spot where her lady waited / That shamed all women for grace'
would have evoked both the 'spot whereon the founders lived and
died' and their last inheritor, gracious Lady Gregory herself. The
felled woods correspond to the 'ancestral trees', goats stray in gardens

like those 'rich in memory' at Coole; the birds have all flown away, the courtyard is flooded by a 'deluge of waters', and *darkness* falls from heaven. It is reasonable to assume, also, that he noted the verbal similarities linking 'Kilcash' with 'Last Lines': 'The earls, the lady, the people / Beaten into the clay'; and the potential *contrast* between the two poems created by the last stanza of 'Kilcash', which envisages a return of what has been lost quite inconceivable to O'Rathaille at the end of his life. Unlike Yeats's poem, neither of these is a ballad, but the folk origins of the anonymous 'Kilcash' may have encouraged him in his use of the form.

Like all the O'Rathaille poems, 'Kilcash' reflects Ireland after the Boyne and Aughrim: the clearance of woodlands was designed to flush out the now landless followers of Sarsfield who had sought shelter in them (*KLC* 98). Yeats's stress on 'Cromwell's house and Cromwell's murderous crew' does not obviously correspond to anything in 'Kilcash' or in the O'Rathaille poems with which we know him to have been familiar. The phrase may have been borrowed from Robert Dwyer Joyce's 'The Blacksmith of Limerick', which includes the line 'He said "The breach they're mounting, the Dutchman's murdering crew,"' but Joyce's ballad is set in the later era.[34] A clue to Yeats's purpose in introducing references to the earlier period is provided by a passage in his essay on Spenser. The passage immediately follows his discussion of Spenser's hostile view of the rebel Irish of Elizabeth's time:

In a few years the Four Masters were to write the history of that time, and they were to record the goodness or the badness of Irishman and Englishman with entire impartiality. They had seen friends and relatives persecuted, but they would write of that man's poisoning and this man's charities and of the fall of great houses, and hardly with any other emotion than a thought of the pitiableness of all life. Friend and enemy would be for them a part of the spectacle of the world. They remembered indeed those Anglo-French invaders who conquered for the sake of their own strong hand, and when they had conquered became a part of the life about them, singing its songs, when they grew weary of their own Iseult and Guinevere. But the Four Masters had not come to understand . . . that new invaders were among them, who fought for an alien State, for an alien religion. Such ideas were difficult to them, for they belonged to the old individual, poetical life, and spoke a language even, in which it was all but impossible to think an abstract thought. They understood Spain, doubtless, which persecuted in the interests of religion, but I doubt if anybody in Ireland could have understood as yet that the Anglo-Saxon nation was beginning to persecute in the service of ideas it believed to be the foundation of the State. I doubt if anybody in Ireland saw that with certainty, till the Great Demagogue had come and turned the old house of the noble into 'the house of the Poor, the lonely house, the accursed house of Cromwell.' He came, ... and the old individual, poetical life went down, as it seems, for ever. (*CA* 242–4)

To a considerable extent, the history of Ireland at the end of the seventeenth century replicated events from the middle of the century and from the turn of the preceding century. Yeats, however, was at pains in the piece on Spenser to isolate something that came into the country *before* the Williamite era: 'The Anglo-Saxon nation was beginning to persecute in the service of ideas it believed to be the foundation of the State.' By the 1930s such persecution had come to be associated in Yeats's mind with Communism – a threat, as he perceived it, to recognition of the primacy of the soul, to order, to rule by the enlightened few, and to his own tradition in literature. In a radio broadcast of 1937, not long after he wrote 'The Curse of Cromwell', Yeats made the equation explicit, declaring that 'Cromwell came to Ireland as a kind of Lenin' (Torchiana 334).

Another implication of the Cromwell allusion, involving a different sort of historical irony, emerges from the piece on Spenser. Cromwell was associated there not only with 'an alien State' but also with 'an alien religion'. In the final sentence quoted, Yeats hedged his bets a bit, suggesting that when Cromwell came 'the old individual, poetical life went down, *as it seems*, for ever'. Ireland under de Valera was proving the wisdom of Yeats's qualification, systematically rooting out the vestiges of the Protestant presence, so that, as Whitaker has noted, 'thanks to the ironic reversal in Irish history, at evening time the Anglo-Irish Yeats could feel, contemplating the new Catholic bourgeois state, that bitter passion which the Jacobite poets had felt as they contemplated in Ireland "the house of the Poor, the lonely house, the accursed house of Cromwell"' (255). So the reference to Cromwell enriches the central symbol of the 'house' in the poem and enables the bardic lament to serve as vehicle for the entire range of foreign and domestic political and literary developments weighing upon Yeats's mind as he sat down to write it.

On 8 January 1937, while 'in the middle of' writing 'The Curse of Cromwell', he wrote to Dorothy Wellesley, who had told him of a recent dream,

> Are not dreams like our poetry – one life in terms of another life? At this moment I am expressing my rage against the intelligentsia by writing about Oliver Cromwell who was the Lennin [*sic*] of his day – I speak through the mouth of some wandering peasant poet in Ireland.

> I find wherever I go; and far & wide I must go
> Nothing but Cromwell's house & Cromwell's murderous crew!
> The lovers & the dancers are beaten into the clay;
> And the tall men & the swordsmen & the horsemen where
>   are they?
> And I without a master wander far and wide
> My fathers served their fathers before Christ was crusefied.

> I send a new *English Review* with a most important article. You must return it for I shall want it when the time comes to reply. It makes it quite plain that you and I are attacked because the greater part of the English intelligentsia are communists. I shall take the challenge but not now. . . . (*LDW* 119–20)

The article, 'Danger of a Dark Age' by Hugh Gordon Porteus, had as its subject 'the encroachment of "left" propaganda on art, thought and letters'.[35] It began by quoting two examples from anthologies of 'Left' writing. The author of one, noting that the Archbishop of Canterbury and W.H. Auden both saw the threat of an imminent Doomsday but that the former deplores Communism and puts his faith in God while the latter 'reads Lenin' and deplores Fascism, asserted that 'nearly every writer, every thinker, every poet of worth stands (whether Mr. Wyndham Lewis and Mr. Yeats and Mr. Eliot like it or not) nearer to Mr. Auden than to the Archbishop in this matter. . . .' The author of the other passage used as an example asserted that Fascism meant the 'torturing of Liberals, Socialists, Communists, Pacifists, Intellectuals, the burning of books and pictures, the negation of art and liberty.' Porteus himself defended Yeats, Eliot and Lewis, claiming that the 'abstract mind, coddled by a "scientific" age on the featherbed of English democracy, is all that is left of our intelligentsia,' and was critical of the Communists' tendency to 'fight to the death, against reason, truth, reality or justice, for the cause they have espoused. . . .' This judgment, and his suggestion that Auden saw it as 'our duty . . . to hasten by fair or foul means the coming of that [Communist] State', must have linked up in Yeats's mind with his own earlier statement that in seventeenth-century Ireland 'the Anglo-Saxon nation was beginning to persecute in the service of ideas it believed to be the foundation of the State.' In the Introduction to the Oxford anthology, although he suggested that 'the men who created the communism of the masses had Stendhal's mirror for a contemporary, believed that religion, art, philosophy, expressed economic change, that the shell secreted the fish,' he had downplayed the doctrinal Communism of the Young English poets and had even had some praise for their work (xxxvi–xxxviii). But attacks on Dorothy Wellesley's poetry in *The Daily Worker* and on his editing of the anthology, supplemented by the Porteus essay, obviously caused him to rethink his attitude and to see in their art more of a threat to his own than he had previously recognised (*LDW* 114; 113, 117). In a letter written a couple of months after completion of the poem he admitted that he 'admired' Auden more than he had said in the anthology, but suggested disagreement with the literary premises of the 'young Cambridge poets' (they 'write out of their intellectual beliefs and that is all wrong'), and indicated that he could not share the optimistic element in their work: 'I have no such pleasant world as they seem to do. Like Balzac, I see decreasing ability and energy and increasing commonness, and like Balzac I know no one who shares the premises from which I work. What can I do but cry out, lately in simple peasant songs that hide me from the curious? ¶ "What are the things I find as far and wide I go – / Nothing but Cromwell's House and Cromwell's murderous crew!"' (*L* 886) Where they pinned their hopes for social regeneration upon economic and political reforms, he would look to eugenics – and to art. Meanwhile, their growing literary prominence had clearly heightened his sense of isolation.

After completing his poem, Yeats told Dorothy Wellesley that it was 'very poignant because it was my own state watching romance & nobility disappear' (*LDW* 122–3). His association of the writers of the Left with a literary realism antagonistic to his own aesthetic principles was involved here, but the disappearance of romance and nobility points also to a specifically modern Irish context for the poem developing from the disappearance of the 'last romantics'

lamented in the final stanza of 'Coole Park and Ballylee, 1931'. As
the Casement ballads demonstrated, Yeats's Irish Nationalist passions
remained intense; he wrote to Ethel Mannin, 'some day you will
understand what I see in the Irish National movement and why I
can be no other sort of revolutionist – as a young man I belonged to
the I.R.B. and was in many things O'Leary's pupil. Besides, why
should I trouble about communism, fascism, liberalism, radicalism,
when all ... are going down stream with the artificial unity which
ends every civilization?' (*L* 869) But by the end of 1936 Ireland had
itself become almost everything he despised, and those domestic
developments cast their shadow over 'The Curse of Cromwell'. The
once dominant Protestant Nation was everywhere in retreat before
resurgent Catholic political and social influence. In a note to 'Three
Songs to the Same Tune' he had already used O'Rathaille's 'My
fathers served their fathers before Christ was crucified' as part of
his 'commendation of the rule of the able and educated, man's old
delight in submission ...' (*VP* 543–4). The relevance of the line and
the associated values had become all the greater by December 1936,
just before Yeats wrote 'The Curse of Cromwell'. The Spanish Civil
War had led to the organisation in Ireland of a movement called the
Christian Front that, as he wrote Dorothy Wellesley, 'is gathering
all the bigots together. We have all been threatened with what can
only mean mob violence by a Catholic preacher. "Those responsible"
ran one sentence "for the outraging of Nuns in Spain are all the intellectuals since the Rennascence who have opposed the supernatural"
& then came sentences, which are supposed to refer to The Irish
Academy of Letters and to myself. We were told we were watched
& that the Catholics of Ireland would not be always patient' (*LDW*
110). The following March he told another correspondent of his fear
that 'my "pagan" institutions, the Theatre, the Academy, will be
fighting for their lives against combined Catholic & Gaelic bigotry'
(*L* 885). The Muses had become things of no account indeed, and
the 'murderous' forces of Cromwell corresponded not only to
international Communism but also – again with grim irony – to the
indigenous Irish Catholic extremists who were so stridently opposing
the Communists in Spain. The Academy had been organised in part
from fear that de Valera would use the censorship laws to silence
dissenting voices among the Irish writers (Krimm 125; see also
LDW 22 and *L* 801, 805); the subsequent developments threatened
to cut Yeats off entirely from Irish audiences, as the growing
strength of the younger generation of English poets and encroach-

ing ' "Left" propaganda' threatened his relationship with English readers. Such anxieties lie behind the crucial importance of 'audience' in 'The Curse of Cromwell' itself.

To call attention to the question of audience, Yeats made 'You' the first word of his poem. This was apparently a late thought, for the version he sent to Dorothy Wellesley had begun 'I find wherever I go ...' and a subsequent draft read 'What are the things I find....' Although the title of O'Rathaille's poem suggested that the poet was writing to 'a friend', there is no evidence of this in the text. The speaker there stresses that 'that great prince who would have heard me call and come / Can come no more', and his repeated use of 'our' in the second stanza emphasises the possessive, in contrast to the claims of the English upstarts. The 'your' in the third stanza literally but implausibly addresses the upstarts themselves, and in a later version of his translation O'Connor changed 'your' to 'their' (*KLC* 107). (The Irish text reads *'an'* – that is, 'the'.) The bard under-scores his own isolation in the fourth stanza, picturing himself as 'a man ... / Who where he wanders weeping no companion hears / But some grave waterfall that has no cause to mourn'. Yeats's speaker uses 'we' in the third stanza to include any other bards who might survive and share his plight, but nothing else in the poem would support the scenario of an encounter with one of them who might then serve as audience. The patrons who represent the bard's natural audience are all in the clay (see *VP* 833). The final image of the poem suggests that the persona has no audience left except 'the dogs and horses that understand my talk'. 'You,' then, ultimately makes most sense as an address from the modern poet to his readers, to that audience without whom artistic power is impossible because it is in their experience of the text that life inter-sects with art and can be changed by it. 'The Curse of Cromwell' shows Yeats in a period during which his confidence about the ability to reach beyond himself was in flux. The stanza he had sent Dorothy Wellesley early in January 1937 stressed solitude (note 'I without a master'), though he says in the letter that in contrast to his 'black mood' of previous weeks he is 'gay now' (*LDW* 120). When he wrote her again after finishing the poem he described his mood somewhat ambiguously: 'I have come out of that darkness a man you have never known – more man of genius, more gay, more miserable' and then followed his observation about the poignance of the poem's personal applicability with a confident assertion: 'I have recovered a power of moving the common man I had in my youth.

The poems I can write now will go into the general memory' (*LDW* 123; see *Au* 262). This claim suggests that if deprived of his select audience of aristocratic patrons, the poet could reach without their intermediary role the broader audience at the other end of the social spectrum. The choice of the ballad form for the poem would be consistent with this ambition. Later in the same letter, though, he had to break off discussion of the contemporary Leftist writers ('the multiple Cromwell') because 'I am upsetting myself'. In March he wrote of the *protective* aspect of the persona (inaccurately insofar as it relates to O'Rathaille, who was scarcely a 'simple peasant' poet, but reflecting what Yeats wished to stress), referring to 'The Curse of Cromwell' as one of his 'simple peasant songs that hide me from the curious' (*L* 886). But he published the poem as a 'Broadside' and included it in one of his BBC broadcasts, both clear signs of his hope of reaching a large audience. Writing of the Broadsides two years earlier he had described the intention of the project thus: 'We want to get new or queer verse into circulation, and we shall succeed. The work of Irish poets, quite deliberately put into circulation with its music thirty and more years ago, is now all over the country. The Free State Army march to a tune called "Down by the Salley Garden" without knowing that the march was first published with words of mine, words that are now folklore' (*LDW* 29). In September 1937 he was gratified by the fact that after he had left the Academy Banquet 'somebody called for the "Curse of Cromwell," and when it was sung a good many voices joined in' (*L* 897; also *LDW* 136–9).

Yeats's third and fourth stanzas themselves offer a sign of emergent positive feeling. Up to that point in the poem the speaker's greatest consolation has been knowing 'the time to die', but as if in answer to the refrain's '*What is there left to say?*' the following lines describe a vision intimating that the vanished culture, the dead patrons, survive and that the poet can be reunited with them. There was nothing comparable to this vision in O'Rathaille's 'Last Lines', but 'Kilcash' had ended with a prayer to Mary and Jesus 'That the great come home again' and Kilcash 'Be lifted on high again'. As Whitaker has observed, Yeats's poem ends 'more ambiguously', perhaps implying 'yet another turn of the gyres' but 'primarily ... the destructive knowledge ... that the poet is, at his peril, serving forces that though "underground" have never been for him more alive than now – forces that alienate him from what others recognize as human life' (256–7). 'Crazy Jane on God' contains a similar vision:

> Before their eyes a house
> That from childhood stood
> Uninhabited, ruinous,
> Suddenly lit up
> From door to top:
> *All things remain in God. (VP* 512)

and it reinforces the view that what Yeats was envisaging in the later poem was not the restoration in Ireland of the era of the 'big house' but rather an opportunity to rejoin the lost masters in a state beyond the cycles of human life.

Even closer in date and in content to 'The Curse of Cromwell' is one of the lyrics in *The King of the Great Clock Tower* (published in 1934):

First Attendant.	O, but I saw a solemn sight;
	Said the rambling, shambling travelling-man;
	Castle Dargan's ruin all lit,
	Lovely ladies dancing in it.
Second Attendant.	What though they danced; those days are gone;
	Said the wicked, crooked, hawthorn tree;
	Lovely lady or gallant man
	Are blown cold dust or a bit of bone.
First Attendant.	O, what is life but a mouthful of air;
	Said the rambling, shambling travelling-man;
	Yet all the lovely things that were
	Live, for I saw them dancing there.
	(*VPl* 1004, LL version, 1934)

The 'travelling-man' who has had the vision anticipates the 'old beggar' poet of 'The Curse of Cromwell', and the counterpointed stanzas correspond to the two conceptions of reality between which he is torn. (The situation will reappear in *Purgatory*.) Accepting that other 'knowledge' need not be so destructive in its consequences as Whitaker suggests. The refrain of 'The Curse of Cromwell' incorporates an echo of one of the most cheerless of all of Yeats's poems, 'Nineteen Hundred and Nineteen':

> But is there any comfort to be found?
> Man is in love and loves what vanishes,
> What more is there to say? (*VP* 429–30, 1928 version)

There the turning of the gyres promises no return of Phidian art but rather the 'insolent fiend Robert Artisson'; and the soul anxious to escape human life entirely faces at best a 'desolate heaven' and at worst the prospect of remorseful purgatorial suffering caused to some extent by the artist's very practise of his trade. The vision in 'The Curse of Cromwell', on the other hand, features a realm characterised by light, love, and music; and the artist will be welcomed 'there', the poet-patron nexus symbolically re-established. What the bardic persona in the poem *does not* foresee is that his own art could bring back to Irish soil the lovers and the dancers, the tall men, swordsmen and horsemen. But behind that mask Yeats himself may have been beginning to entertain such a view with renewed conviction. He had recently explored related thoughts in the generalised context of 'Lapis Lazuli'. Although at one level *'What is there left to say?'* as the *final* line of the poem answers its own question negatively, at another it creates an open-ended ending that encourages the reader to bring to mind relevant responses. Yeats had begun the poem by calling attention to his own quest for an audience; and had recounted with pleasure the story of how his ballad, sung *after* he had left the Banquet, thereby showed signs of passing into 'the general memory'. In the remaining years of his life, his resurgent faith in artistic power would prove a chief source of the strength with which he faced the threat of another world war and the prospect of his own death.

VI. 'LAPIS LAZULI' (1936), 'THE GYRES' (1937), 'THE MUNICIPAL GALLERY RE-VISITED'(1937)

On 4 March 1935, Yeats wrote a letter warning Ethel Mannin not to let propaganda come too much into her life because it would embitter her soul with hatred as it had his: 'Bitterness is more fatal to us than it is to lawyers and journalists who have nothing to do with the feminine muses. Our traditions only permit us to bless, for the arts are an extension of the beatitudes. Blessed be heroic death (Shakespeare's tragedies), blessed be heroic life (Cervantes), blessed be the wise (Balzac). Then there is a still more convincing reason why we should not admit propaganda into our lives. I shall write it out in the style of *The Arabian Nights* (which I am reading daily). There are three very important persons (1) a man playing the flute (2) a man carving a statue (3) a man in a woman's arms' (*L* 831–2).

Yeats glossed the enigmatic final images in a letter to Olivia Shakespear, saying 'we must keep propaganda out of our blood because three important persons know nothing of it ...' (*L* 833). These observations were perhaps the germ of 'Lapis Lazuli', with 'Shakespeare's tragedies' anticipating the second stanza,[36] while 'heroic life', 'the wise', and the 'three very important persons' found counterparts in the Chinamen on the carved stone. The attitudes of the first triad towards propaganda would correspond to the gaiety of the latter in the face of the 'tragic scene' they contemplate. In echoing the concept of the artist as bestower of blessings from 'Blood and the Moon' Yeats was perhaps reaching back towards the positive view of artistic power that had infused the opening sections of that poem but that in the third and fourth parts of it had given way to the more pessimistic attitude that dominated his work for the next several years. The reference to bitterness anticipates the letter of 6 July 1935 to Dorothy Wellesley in which Yeats quoted Dowson in support of the assertion that 'people much occupied with morality always lose heroic ecstasy':

> Wine and women and song
> To us they belong
> To us the bitter and gay.

identifying 'bitter and gay' as 'the heroic mood' and adding that 'when there is despair, public or private, when settled order seems lost, people look for strength within or without. Auden, Spender, all that seem the new movement *look* for strength in Marxian socialism, or in Major Douglas; they want marching feet. The lasting expression of our time is not this obvious choice but in a sense of something steel-like and cold within the will, something passionate and cold' (*LDW* 7). As he himself contemplated the loss of settled order, he was looking for strength to the values championed in 'The Fisherman', which had likewise originated as a response to feelings of bitterness and presented an ideal image intended to change grim reality. Later in the same letter he offered the description of the lapis itself that led to further efforts to define 'the heroic cry'.

In April of the following year Yeats was pressed by Mannin to intervene in the affair of the German poet Ossietsky, lying ill in a Nazi concentration camp. In refusing he suggested that he *had* been engaging the crises of his time, through his art: 'Communist, Fascist, nationalist, clerical, anti-clerical, are all responsible according to the number of their victims. I have not been silent; I have used the only vehicle I possess – verse. If you have my poems by you, look up a poem called *The Second Coming*. It was written some sixteen or seventeen years ago and foretold what is happening. . . . This will seem little to you with your strong practical sense, for it takes fifty years for a poet's weapons to influence the issue' (*L* 850–1). Significantly, the concept of artistic power as he presented it here stressed the long-term nature of the impact. It was apparently shortly after this that he wrote 'Lapis Lazuli', which he finished on 25 July 1936 (*LDW* 83). There, as in the letter, we can detect a revival of faith in the artist's central role in the shaping of civilisations, coupled with an emphasis upon his limitations. Nothing he can do will prevent war and destruction. (The reference to 'King Billy' anticipates 'The Curse of Cromwell', set in the wake of that specific instance of destruction.) 'Wisdom' itself must inevitably go 'to rack'. The artist can only exemplify in his own behaviour the appropriate response, tragic gaiety, and build things again. His own courage might also serve as a model that could make at least some of those coming after him 'indomitable'. Undoubtedly Yeats was thinking not only of Dowson but also of O'Shaughnessy, whose 'dreaming and singing' poets were 'Ceaseless and sorrowless'. Having 'Built Nineveh . . . / And Babel . . .' they had also overthrown them 'with prophesying / To the old of the new world's worth' and had hailed a great race yet to come. In the darkness of Europe in 1936 Yeats could not share that exultation in destruction or so confidently anticipate the better era to follow. Perhaps writing 'The Curse of Cromwell' was cathartic, for in 'The Gyres', which he seems to have written a few months after it, he was able to feel both the exultation and the anticipation.

A.N. Jeffares, citing no evidence, suggests July 1936 – January 1937 for the composition of 'The Gyres', but Yeats dated the 'final draft' of the poem 'April 9'.[37] Most probably he conceived the poem very late in December 1936. Writing to Dorothy Wellesley just before the new year that he had been exhausted by overwork and mental strain, he listed as causes of that strain his rage at the Casement 'forgeries'; 'Catholic threats against self & friends'; 'Attacks on Anthology (Feeling that I have no nation'; and 'The present state of Europe. (Europe is in the waning Moon, are all those things that we love waning?)' He copied out a draft, written the day before, of 'Imitated from the Japanese', with its final line 'And never have I danced for joy'. Then he added what seems the first conception of

'The Gyres': 'My emotional crisis has given me a theme for one or my more considerable poems, in the metre of *Sailing to Byzantium* but I must not attempt it until quite recovered' (*LDW* 116–17). The fading of all the values dearest to him, the grim political situation, the concern with 'joy' would all get into the poem, which he may have begun actually composing around 29 March, when he told Dorothy Wellesley that no more ballads were coming to him and he would therefore have to 'go back to the poems of civilisation' (*LDW* 134).

The statement that 'Europe is in the waning Moon' suggests that one of the multiple identities of 'Rocky Face' may in fact be the moon, the White Goddess, the poet's Muse. Although at one point in the drafts the figure is referred to as 'Old cavern man' (*YW* 145), in the final text no gender is indicated. The moon does have a 'face', and 'rocky' might suggest its craterous surface. As its phases were Yeats's favorite symbol for the gyring movements of history, it would be addressed appropriately immediately after the opening 'The gyres!'; and 'look forth' recalls the last lines of 'Blood and the Moon', where 'the stain of blood' (compare 'streams of blood') is contrasted with 'the visage of the moon / When it has looked in glory from a cloud.' One manuscript includes the line 'From dark and bright that Rocky Face holds dear,' suggesting no moon and full moon, Phases One and Fifteen (*YW* 147). It may indeed be the voice of the Delphic Oracle that utters from a cavern the command ' "Rejoice!" ' but Richard Ellmann's claim that the Oracle 'is a proper muse for a prophetic poem' is more convincing in regard to prophecy than to poetry.[38] O'Shaughnessy's artists wander under the 'pale moon'. Yeats had warned Ethel Mannin that bitterness was fatal to those who have to do with the Muses, and in 'The Curse of Cromwell' they had become 'things of no account'. What might at first seem a comparable irreverence in the epithet 'Old' *can* be taken as part of the almost jocular tone with which the poet confronts his plight, and is balanced by the later tenderness of 'holds dear' as well as recalling the primal antiquity of the Goddess-Muse. The 'Lovers of horses and of women' are clearly the artists, and it is the Muse who holds *them* dear. Under her sponsorship they will usher in the new cycle of civilisation.

A draft of line 17 read 'Perfection of the work, the life the soul!' (*YW* 146), alluding more clearly than the published version to 'Coole Park and Ballylee, 1931' and 'The Choice', where art had seemed at best impermanent, at worst destructive to the artist's own soul, and the artist himself had felt not tragic joy but despair. In 'The Gyres' no bleakness can shake the poet's confidence, a confidence underscored by the strategically emphatic placement of 'shall' in line 19. Nightmare rode on top in the second stanza, but the end of the poem envisages the time when the high horse will be mounted once again. Instead of fruitlessly sighing for the past, the artist will bring it back, as 'disinter' suggests. The 'darkness' in which its avatars reside combines that of the grave and that of the end of the lunar cycle, a supernatural phase by way of which the visionary artist can reach the archetypes, models for the era to come. In 'Parnell's Funeral' the lines 'Leave nothing but the nothings that belong / To this bare soul' may have been meant to recall Lear's 'Nothing will come of nothing'; in 'The Gyres' the word has the same positive force as in 'Where there is Nothing, there is God': from it will come the new world order. 'The workman, noble and saint' may owe something to O'Shaughnessy's 'Ode', in which

> The soldier, the king, and the peasant
> Are working together in one,
> Till our dream shall become their present
> And their work in the world be done. . . .

They certainly anticipate the catalogue of approved poetic 'types' in 'Under Ben Bulben' V, porter-drinkers, lords and ladies, holy clerics; and their function is the same. Unlike the paradigmatic figures there, however, those in 'The Gyres' lack a *national* identity. A few months later Yeats would combine his revitalised sense of art's power to shape life with a specifically Irish milieu in 'The Municipal Gallery Re-visited'.

At the end of 1936 Yeats had felt he had 'no nation'; his poem on the Gallery, which he finished in September 1937 (*L* 897), presents a strongly affirmative vision of Ireland. Such a vision comes at first as a surprise, for the country itself had certainly not, in Yeats's eyes, changed for the better since de Valera had taken up the reins of state. Perhaps the single most important factor behind that shift in feeling was Yeats's relationship with the American Fenian Patrick McCartan. McCartan had supported his fund-raising efforts for the Academy; at the time of the uproar over the Casement ballads he had praised Yeats's work and defended it against attacks (McCartan 379), creating so supportive an atmosphere for him that Yeats, thanking him for a dinner party, wrote 'the freedom of speech and the lack of party bitterness made up a combination I never thought to see in Ireland' (382); and he was instrumental in establishing a fund designed to relieve him of all financial worries for the rest of his life, a project about which Yeats learned early in 1937 (384). But his really crucial gift to Yeats was in fact his insistence that the poet had *always* been looked upon by the IRB as 'a Fenian in practice', 'working on parallel lines and doing well work none of us were capable of even attempting . . .' (411, 428). Such praise was a powerful counterforce to Yeats's feelings of isolation. In thanking McCartan for his role in putting together the endowment Yeats said 'I have had honours from other countries, but have sometimes wished they were from my own. Do you remember that song where Raftery describes himself as sitting among his people playing a fiddle with his face to the wall? Henceforth I shall think of myself as sitting among my people, but you who remember the song know the reason why I am more fortunate than Raftery' (411). As a sort of O'Leary redivivus, McCartan made present for Yeats what might otherwise have seemed merely the object of nostalgic longing, made him feel once again at the heart of the Nationalist movement. 'The Municipal Gallery Re-visited' dramatised that change. 'The Curse of Cromwell' had been set in the past and used one of the poet's predecessors as a mask, while 'The Gyres' was generalised in place and even – through the references to Empedocles and Troy – in time; in the new poem, which Yeats announced at the Academy Banquet honouring McCartan that he would send to the benefactors who had made the gift to him, he chose a highly particularised Irish setting and emphasised his *present* experience of it. In his speech at the Banquet Yeats had projected that the poem would be 'about the Ireland that we have all served, and the movement of which I have been a part' (410). In the poem itself he used the situation of walking through the gallery, surrounded by paintings depicting Irish experience, as a way of dramatising his feeling of being part of that experience rather than an outsider; and using 'I say', 'I sink down', 'And here's' constructions to create a sense of immediacy. Both setting and response led naturally to thoughts of the relationship between art and life.

Despite Yeats's notorious vagueness about dates, the emphasis he gave 'thirty years' by placing it at the end of the poem's first line encourages us to recall 1907, the years of the *Playboy* riots and of O'Leary's death, a dark year for Yeats. However it was also, as he may or may not have known, the year in which Fenian exile Tom Clarke returned to Ireland and provided leadership for a younger, more militant wing of the IRB, and thus a crucial point in the progress of events leading towards the Rising and the establishment of the Free State.[39] Some of the individuals and events depicted in the paintings referred to in the first ten lines were unquestionably more to Yeats's liking than others, but that was not the point. The opening catalogue of pictures ends, significantly, with an act of blessing that recalls the poet's similar act at the beginning of 'Blood and the Moon'. At the Banquet Yeats had spoken of 'Ireland not as she is displayed in guide book or history, but, Ireland seen because of the magnificent vitality of her painters, in the glory of her passions. For the moment I could think of nothing but that Ireland: that great pictured song' (*VP* 839–40). The final phrase suggests literature as well as painting and thus points towards the text itself, which emphasises not only the paintings but also the poems that lay behind them. 'Images' could refer to either, and in the second stanza the poet speaks specifically of his own art:

> . . . 'This is not', I say,
> 'The dead Ireland of my youth, but an Ireland
> The poets have imagined, terrible and gay.' (*VP* 601–2)

In the context of his work, 'terrible' would evoke 'Easter, 1916' and 'gay' echoes 'Lapis Lazuli'. In 1907 Yeats had been forty-two years old; for the 'dead' Ireland of his youth we have to go back much further, probably to a time before the beginnings of his literary activities in the 1880s. From that point on he had devoted himself to creating an art that would change his country. During a period of discouragement not long after 1907 he had doubted the efficacy of his efforts, writing in his journal that he was 'un-national in any sense the common man can understand' and adding 'I must therefore be content to be but artist, one [of] a group, Synge, Lady Gregory – no, there is no other than these – who express something which has no direct relation to action. We three have conceived an Ireland that will remain imaginary more powerfully than we have conceived ourselves' (*Mem* 251). In 1937 his tone was more positive. Although he and his fellows had not yet actually transformed the country, at least they had created the ideal image embodied in the paintings he had seen, which had shown him 'Ireland in spiritual freedom' (*VP* 839–40). And pictures as well as poems might yet make that ideal a reality, as his poems on the Lane controversy had long ago suggested.

In January 1937 Yeats had written to de Valera himself, encouraging him to pursue the return of the pictures in his current negotiations with the British government (*L* 877–8). In Yeats's speech in August he devoted considerable attention to the controversy, concluding with the information that the Government had 'undertaken to press Ireland's demand for those pictures at the first possible opportunity' and suggesting confidently that if his audience and the country stood behind their leader's efforts 'the demand will be successful' (McCartan 408–9). He returned to this thought at the end of his prose account of his visit to the Gallery: 'The next time I go, I shall stand once more in veneration before the work of the great Frenchmen' (McCartan 410; *VP* 840). His optimism on this score proved premature, but at the time it reinforced his recovered confidence. A good index to the strength of that confidence is his new ability to accept what in 'Coole Park and Ballylee, 1931' had seemed apocalyptic, the death of Lady Gregory. No thought or theory could keep him from momentarily experiencing 'despair' anew at the realisation 'that time may bring / Approved patterns of women or of men / But not that selfsame excellence again.' Both poems and pictures contained 'approved patterns', paradigms of the ideal like the workman, noble and saint in 'The Gyres', and in the fullness of time there would be Irishwomen with pride and humility comparable to Lady Gregory's, but they would not *be* Lady Gregory. But he moved on to contemplate without tears the destruction of Coole Park; no later degradation of the actual place could harm the paradigms, which would survive in the writers' own art and in the pictures in the Gallery. There they would shape the experiences of his children and the Ireland of the future. Thus the 'glory' seen in 'Coole Park and Ballylee, 1931' as 'spent' reappears twice in the last two lines of 'The Municipal Gallery Re-visited'.

Although rhetorically the emphasis of the poem's final stanza is on friendship, the ultimate source of comfort for the poet lies in that renewed faith in the power of art. By the end of the poem the Gallery has become the sort of 'hallowed place' that the poet had sought through his act of blessing to make the tower in 'Blood and the Moon'. Addressed directly to readers, present and future, the closing lines employ an image Yeats would soon develop more fully in 'The Statues'. The reader who will visit the Gallery – or read of it in the 'pictured song' of the poem – and 'trace' the history of Ireland in the 'lineaments' of Yeats's friends, will be performing essentially the same act as those Irish boys and girls, unconsciously seeking approved models of the men and women they will become, who in the later poem trace the lineaments of a plummet-measured face and thereby create in Dublin a culture comparable to Phidian Athens. Such thoughts would sustain Yeats till his death and play a major role in the book that would prove to be his literary testament, *Last Poems and Two Plays*.

VII. *LAST POEMS AND TWO PLAYS* (1938–39)

Shortly before his death Yeats drew up a table of contents for a volume of poems and plays to be published by the Cuala Press.[40] In recent years that list has been used to justify printing the 'Last Poems' in the order followed there, beginning with 'Under Ben Bulben' and ending with 'Politics'.[41] However, Yeats died before *Last Poems and Two Plays* went to press, and left behind no statement or other documentary evidence that he intended to print the same poems in the same order when including them (as he would eventually have done) in his *Collected Poems*; there is in fact good reason to *doubt* that he meant to do so. In such circumstances, the only secure foundation for critical analysis of the poems in question as an authorially ordered sequence is to follow the order and contents of *Last Poems and Two Plays*, which ends not with 'Politics' but with *The Death of Cuchulain* and *Purgatory*. The sequence as a whole reveals that Yeats arranged his last volume to give particular emphasis to the question of art's shaping power. He began with 'Under Ben Bulben', placed 'The Statues' approximately half-way (in terms of pages) among the poems, and ended with the plays, which offer antithetical prospects for the future as the artists prevail or fail. In order of composition *Purgatory* had come first, then 'The Statues', on the final stages of which he was still at work when he began 'Under Ben Bulben' in August 1938;[42] *The Death of Cuchulain* was well under way by early October and still being polished in the last days of his own life (*DCU* 4). Considered from a chronological perspective *Purgatory*, which contained no explicit concern with artistic power, would seem to reflect a despairing mood left behind, while the other three texts affirm such power and draw much of their strength from it. But *Last Poems and Two Plays* tells a different story.

In Yeats's Preface to *Gods and Fighting Men* (1904) he had referred to 'Benbulben, the great mountain that showed itself before me every day through all my childhood and was yet unpeopled' and suggested that it was precisely such books as Lady Gregory's retellings of the 'old stories', the legends of the Irish heroic age, that could make the holy mountains of the land 'populous with memories' for modern readers (xxiv). Making the land 'begin again to be a Holy Land' (*CM* xvii) was of course a central part of Yeats's plan for the transformation of the entire culture: 'If we would create a great community . . . we must recreate the old foundations of life, . . . as they must always exist when the finest minds and Ned the beggar and Seaghan the fool think about the same thing' (*GFM* xxiii). Such criteria were in Yeats's mind thirty-four years later, as the manuscripts of 'Under Ben Bulben' reveal:

> I believe as did the old sages
> Who sat under the palm trees
> the banyan trees, or among
> those snow bound rocks, ~~and~~
> a thousand years before ~~Chri~~ Christ
> was born; I believe as did the
> monks of the Mareotic sea,
> as do ~~every n~~ country men
> who see the old fighting men
> & their fine women coming out
> of the mountain, moving from
> mountain to mountain (*VR* 154–5)

Suggesting as he did in regard to his fictitious hermit persona Ribh that 'Saint Patrick must have found in Ireland, for he was not its first missionary, men whose Christianity had come from Egypt, and retained characteristics of those older faiths that have become so important to our invention,' Yeats had no trouble naturalising banyans to an Irish climate, merging the Egyptian desert with fertile Irish soil (*VP* 837; see also *E&I* 513–14). The drafts of 'Under Ben Bulben' show him thinking himself back into the world of those older faiths:

> God comes to us in all things – in our
> passing thoughts in the sun in the leaves
> he is in all this morning & (.) Yet I

<pre>
          I would   could
       ~~would~~ not ask him for anything & I ~~will~~
       be satisfied by death did I not know
       that it is he who asks who refuses to ask.
       But I throw from my heart all images of
       submission – I have found the great
       Cuchullain in my arrogant heart. There
       is nothing that I have not ~~will~~ willed (*VR* 153)
</pre>

Cuchulain was as much in Yeats's thoughts at this time as he had been in Pearse's, having appeared in the final stanza of 'The Statues' and becoming the central figure in *The Death of Cuchulain*, where his assertion 'I make the truth' voices what Yeats had chosen to eliminate from the final draft of 'Under Ben Bulben' (*DCU* 9–10). Yeats may have decided to omit the specific reference to Cuchulain because *his* topographical associations lay elsewhere, 'Dundealgan and Emain Macha and Muirthemne' (*GFM* xxiv). (In the play, Cuchulain himself appears among the supernatural horsemen in the song the 'harlot / Sang to the beggarman'.)

To 'create a great community' by bringing the wisdom of 'older faiths' to bear upon the present was the task not of the sages but of the artist. The pantheism or animism Yeats described in the manuscripts, yoked with a proud 'subjective' identification of the self with the Divine Being, had appeared also in the famous 'Song of Amergin', Amergin being the archetypal Irish bard, a Celtic Homer:

> I am the wind on the sea;
> I am the wave of the sea;
> I am the bull of seven battles;
> I am the eagle on the rock;
> I am a flash from the sun;
> I am the most beautiful of plants;
> I am a strong wild boar;
> I am a salmon in the water;
> I am a lake in the plain;
> I am the word of knowledge;
> I am the head of the spear in battle;
> I am the god that puts fire in the head;
> Who spreads light in the gathering on the hills?
> Who can tell the ages of the moon?
> Who can tell the place where the sun rests?[43]

In the final version of 'Under Ben Bulben' the doctrine featured is reincarnation, which Yeats knew to be found in a poem by the medieval Welsh bard Taliesin that the French Celticist Arbois de Jubainville had linked with the 'pantheistic' verses of Amergin.[44] 'Pantheism' as Yeats saw it was organically linked to reincarnation. In his 1930 Diary he had suggested that

> two conceptions, that of reality as a congeries of beings, that of reality as a single being, alternate in our emotion and in history.... I am always, in all I do, driven to a moment which is the realisation of myself as unique and free, or to a moment which is the surrender to God of all that I am. I think that there are historical cycles wherein one or the other predominates, and that a cycle approaches where all shall [be] as particular and concrete as human intensity permits. Again and again I have tried to sing that approach, *The Hosting of the Sidhe*, 'O sweet everlasting voices', and those lines about 'The lonely, majestical multitude', and have almost understood my intention. Again and again with remorse, a sense of defeat, I have failed when I would write of God, written coldly and conventionally. Could those two impulses, one as much a part of truth as the other, be reconciled, or if one or the other could prevail, all life would cease. (*D* 18–19)

Yeatsian 'pantheism', then, would involve the conception of reality as a congeries of beings, each individual soul divine but 'unique and free', and historically would predominate in the eras before and after the Christian. In the Diary he went on to link this concept with reincarnation: 'If men are born many times, as I think, that must originate in the antinomy between human and divide freedom. Man incarnating, translating "the divine ideas" into his language of the eye, to assert his own freedom, dying into the freedom of God and then coming to birth again' (*D* 20).

Plotinus, 'as he was compelled to at his epoch, thought of man as re-absorbed into God's freedom as final reality' (*D* 21). In this light it is easy to see why Yeats had mocked Plotinus's thought in Part III of 'The Tower', which (as Curtis Bradford has noted) anticipates 'Under Ben Bulben' as a declaration of faith and a testament to the poet's heirs (*YW* 95–6). To assert that 'Death and life were not / Till man made up the whole, /... / Aye, sun and moon and star, all ...' was to assert human freedom and creative power. Amergin, embodying 'the primeval unity of all things', was appealing partly because as such 'he has the power to bring a new world into being, and his poems are in the nature of creation incantations' (Rees 99). (In a note to 'The Tower' Yeats had cited a passage from the *Enneads* that seemed to place Plotinus on his side:

> "Let every soul recall, then, at the outset the truth that soul is the author of all living things, that it has breathed the life into them all, whatever is nourished by earth and sea, all the creatures of the air, the divine stars in the sky; it is the maker of the sun; itself formed and ordered this vast heaven and conducts all that rhythmic motion – and it is a principle distinct from all these to which it gives law and movement and life, and it must of necessity be more honourable than they, for they gather or dissolve as soul brings them life or abandons them, but soul, since it never can abandon itself, is of eternal being." (*VP* 826; see *YL* 1592)

For this reason he is perhaps after all to be included among the Egyptian 'sages' whose views harmonise in Part I of 'Under Ben Bulben' with the philosophy underlying Irish fairy belief. In 'The Hosting of the Sidhe' Yeats had described 'the gods of ancient Ireland' riding over Sligo mountains (*VP* 800); in setting superhuman horsemen to ride 'the wintry dawn/ Where Ben Bulben sets the scene' in his new poem he was again singing the approach of the cycle in which the values of self-realisation and creative power would be the norm. The sidhe and their dwellings were traditionally associated with poetic inspiration.[45] Similarly the Witch of Atlas, associated by Yeats with Neoplatonism and with poetry, presides as a sort of Muse (*IGE* 118–25), and the 'high horse' of art, 'riderless' in 'Coole Park and Ballylee, 1931', carries horsemen and women again. According to Graves, who linked the Song of Amergin with fertility rituals, an incident in the tale of 'The Boyhood Deeds of Fionn' suggests that the entrances to Irish prehistoric burial mounds 'were left open at *Samhain*, All Souls' Eve, which was also celebrated as a feast of the Dead in Ancient Greece, to allow the spirits of the heroes to come out for an airing; and that the interiors were illuminated until cockcrow the next morning' (*WG* 12–13, 103). Lady Gregory's version of the story does not mention the cocks, but three times refers to 'breaking of day' or 'rising of the sun' as the time at which the spirits have retired (*GFM* 164–7). Samhain signalled the beginning of winter in the fertility-oriented calendar of the early Irish. W.Y. Evans Wentz, whose work Yeats knew, had argued that 'to the pre-

Christian Celts, the First of November, or the Festival of *Samain*, which marked the end of summer and the commencement of winter, was symbolical of death. *Samain* thus corresponds with the Egyptian fête of the dead.'[46] Samhain was also the time when the bard's role as spiritual protector of the king and kingship came to the fore; according to a medieval law text, 'it is the poet's duty to be with the king on Samain and protect him against enchantment' (Nagy 298–9). It is scarcely surprising that such thoughts as underlie Part I of 'Under Ben Bulben' loomed so large for Yeats as he neared the end of his own life. A belief in the primacy and creative power of the individual human soul, linked with reincarnation and seasonal and historical cycles and preserved in the Irish bardic tradition, was crucial to his own response to death.

It would also be crucial to Ireland in the era about to begin. In 'A General Introduction for my Work' Yeats, returning to the subject he had explored in the Diary of 1930, took issue with Arnold Toynbee's suggestion that what he called 'Irishry' would 'cease to be "the relic of an independent society . . . the romance of Ancient Ireland has at last come to an end. . . . Modern Ireland has made up her mind, in our generation, to find her level as a willing inmate in our workaday Western world"', and asserted that on the contrary 'if Irish literature goes on as my generation planned it, it may do something to keep the "Irishry" living. . . . It may be indeed that certain characteristics of the "Irishry" must grow in importance' (*E&I* 517). Yeats and the writers of his school, believing that 'ancient Ireland knew it all' but unwilling to acquiesce in the loss of that indigenous wisdom, had given continued life to legends from an era in which it was impossible to say 'where Christianity begins and Druidism ends' (513–14) and Irish Christianity itself preserved much of the older faith, as well as incorporating elements from Neoplatonism and Cabbalistic thought; thus the Irish tradition might now combine with psychical research to make clear 'in two or three generations' that 'the mechanical theory has no reality, that the natural and supernatural are knit together . . .' (518). He went on to profess his own belief: 'I was born into this faith, have lived in it, and shall die in it; my Christ, a legitimate deduction from the Creed of St. Patrick as I think, is that Unity of Being Dante compared to a perfectly proportioned human body, Blake's "Imagination", what the Upanishads have named "Self"; nor is this unity distant and therefore intellectually understandable, but imminent, differing from man to man and age to age, taking upon itself pain and ugliness . . .' (*E&I* 518).[47] In the earliest stages of composition 'Under Ben Bulben' was titled 'Creed' and sprinkled with 'I believe . . .' phrases (*VR* 150–1). But at the beginning of the 'General Introduction' Yeats had stressed how the poet, no matter how personal he is being, 'never speaks directly as to someone at the breakfast table, there is always a phantasmagoria.' He 'has been reborn as an idea, something intended, complete'; thus he is inevitably 'part of his own phantasmagoria, and we adore him because nature has grown intelligible, and by so doing a part of our creative power. . . . The world knows nothing because it has made nothing, we know everything because we have made everything' (*E&I* 509–10).[48] As the writing of the poem proceeded, Yeats's persona became less confessional, more assertive, eliminating 'I' and frequently addressing his audience in emphatic commands. Not content to leave the prospect of change to the reversal of the gyres, Yeats, his confidence in the power of art resurgent, naturally chose once more the role of unacknowledged legislator in order 'to keep the "Irishry" living'.

The first reference to Unity of Being in the drafts of 'Under Ben Bulben' appeared in an early, enigmatic passage:

> armed philosophers seek each other in
> air, where the conflict is has be
> becomes nobility of body (*VR* 151)

A revised version of these lines linked the concept to man's 'two eternities':

> I declare that man serves these
> sword in hand or with armed
> mind & with an armoured mind That
> a race is born only so armed does
> man pick the right mate, & only
> when only in the midst in the midst
> of a conflict, not [?] straining all his
> mind & his body & to the utmost
> has he wisdom enough to choose
> his right mate. The wisdom I
> seek is written on a sword (*VR* 155–6)[49]

The antinomies here evoke Yeats's 'choice' poems from *The Wanderings of Oisin* through 'A Dialogue of Self and Soul' and 'Vacillation', as well as the pervasive concern in his oeuvre with wisdom and power. The cancelled 'race is born' (which has connections with 'the great race that is to come' from *The King's Threshold*) was a sign that Yeats was thinking not merely of personal self-realisation but of Unity of Culture as well. The question of choosing one's mate also has general implications, as *Purgatory* and the concern with eugenics in *On the Boiler* suggest. But in the concept that art can shape life Yeats had an alternative to eugenics that was attractive not only because it offered a way to avoid the repugnant features of 'selective breeding' but also because it made the artists rather than the politicians or scientists the primary force for improvement. Part III of the published version focussed mainly upon Unity of Being, Part IV upon the artists' role in effecting its cultural equivalent.

Yeats said in a letter that the poem contained his thoughts about 'the breach between ancient & modern art.'[50] In 1909 the work of Augustus John had led him to reflect upon a similar distinction, for it broke 'with violence the canons of measurement which we derive from the Renaissance.' A gymnast contemplating the figures in John's etchings would have striven to bring them 'nearer to that ancient canon which comes down to us from the gymnasium of Greece, and which when it is present marks . . . a compact between the artist and society, a purpose held in common with his time to create emotions or forms which Nature also desires. John is interested not in the social need, in the perpetual thirst for ever more health and physical serviceableness, for bodies fitted for the labour of life, but in character, in the revolt of the individual from all that makes it like others. The old art, if it [had] gone to its logical conclusion, would have led to the creation of one single type of man, and one single type of woman, in whom would have been concentrated, however, by a kind of deification, the capacity for all energy and all passion, a Krishna, a Christ, a Dionysus, or a drawing of all into a single mind as at the end of the cycles. . . .' John's was thus 'a powerful but prosaic art, celebrating the fall into division not the resurrection into unity' (*Mem* 187–9). In contrast to his position in 'Blood and the Moon' Yeats did not in 'Under Ben Bulben' assume that *every* modern nation has to remain half-dead at the top; the urgency of his address to the artists came directly from his sense that their work *could* make a difference, in the present and in the future. Had the allusions to the sword been carried over into the final text, they would have called to mind the dilemma of the artist whose 'work' can bring the souls of others to God but only at the expense of his own; although clearly Yeats had not lost sight of that troubling possibility, he chose not to focus on it here. Similarly, he had explored in poems such as 'The Dolls' the potential for conflict between bringing the soul of man to God and making him fill the cradles right. From a Neoplatonic point of view, the desirable course would be to escape from *all* cradles, to return to the Divine source; and possibly 'right' means 'so as to lead to' such an escape. However, the later line 'Profane perfection of mankind' makes clear that Yeats was not opting for any doctrine that would devalue human life. Given the terms of the Diary of 1930, where the 'subjective' definition of 'God' is the individual soul in its highest state, lines 40 and 41 would in fact have essentially the same meaning. (The soul in 'A Prayer for my Daughter' discovering that 'its own sweet will is Heaven's will' embodies a comparable position.)

In the light of this modification of Neoplatonism it may at first seem surprising that 'Forms a stark Egyptian thought' has been taken as a reference to Plotinus, but as we saw in Chapter Two, his claim that the artists 'add where nature is lacking. Thus Pheidias wrought the Zeus upon no model among things of sense but by apprehending what form Zeus must take if he chose to become manifest to sight' was part of the tradition behind Yeats's own aesthetic, and he had perhaps already found a place among the 'sages' in Part I.[51] Phidian statues and the Sistine Chapel frescoes both offer Edenic images comparable to those Seanchan had sought to hang about the childbed of the world to make it bear triumphant children. The image of 'globe-trotting Madam' with her bowels in heat is Yeats's most dramatic transformation of the passages from Wilde and Pater about the brides affected in their passion by statues in the bridal chambers. All this material is given much fuller expression later in *Last Poems and Two Plays* in 'The Statues'. And there, as in Part V of 'Under Ben Bulben', the focus in the present turns to *Irish* art and culture.

In the Diary of 1930 Yeats had followed his thoughts about the nature of God and reality with some speculations about the historical era to come, asking specifically 'what idea of the State ... will serve our immediate purpose here in Ireland?' (*D* 53) His answers could almost serve as a scenario for 'Under Ben Bulben', especially Part V. The essential underlying convictions or postulates would be 'Freedom, God, Immortality' (49), and because these were currently out of favour, 'realism' and 'Stendhal's "mirror dawdling down a lane"' had taken over and there was no basis for 'legitimate' tragedies –

'those that are a joy to the man who dies' (50). In the eighteenth century Bishop Berkeley had caused the defeat of English material-ism, 'the Irish Salamis' (51); another such moment was approach-ing, the national intellect lay ready for another defining experience. What that experience might be was subject to influence by thinkers or artists, for 'history is necessity until it takes fire in some one's head and becomes freedom or virtue. Berkeley's Salamis was such a conflagration, another is about us now?' (54) As a 'practical rule' for shaping the Irish nation he offered, 'serve nothing from the heart that is not its own evidence, what Blake called "naked beauty displayed", recognise that the rest is machinery and should [be] used as such' (D 54). To illustrate this he contrasted Douglas Hyde's Gaelic League propaganda with his early lyric poetry in Irish:

> One day thirty years ago, walking with Douglas Hyde I heard haymakers sing what he recognised as his own words and I begged him to give up all coarse oratory that he might sing such words. The factories will never run short of hands, and yet
>
> > We built Nineveh with our sighs,
> > And Babel itself with our mirth. (D 54; see also Au 217)

The quotation from O'Shaughnessy was of course one of his touch-stones of artistic power, and signalled that the following sentence, 'Preserve that which is living and help the two Irelands, Gaelic Ireland and Anglo Ireland so to unite that neither shall shed its pride', was addressed to the artists themselves (D 54–5; see also Au 101–2); he went on to advise them to study 'the re-birth of European spirituality in the mind of Berkeley, the restoration of European order in the mind of Burke', and the educational philosophy of Gentile (D 55). In an Ireland with Unity of Culture, 'all classes' would support the government in an invasion and grant its right to take life (D 55). Such a synthesis had almost been achieved at the end of the eighteenth century, until Protestant refusals to grant Catholic emancipation had brought 'disorder and the Act of Union'; now in modern Ireland something like the reverse of this situation obtained, with the attendant danger that the now-dominant Catholics might marginalise the Anglo-Irish Protestants (D 56). Again, art might help establish the necessary bond, for 'our moral unity is brought nearer by every play, poem or novel that is characteristically Irish' (D 57). He offered the example of O'Casey's *The Silver Tassie*. When working with Irish material O'Casey had contributed to the realisation of the future state, but then he had 'caught the London contagion' and created a play with the defects of English materialist philosophy (*D* 50, 57).

During the years that passed between the writing of the diary and the poem, de Valera's party had taken over the government and the position of Protestants in the new state had further deteriorated, while the Catholic masses, in Yeats's eyes generally inferior intellectually and even physically, had acquired more and more power; the 'Irish Renaissance' had come to an end, and virtually everything Yeats had stood for was under attack. These developments only increased the need for Irish writers to produce art that would act as a force for 'moral unity'. One of the immediate stimuli for Part V of 'Under Ben Bulben' had been an Abbey actor who was threatening to resign because he 'hates the misshapen lot – "ear wigs" – who are growing up now'; Yeats informed Dorothy Wellesley that his complaints were 'the origin of a passage' in the poem.[52] In poem as in diary Yeats looked to the Irish writers to use their art to forge a unified Irish culture in the era ahead, urged them to turn to the past, from 'ancient Ireland' to the 'seven heroic centuries', for paradigmatic ideals, and stressed that such ideals should foster a synthesis of classes and religions. And in using the phrase 'other days' he may have intended to remind readers of the lost opportunity that had led to '98 and the Union. The same phrase appears in two of the most famous lyrics of Tom Moore. In 1937 L.A.G. Strong had dedicated to Yeats his biography of Moore, and in thanking him for the honour Yeats had written that he 'immensely' admired two of Moore's poems (*L* 877). Allan Wade may have been right in his conjecture that the two were 'At the Mid Hour of Night' and 'The Light of Other Days' (more commonly known as 'Oft, in the Stilly Night'), which Yeats had chosen decades before to represent Moore in *A Book of Irish Verse*. The second verse of the latter might seem poignantly appropriate to Yeats's own state at the end of his life:

> When I remember all
>   The friends, so link'd together,
> I've seen around me fall,
>   Like leaves in wintry weather;
>   I feel like one
>   Who treads alone
>   Some banquet-hall deserted,

> Whose lights are fled,
> Whose garlands dead,
> And all but he departed!
> Thus, in the stilly night,
> Ere Slumber's chain has bound me,
> Sad Memory brings the light
> Of other days around me. (11)

But in fact the *tone* of 'Under Ben Bulben' is far different from the sentimental nostalgia of Moore's poem, energetic and defiant rather than passive and acquiescent. The other Moore poem in which 'other days' appears, 'Let Erin Remember the Days of Old', is more public and political in its concerns:

> Let Erin remember the days of old,
>   Ere her faithless sons betray'd her;
> When Malachi wore the collar of gold,
>   Which he won from her proud invader,
> When her kings, with standard of green unfurl'd,
>   Led the Red-Branch Knights to danger; –
> Ere the emerald gem of the western world
>   Was set in the crown of a stranger.
>
> On Lough Neagh's bank, as the fisherman strays,
>   When the clear cold eve's declining,
> He sees the round towers of other days
>   In the wave beneath him shining;
> Thus shall memory often, in dreams sublime,
>   Catch a glimpse of the days that are over;
> Thus, sighing, look through the waves of time
>   For the long faded glories they cover.[53]

Here the mood is post-Union melancholy, and although the opening line seems to urge recollection for some purpose, the remainder of the poem does no more than look back nostalgically at an un-recoverable past. It was this very sense of unrecoverability, with corresponding implications of literary impotence, that 'Under Ben Bulben' V rejects. In contrast to Moore, the Irish writers of Yeats's day were to *bring back*, unfaded, all that was best in the Irish past and use it to transform the future.

Yeats's recognition that he was not going to see Ireland 'in coming days' provides a natural bridge to Part VI of 'Under Ben Bulben', but other connections are discernible as well. One of these involves the phrase 'indomitable Irishry'. In the 'General Introduction', after arguing against Toynbee's prediction of the assimilation of Ireland into Western culture and professing his own faith in Unity of Being, Yeats returned to the subject of the 'Irishry', who had preserved their identity 'through wars which, during the sixteenth and seventeenth centuries, became wars of extermination; no people, Lecky said at the opening of his *Ireland in the Eighteenth Century*, have undergone greater persecution, nor did that persecution altogether cease up to our own day. No people hate as we do in whom that past is always alive ...' (*E&I* 518–19). The strong language reflected Yeats's own feelings here, for, as he went on to say, 'there are moments when hatred poisons my life and I accuse myself of effeminacy because I have not given it adequate expression. It is not enough to have put it into the mouth of a rambling peasant poet.' Yeats's drafts indicate that he had planned to quote the first stanza of 'The Curse of Cromwell' here; but in contrast to the singleminded antipathy of a bard such as O'Rathaille, Yeats's feeling were divided. He went on to remind himself that 'all my family names are English, and that I owe my soul to Shakespeare, to Spenser and to Blake, perhaps to William Morris, and to the English language in which I think, speak, and write, that everything I love has come to me through English; my hatred tortures me with love, my love with hate.' The dilemma was national as well as personal: 'This is Irish hatred and solitude, the hatred of human life that made Swift write *Gulliver* and the epitaph upon his tomb, that can still make us wag between extremes and doubt our sanity.' His own vacillation continued to the end of the essay, where, when contrasting his artistic vision with that of the 'young English poets', he declared 'I am joined to the "Irishry" and I expect a counter-Renaissance'; but then professed to be 'no Nationalist, except in Ireland for passing reasons; State and Nation are the work of intellect, and when you consider what comes before and after them they are ... not worth the blade of grass God gives for the nest of the linnet' (525–6).

The progression from the patriotic stance of 'indomitable Irishry' to an epitaph yoked with a tension between opposites and a final perspective looking beyond life itself is repeated at the end of 'Under Ben Bulben'. Precisely what Yeats meant by that epitaph has been the subject of much debate. Possibly its emotional content derives at least to some extent from a recognition of the implications pointed towards in the 'General Introduction'. Given that 'no people hate as we do in whom that past is always alive', the poet whose work preserves that past and brings it to bear upon the present is *responsible for* the perpetuation of hatred and, very probably, for further persecution and violence (see 526); but if his nation is allowed to forget its history, it will lose its distinctive identity, fulfilling Toynbee's prediction. In Part V Yeats had obviously chosen the former course, and had the poem ended there it would have exceeded in patriotic affirmation even such a text as Corkery's story 'Rock-of-the-Mass' (1929), the Gaelic Catholic peasant protagonist of which is called 'indomitable',[54] or Robert Flaherty's lyrical romanticising of Western life in *Man of Aran* (1934), in which the Islanders are praised with the same term. The presence of Part VI leaves the reader less certain, the cold eye cast from beyond the grave suggesting reconsideration of the unqualified assertion of national pride preceding it. A draft of the lines leading up to the epitaph shows that in describing what the choice of monument and inscription was designed to *avoid* Yeats considered both 'braggs of the country's loss' and 'man's loss' – the national and assimilative alternatives (*VR* 169). Taken in the context of *Last Poems and Two Plays* such doubts would be overshadowed when the reader came to 'The Statues', which does end with an unqualified affirmation of the 'national being' and its key role in the historical cycle to come; then 'The Man and the Echo' would revive them; but the two plays, despite their contrasting moods, both take up once more the concern with the future of the 'Irishry'.

There is no indication in the published text of 'The Statues' that Yeats had in mind in the first stanza any particular statue or even any specific identity for the figure depicted. However, the manuscripts of the poem contain the line 'Apolo forgot Pythagoras & took the name of Buddha' (*VR* 125). 'Apolo' in fact provided an important organisational principle for Yeats's almost bewilderingly complex array of materials and though unnamed in the final version remains a significant presence.

In *The Birth of Tragedy* Nietzsche had treated sculpture as the 'Apollonian' art.[55] At the most general level, the statues in the poem are Apollonic – using the Nietzschean term, as Yeats had done in 1903, to suggest Incarnation, the creation of forms embodying the soul, 'the realization of beauty'. In the later terminology of *A Vision* they would correspond to Phase 15, a superhuman phase in which 'the soul / Becomes a body' (*VP* 374). The process involved in their creation is comparable to the visionary poet's use of symbol and myth to give body to and present for the experience of others what

Yeats variously termed the Moods, the archetypal ideas, heroic images. As Blake had put it, 'the Venus, the Minerva, the Jupiter, the Apollo, which they admire in Greek statues are all of them representations of spiritual existences, – of Gods immortal, – to the ordinary perishing organ of sight' (II, 373). In seeing Phidian sculpture in this way Yeats may have been indebted not only to Plotinus's assertion that 'Pheidias wrought the Zeus upon no model among things of sense but by apprehending what form Zeus must take if he chose to become manifest to sight' but also to Pater (a major influence on the whole poem), who had written of '*Allgemeinheit* – breadth, generality, universality –' as 'that law of the most excellent Greek sculptors, of Pheidias and his pupils, which prompted them constantly to see the type in the individual, to abstract and express only what is structural and permanent, to purge from the individual all that belongs only to him' (*Renaissance* 51). It was precisely the universal quality of those statues that made them appropriate models for the profane perfection of mankind.

If the soul's urge to transcend forms might well prove ultimately inimical to art, the opposite impulse would seem to find its natural fulfillment there, and thus it is appropriate that Apollo should have been 'leader of the Muses'. Pater had suggested a more complex connection: 'The Dorian worship of Apollo, rational, chastened, debonair, with his unbroken daylight, always opposed to the sad Chthonian divinities, is the aspiring element, by force and spring of which Greek religion sublimes itself. Out of Greek religion, under happy conditions, arises Greek art, to minister to human culture. It was the privilege of Greek religion to be able to transform itself into an artistic ideal' (*Renaissance* 162–3). Pater had also written in *Greek Studies* of the pre-Phidian sculptor Canachus, whose colossal statue of Apollo had been carried away to Ecbatana by the Persian armies in the era of the Battle of Salamis, and elsewhere implied the symbolic significance of such an event by arguing that 'in the East from a vagueness, a want of definition, in thought, the matter presented to art is unmanageable, and the forms of sense struggle vainly with it. The many-headed gods of the East ... are at best overcharged symbols, a means of hinting at an idea which art cannot fitly or completely express, which still remains in the world of shadows.'[56]

Although Pythagoras was one of the most important early figures in the tradition of the 'perennial philosophy' and thus might seem to fall into the 'Dionysiac' category, he was in fact said in several early accounts to have been the *son* of Apollo, of which parentage he offered his famous 'golden thigh' as a sign; and 'the only altar at which he worshipped was that of Apollo.'[57] The manuscripts make clear that this connection was in Yeats's mind as he wrote the poem, which might in a sense be seen as a series of transformations or incarnations of Apollo, starting with his link to Pythagoras; thence to Phidian sculpture; then, in the next cycle, carried by Alexander to the East to affect the depiction of the Buddha in Gandhara art; and finally back to the West in the era about to begin. The juxta-positions of the third stanza also allow for a residual Apollonic influence remaining in the West during the Middle Ages and the Renaissance. Pater had quoted Heine's description in *Gods in Exile* of

> how the gods of the older world, at the time of the definite triumph of Christianity, ... fell into painful embarrassments. ... They had then to take flight ignominiously, and hide themselves among us here on earth, under all sort of disguises. ... Just in the same way, they had to take flight again, and seek entertainment in remote hiding-places, when those iconoclastic zealots, the black brood of monks, broke down all the temples, and pursued the gods with fire and curses. ... Apollo seems to have been content to take service under graziers. ... Here, however, ... he was recognised by a learned monk as one of the old pagan gods, and handed over to the spiritual tribunal. On the rack he confessed that he was the god Apollo. ... Some time afterwards the people wished to drag him from the grave again, that a stake might be driven through his body, in the belief that he had been a vampire. ... But they found the grave empty. (*Renaissance* 24–5)

Pater himself had dramatised such a survival in his story 'Apollo in Picardy'(1893), depicting a medieval monk whose orthodox schol-asticism is undercut by the influence of the god, disguised as a herd, at the grange where the monk has gone to restore physical health broken by years of arduous religious study.[58] During the Renaissance, with its emphasis on reconciling the religions of antiquity with Christianity, the pagan gods emerged from hiding and figured prominently in art, Apollo having an important iconographic place, for example, in the decoration of the Stanza della Segnatura, and sometimes even being depicted as a 'type' of Christ.[59] Such an equation was comparable to his Eastern metamorphosis as the Buddha.

In the centuries between the Renaissance and Yeats's own day, Blake, Shelley and Wilde had all evoked Apollo in the context of their theories of the power of art to shape life. For Blake, he was the type of the 'Beautiful Man', the Beauty in question, that 'proper for sublime art', being 'lineaments, or forms and features that are capable of being the receptacles of intellect': Shelley had written of 'the statues of Apollo and the Muses', having been 'endowed with life and motion', walking 'forth among their worshippers, so that the earth became peopled by the inhabitants of a diviner world'; and Wilde suggested 'Hermes' or 'Apollo' as subjects of the statues placed in those Grecian bridal chambers. Nietzsche's work, too, undoubtedly seemed to extend the tradition; for example, his suggestion that it was in the Apollonic realm of dreams that 'the glorious divine figures first appeared to the souls of men, in dreams the great shaper beheld the charming corporeal structure of superhuman beings' anticipates the images in 'The Statues' of the boys and girls, 'pale from the imagined love / Of solitary beds', who recognised the plummet-measured faces, and of Phidias giving 'women dreams and dreams their looking glass.'[60]

Apollo's final embodiment in the poem, as Cuchulain, may at first seem surprising. But Yeats as a young man had encountered theories that identified Cuchulain as a euhemerised solar deity, and thus a sort of Celtic equivalent for Apollo (*VP* 807). He had also read Alfred Nutt's account of similarities between Celtic and Pythagorean doctrines of rebirth, which included extensive testimony from Classical sources that Pythagoras had drawn his ideas from the Druids, or they theirs from him.[61] (Yeats treated the subject with comic irreverence in 'News for the Delphic Oracle', which followed immediately after 'The Statues' in *Last Poems and Two Plays*, putting Pythagoras beside Niamh and Oisin among the 'golden codgers'.) Like Apollo, Cuchulain also had a connection with Christ, for Irish monks anxious to reconcile sacred and indigenous history had synchronised their lives in the medieval Annals.[62] For Yeats the Irish bards were 'greater' than the Druids for they, like the Phidian artists, had drawn upon divine images in order to create the works that, as O'Grady had argued, had actually given their society its distinctive shape. Thus the 'ancient sect' into which the modern Irish were born could refer to both early Greek and early Irish cultures.

Although 'The Statues' is a poem centrally concerned with the cycles of history it is only in its final stanza, in the phrase 'proper dark', that Yeats introduced the lunar symbolism that he generally used to represent such cycles. The early prose draft of the poem began 'They went out in broad day or under the moon / Moving with ~~the~~ dream certainty, somebody calls them / divinities', and other drafts contained lunar references; but the Apollonic associations pervading the final text make it primarily 'solar' (*VR* 125, 129, 133–4). It is possible to see in such an emphasis a connection with yet another mythic interpretation of Apollo, that elaborated by Graves soon after Yeats's death. In Graves's scenario, 'the Battle of the Trees was fought between the White Goddess ("the woman") for whose love the god of the waxing year and of the waning year were rivals, and "the man", Immortal Apollo, or Beli, who challenged her power' (*WG* 341). In cultural terms, when early matriarchal society fell under the domination of patriarchal invaders, the male divinity Apollo 'took over the charge of poetry from the Triple Muse' (390, 391–3; 475–6). His domination, Graves lamented, had lasted into the present age: 'This is an Apollonian civilization' (458). If 'The Statues' picks up the 'one myth' at the point where patriarchal values are already in the ascendant, Yeats did not allow them to stand unchallenged. In *Last Poems and Two Plays* he balanced against the emphasis of 'The Statues' more 'news' for Apollo's Delphic Oracle, a last portrait of the Goddess and her doomed lover in *The Death of Cuchulain*.

Pater had concluded his chapter on Winckelmann in *The Renaissance* by exploring the question of whether the ideal embodied in the Phidian statues could be carried over into 'the gaudy, perplexed light of modern life': 'Certainly, for us of the modern world, with its conflicting claims, its entangled interests, distracted by so many sorrows, with many preoccupations, so bewildering an experience, the problem of unity with ourselves, in blitheness and repose, is far harder than it was for the Greek within the simple terms of antique life. Yet, not less than ever, the intellect demands completeness, centrality' (181–2). He offered the work of Goethe as evidence that it was possible to communicate the Classical ideal to artistic productions that would also contain 'the fulness of the experience of the modern world', suggesting, however, that sculpture, appropriate to 'the unperplexed, emphatic outlines of Hellenic humanism', was a less viable medium than 'music and poetry' for contemporary life (182–5). 'The Statues', at least at a literal level, would seem to challenge this view; but in *The Death of Cuchulain* Yeats would attempt to bring to bear upon a modern world far more grimly conceived than Pater's not the *statue* of Cuchulain erected in the GPO but rather a literary substitute, the protagonist of his play, who could be both ancient hero and a mask for the modern author, doing justice to the complexity of experience in 1938–9 and simultaneously functioning as a type or ideal that could also help provide the basis for Irish Unity of Being and Unity of Culture and a corresponding importance for the 'Irishry' in the era about to begin.

'The Man and the Echo', placed in *Last Poems and Two Plays* between 'The Statues' and *The Death of Cuchulain*, is one of the most pessimistic poems Yeats ever wrote. Not surprisingly, it presents the question of artistic power unfavourably, as one of several causes for the dirtiness of the artist's spiritual slate. In the earliest stages of composition, the source of guilt was not limited to a single text: 'My [word illegible] words my books & words / All that I have done seems evil ...' (*VR* 60). In choosing to allude specifically to *Cathleen ni Houlihan* Yeats was focusing attention upon the power of art at its most problematical, when it might have led to widespread death and destruction. Of course it was possible also to see among the 'consequences' of that play and his other work the emergence of an independent Ireland – though one that certainly had not yet become the great nation that Yeats had long imagined.[63] No thought of the sort lightens the gloom of 'The Man and the Echo', but 'The Statues' had ended with such a prospect and so did *The Death of Cuchulain*.

The scorn and vituperation that constitute the dominant note of the prologue offer little indication that the play will be more positive than 'The Man and the Echo'. But the final lines of the text provide a perspective that forces us to re-evaluate all that has come before:

> No body like his body
> Has modern woman borne,
> But an old man looking back on life
> Imagines it in scorn
> A statue's there to mark the place
> By Oliver Sheppard done
> So ends the tale that the harlot
> Sang to the beggarman. (*DCU* 180)

In 'The Adoration of the Magi' Yeats had already associated the harlot, an outcast from the present cycle of civilisation, with the new cycle and its avatar, about to be born. The act about which she sings here replicates the pattern of 'The Fisherman' and 'Blood and the Moon'. In all three cases, the spiritual bankruptcy of the present moment is taken for granted and the artist's task is to use his art to ensure that the future will be better.[64] In the earlier poem the speaker, 'In scorn of' his audience, had been 'Imagining a man' who embodied ideal qualities that audiences would eventually emulate and come to share. 'In mockery of' the present, the speaker in 'Blood and the Moon' had turned for an ideal to the tower and the Anglo-Irish culture of the eighteenth century that he wished it to symbolise. In a draft of the lyric in *The Death of Cuchulain* Yeats had suggested that *Swift* 'may have imagined' such a figure as Cuchulain 'to mollify his scorn' (*DCU* 119). Although this reference was deleted, the concern with the process of casting one's mind on other days for an ideal remained. Yeats thought Sheppard's Cuchulain 'a bad statue' (*DCU* 15); it had been placed in the Post Office in 1938 by a government from which he was alienated, to commemorate rather than to inspire; and perhaps, as Pater had suggested, literature was in any case more adequate than sculpture as a vehicle for dealing with modern complexity while helping to realise personal and cultural 'complete-ness'. *The Death of Cuchulain* thus became Yeats's last effort to carry out the task he had announced in 1903: to 're-create an heroical ideal [in] manhood – in plays of old Irish life'.

In more general terms, as we have seen, such had been Yeats's goal since his initial commitment to national literature in the mid-1880s. In the Introduction to *Fighting the Waves* he had identified O'Grady, who had 'retold the story of Cuchulain that he might bring back an heroic ideal', as the inspiration that had led him to write *On Baile's Strand, Deirdre, The Green Helmet, At the Hawk's Well*, and *The Only Jealousy of Emer*; he 'would have attempted the Battle of the Ford and the Death of Cuchulain, had not the mood of Ireland changed.' During the early years of the literary movement 'Irish imagination fled the sordid scene' of parliamentary politics in the years after the fall of Parnell: 'Repelled by what had seemed the sole reality, we had turned to romantic dreaming, to the nobility of tradition' (*WB* 70–7). The phrase 'sole reality' reappears in the lyric that ends *The Death of Cuchulain*:

> Are those things that men adore and loathe
> Their sole reality? (*DCU* 180)

The context in each case involves the power of art to influence life, with specific reference to the impact of an ideal Cuchulain upon the

204 Yeats And Artistic Power

course of modern Irish history; and the Introduction suggests as the answer to the enigmatic question posed in the lyric that there was indeed *another* 'reality', outside of and not mixed with loathing like mere mundane experience, a reality made accessible, embodied in a heroic character, in the work of romantic artists wedded to tradition. (Thus *The Death of Cuchulain* is 'antequated romantic stuff', as the Old Man calls it.) The 'Cork Realists', who, 'instead of turning their backs upon the actual Ireland of their day, ... attacked everything that had made it possible,' were soon followed by Joyce as the climate for the earlier sort of literature became less and less favourable. But by the 1930s the beginning of a new cycle was drawing nearer, anticipated by the psychical research of Sir William Crookes, which seemed to herald 'a revolution that may ... establish the scientific complement of certain philosophies that in all ancient countries sustained heroic art.' (In an unpublished passage once intended for *A Vision* Yeats said of the coming cycle that 'its Schools and Universities would combine some Asiatic philosophy with the latest results of that psychical research founded by William Crookes, preparing all to face death without flinching, perhaps even with joy.'[65]) Yeats was ostensibly bringing these signs of change to the attention of 'the Garrets and Cellars' in order that they might 'shape things at their beginning, when it is easy, not at the end, when it is difficult' (74); but of course he was also thinking of his own art 'Since my twentieth year,' he noted with surprising precision, 'these thoughts have been in my mind' [77], and *its* impact was his primary concern.

At this point in the Introduction he made the distinction between sacrifice as the act of some man when he is least himself, most completely 'the crowd', and 'the heroic act, ... an act done because a man is himself, because, being himself, he can ask nothing of other men but room amid remembered tragedies; a sacrifice of himself to himself, almost, so little may he bargain, of the moment to the moment' (75) that in 1934 may have applied primarily to 'Parnell's Funeral' but would come to assume an obvious relevance to *The Death of Cuchulain* as well (see also *Au* 465). He went on to describe the loneliness of that ancient act, the great 'pathos of its joy', which he associated with a passage in *Sigurd the Volsung*, 'the best sprung from the best', and confessed his own emotion: 'How could one fail to be moved in the presence of the central mystery of the faith of poets, painters, and athletes? I am carried forty years back and hear a famous old athlete wind up a speech to country lads –

"the holy people have above them the communion of saints; we the communion of the *Tuatha de Danaan* of Erin"' (75–6). The lyric that closes the play juxtaposes the pious Catholic Pearse, like Christ a 'type' of 'objective' sacrifice, with Cuchulain, whose death was clearly a 'subjective' sacrifice of himself to himself. That death had taken place as the pre-Christian cycle was about to be supplanted by its opposite; twenty centuries had run their course, and the time had come for a new subjective avatar. Sheppard's statue had depicted Cuchulain in a pose inescapably reminiscent of Christ on the cross; Yeats's play would show him facing death unflinchingly, even with joy. Echoing Pater, Yeats warned that the new era would not be identical to the pre-Christian one, 'not the old simple celebration of life tuned to the highest pitch, ... something more deliberate than that, more systematised, more external, more self-conscious ...' (*WB* 74). His literary 'statue' would allow the necessary doubleness in the protagonist. He had asserted in the Introduction that it was science's current task to show that 'states are justified, not by multiplying or, as it would seem, comforting those that are inherently miserable, but because sustained by those for whom the hour seems "awful", and by those born out of themselves, the best born of the best' (77); and of course he elaborated his interest in eugenics in *On the Boiler*. But writing *The Death of Cuchulain* was an expression of 'the faith of poets', another effort, as he faced his own death, to mould an indomitable Irishry through his own art. The drafts of the lyric refer to 'the fight that gave us freedom' and 'the fight / That set their country free' (*DCU* 117). Yeats was clearly struggling here with the question of how fully he could identify with Ireland after the Revolution or consider it – partitioned, suspicious of art, hostile to the Protestant tradition – in any meaningful sense 'free'. Also on his mind was the question of causality: another manuscript line read 'What singer had filled their thought' (*DCU* 121); and though the line itself was dropped, the concern remained. Pearse had had three main models for his sacrifice: Christ, Robert Emmet, and Cuchulain. Of these three only the last could serve Yeats's purposes; newly embodied, he might bring to realisation what the Rising and its aftermath had left unfinished.

Given Yeats's half-century of identification with Cuchulain and his sense that his own life was nearing its end, the choice of Cuchulain's death as the subject of the play seems inevitable. Its appropriateness was increased by the hero's traditional association with bravery against hopeless odds and Yeats's own association of him with a subjective era at cycle end, as well as by his importance in O'Grady's and Lady Gregory's work, by what Yeats called Pearse's 'cult of Cuchulain', and by the decision of the de Valera Government to commemorate the Rising with the statue (*L* 911). The legend also offered potential correspondences with aspects of occult thought that Yeats had recently been exploring. On 9 October 1938, while at work on the play, he had written Ethel Mannin about Rilke's idea of death and that in her novel *Darkness My Bride* as compared with

> the same thought as it is in what I call my 'private philosophy' (The *Vision* is my 'public philosophy'). My 'private philosophy' is the material dealing with individual mind which came to me with that on which the mainly historical *Vision* is based. I have not published it because I only half understand it. . . . According to Rilke a man's death is born with him and if his life is successful and he escapes mere 'mass death' his nature is completed by his final union with it. Rilke gives Hamlet's death as an example. In my own philosophy the sensuous image is changed from time to time at predestined moments called *Initiationary Moments* (your hero takes ship for Bordeaux, he goes to the Fair, he goes to Russia and so on). One sensuous image leads to another because they are never analysed. At *The Critical Moment* they are dissolved by analysis and we enter by free will pure unified experience. When all the sensuous images are dissolved we meet true death. Franz will follow the idea of liberty through a series of *initiationary* moments . . . but will never I think analyse the meaning of 'liberty' nor the particular sensuous image that seems to express it, and so will never meet true death. This idea of death suggests to me Blake's design (among those he did for Blair's *Grave* I think) of the soul and body embracing. All men with subjective natures move towards a possible ecstasy, all with objective natures towards a possible wisdom. . . . (*L* 916–17)

There is no explicit reference here to *The Death of Cuchulain*, but the question of whether various literary heroes meet 'true death' implies it, and in Yeats's next letter to Mannin he did say specifically about the play that 'my "private philosophy" is there', guiding him to certain conclusions and giving him 'precision' but never visible (*L* 917–18). From this it would seem that he structured the play around a series of 'critical moments' in which various 'sensuous images' from Cuchulain's past are analysed and presumably dissolved, resulting in 'pure unified experience' and 'true death'. Furthermore, Blake's design, 'The Reunion of the Soul and the Body', depicts the soul as a female figure embracing the body, a male figure, amidst flaming tombstones. This image and the number of female figures from Cuchulain's past with which Yeats chose to surround him suggest that the broadest context in which Yeats saw the events of his play was that of the Goddess-Muse and her lover (both sacrificial victim and poet), a subject that had long preoccupied him and that, in addition to complementing the Apollonic emphasis of 'The Statues', represented the sort of archetypal pattern that might affect audiences unable to comprehend such a subject analytically.[67] In the Introduction to *Fighting the Waves* he had actually alluded to Jung's effort to trace 'the "mother complex" back to our mother the sea', the sea itself pointing, as Jung saw it, to 'the great primitive idea of the mother.'[68]

In a note to *The King of the Great Clock Tower* (1934) Yeats suggested that the dance with the severed head was 'part of the old ritual of the year: the mother goddess and the slain god' (*VPl* 1010). In that play and in the rewritten version of it entitled *A Full Moon in March* he represented the Goddess through the Queen, the single female character. Historically, however, the Goddess was both the One and the Many, taking on various roles corresponding to different stages in the life cycle of women: young maiden, birth-giving matron, and old woman or crone. The 'Triple Goddess' was associated with the phases of the moon – waxing, full, waning – and with growth, love and battle, and death ('the inevitable destruction or dissolution that must precede regeneration'[69]). In *The Death of Cuchulain* Yeats suggested something similar through the prominent group of female characters with overlapping associations.[70] The earliest stage is represented by the young Aoife, who lays her 'virgin body' at Cuchulain's side; Eithne, young but no longer the maiden, marks another gradation; Emer plays the matronly role, as well as actually performing the ritual dance; this stage is also evoked by Aoife asking Cuchulain how their *son* had fought and by her own former Amazonian warrior prowess. Her associations with battle and her white hair in the play's present link her with the Morrigu, who as battle goddess had loved Cuchulain and tried to warn him of the danger he was facing but who as death goddess arranges the dance associated with his own death and rebirth. The Blind Man finds Cuchulain strapped to the pillar stone with Aoife's veil, 'some womanish stuff'. Even Maeve, though she never actually appears on the stage, is part of the pattern: 'Though when Cuchulain slept with her as a boy / She seemed as pretty as a bird she has changed / She has an eye in the middle of her for head' (*DCU* 172). It is she whose forces bring about Cuchulain's death and who offers the Blind Man twelve pennies for his head. In the *Táin* there are many vestigial traces of her origins as a fertility goddess, including her 'friendly thighs' (evoked in the harlot's song, ll.200–3), her great bladder capacity, and the succession of lovers, always a new one waiting in the shadow.[71] Yeats recalled this aspect of her identity in the Morrigu's account of Cuchulain's slayers:

> . . . this man came first,
> Youth lingered though the years ran on, that season
> A woman loves the best, Maeve s latest lover;
> This man had given him the second wound
> He had possessed her once. . . . (*DCU* 178)

Such figures suggest the paradigm of the fertility gods of the waxing and waning year. Cuchulain links himself to this paradigm when he tells Eithne 'You need a younger man, a friendlier man' (*DCU* 172); and later in the same scene he excuses her supposed treachery by saying

> You thought that if you changed I'd kill you for it
> When everything sublunary must change
> And if I have not changed that goes to prove
> That I am monstrous (*DCU* 173)[72]

– thereby introducing the lunar symbolism and associating his own 'waning' with it. Even the final lines of the play take on a new meaning when seen from this perspective, for if 'No body like his body / Has modern woman borne', the paradigm assures us that the time *will* come.

The association of Goddess and lover with Muse and artist was already well established in Yeats's work. *The Wanderings of Oisin* had featured a hero who was both warrior and poet; his romance with Niamh may suggest supernatural sources of inspiration, the pull of Ireland corresponding to the artist's inescapable need to immerse himself or herself in the life of the ordinary world. In 'The Binding of the Hair' the head of the decollated bard sang to the beloved queen who had inspired his verses; and Hanrahan, compared overtly to the Fenian warrior-bard who 'knew unappeased three hundred years of dæmonic love' (*VSR* 198), had proved unable to escape the love of Cleena the *leannán sidhe* (defined by Yeats elsewhere as a being who 'lives upon the vitals of its chosen, and they waste and die. . . . To her have belonged the greatest of the Irish poets, from Oisin down to the last century').[73] 'The Grey Rock', in which the warrior Dunlaing's unfaithfulness to the goddess Aoife had been contrasted with the poet's fidelity, in spite of trials, to the 'rock-born, rock-wandering foot', had made the equation explicit. The first edition of *A Vision* contained some passages that seem relevant. For example, we are told there that

> man's *Daimon* has . . . her energy and bias, in man's *Mask*, and her constructive power in man's fate, and man and *Daimon* face each other in a perpetual conflict or embrace. This relation (the *Daimon* being of the opposite sex to that of man) may create a passion like that of sexual love. . . . The *Daimon* carries on her conflict, or friendship with a man, not only through the events of life, but in the mind itself. . . . [W]hen . . . in antithetical man the *Daimonic* mind is permitted to flow through the events of his life (the *Daimonic Creative Mind*) and so to animate his *Creative Mind*, without putting out its light, there is Unity of Being. A man becomes passionate and this passion makes the *Daimonic* thought luminous with its peculiar light – this is the object of the *Daimon* – and she so creates a very personal form of heroism or of poetry. (*AV A* 26–30)[74]

Here, as in the play, the relationship between male and female paradoxically combines attraction and antagonism; in one manuscript passage Cuchulain had told Aoife 'I had loved & hated you' (*DCU* 12), and 'adoration' and 'loathing' are central in the Harlot's song (see also *DCU* 121). Exterior ('the events of life') and interior ('in the mind itself') are paralleled; and the twin effects of *Daimonic* animation of the man's *Creative Mind* are 'heroism' and 'poetry'. Yeats himself evidently found the concept of the *Daimon* a problematic one, for this passage was dropped when the book was revised, and the *Daimon* defined differently. But as Helen Vendler has shown, during the 1930s Yeats was continuing to explore the Goddess-Muse / Lover-Poet equation in *The King of the Great Clock Tower* and *A Full Moon in March*.[75] The bizarre comedy of *The Herne's Egg* may also conceal such concerns (Vendler 158–9; Krimm 178–82). As the 'plot' of the 'one story' inexorably moves towards apparent defeat and death for the male protagonist, Yeats virtually had to return to it as he neared that point in his own experience, determined to embody truth in the conclusion of his life (*L* 922).

As Graves was to formulate it, that plot involved 'the birth, life, death and resurrection of the God of the Waxing Year; the central chapters concern the God's losing battle with the God of the Waning Year for love of the capricious and all-powerful Threefold Goddess, their mother, bride and layer-out. The poet identifies himself with the God of the Waxing Year and his Muse with the Goddess; the rival is his blood-brother, his other self, his weird' (*WG* 24). In *The Death of Cuchulain* the 'end' of the (circular) story has been reached. The hero, having assigned his mistress to Conal Caernach 'because the women / Have called him a good lover' (*DCU* 174), goes forth to a losing battle against the forces of the Goddess and is given his first mortal wound by her 'latest lover'. Christ, His reign supposed to have begun about the time of Cuchulain's death, could be, by way of Frazer, another image of the 'other self'. The Blind Man, who finishes Cuchulain off, is perhaps also an image of that self, for he alludes to the events of *On Baile's Strand*, where he was paralleled with Conchobar as his opposite number, and the Fool was paralleled with Cuchulain; Maeve and the reigning lover will reward him for bringing the head. But instead of that 'desecration' Emer dances with it, 'as if in adoration or in triumph' (*DCU* 179); the bird notes she hears, validating Cuchulain's assertion about his soul in his last words, 'I say it is about to sing', signal his survival.[76] The dance has been 'arranged' by the death goddess; she, too, had loved Cuchulain and thus she exults that his death has been avenged. Finally, the Harlot sings of his 'reincarnation', perhaps metaphorical, a transition from a state of inaccessibility to one of renewed power in the world of men. 'Who thought Cuchullain till it seemed / He stood where they had stood'? (*DCU* 180) The artist, identifying with the hero, imagining him anew in order to bring back a heroic ideal.

It remains to consider in what specific ways Yeats's Cuchulain represents a model for the Irish people in the era about to begin. One significant feature is surely his embodiment of 'subjective' values, as manifested in the line 'I make the truth' (*DCU* 9–10, 174). A second is suggested by the reference to Unity of Being in the passage about the *Daimon* in *A Vision*. Yeats went on in the same passage to define the man who attains Unity of Being as 'some man, who, while struggling with his fate and his destiny until every energy of his being has been roused, is content that he should so struggle with no final conquest. For him fate and freedom are not to be distinguished; he is no longer bitter, he may even love tragedy like those "who love the gods and withstand them"; such men are able to bring all that happens, as well as all that they desire, into an emotional or intellectual synthesis and so to possess not the Vision of Good only but that of Evil' (*AV A* 28–9). This process seems comparable to that of achieving 'pure unified experience' and 'true death' in the 'private philosophy' that Yeats admitted incarnating in the play; the 'embrace' of soul and body beyond the grave in the Blake picture Yeats referred to in the same letter provides a further link. Hence the hero offers an image of Unity of Being, the fullest self-realisation available in human life, 'profane perfection'. In Yeats's first piece on Ferguson, published in 1886, he had claimed that a modern literature based on the old Irish legends could 'arouse the whole nature of man' (*UP1* 84; also *Au* 193–4), and such was still his goal. And finally, if, dying on his feet, with a defiant assertion on his lips, he seems superior to 'living men' – seems, like William Faulkner's 'indomitable' Bear to dwarf the 'little puny humans' hacking at him 'in a fury of abhorrence and fear'[77] – copies of the play placed in Irish bridal chambers would reverse the process of degeneration, providing the sexual instinct of the nation with its 'fixed type', giving Irish women dreams and dreams their looking-glass.

Such implications explain why Yeats placed *Purgatory*, in which the subject of art's shaping power is conspicuously absent, at the very end of *Last Poems and Two Plays*, in which the subject had bulked so large. The play had very recently appeared, also last in the volume, in *On the Boiler*. Three lyrics in that volume were not carried over. By using *Purgatory*, which had provided the conclusion to a volume centrally concerned with eugenics, as the final piece in the new book, he not only contrasted two solutions to the same perceived problem but also suggested what would happen if his own books were not read and a younger generation of Irish writers failed to learn their trade. *Purgatory* dramatises a world with no artists and no art, thus a world in which degeneration has continued and the mood is one of utter despair.

On the Boiler itself ('a policy for young Ireland' [*L* 901]) had adumbrated this juxtaposition, for the penultimate expository section had contained a prose statement of the thought that art would once again be based on 'those Greek proportions which carry into plastic art the Pythagorean numbers, those faces which are divine because all there is empty and measured,' and contrasted such art with the 'red patches' on human flesh 'whereby our democratic painters prove that they have really studied from the life' (*OB* 37). This was followed in the final expository section by the assertion that 'artists of all kinds should once again praise or represent great or happy people.'[78] To end this section Yeats printed the poem later titled 'The Statesman's Holiday', the refrain of which, '*Tall dames go walking in grass green Avalon,*' links it, with considerable irony, to the preceding passage. Then came *Purgatory*, in which no one is great or happy.

In *Last Poems and Two Plays* the plays were connected and contrasted by the presence in each of an Old Man.[79] In response to the degeneracy of modern life the Old Man in *The Death of Cuchulain* had 'imagined' the epic hero; the Old Man of *Purgatory*, obsessed by his mother's debasing marriage, hoped to end the consequences of her transgression by killing his own son before he could beget and pass pollution on. But as Yeats had written in 'If I were Four-and-Twenty', 'a single wrong choice may destroy a family, dissipating its tradition or its biological force, and the great sculptors, painters, and poets are there that instinct may find its lamp' (*Ex* 274, noted by Torchiana 343). They are *not* 'there' in *Purgatory*: 'the bride sleep fell upon Adam' but there was no Seanchan to bring Edenic images to bear upon the development of the family, so the mother, her bowels in heat, chose the drunken groom (a debased reminder of 'Hard-riding country gentlemen') as her mate.[80] To the extent that the Old Man seems a projection of Yeats himself he represents a sort of alter ego, an image of the impotent rage he might have felt if his own creativity had dried up. This note had been sounded at the beginning of *On the Boiler*, associated with the persona of the haranguing ship's carpenter and the lyric later titled 'Why should not Old Men be Mad?'[81] The ruined country house with the moonlight falling on it evokes 'Blood and the Moon', in which hope of improvement had been raised, then dashed; in *Purgatory* the Old Man's recollection of the past glory of the house is futile nostalgia. Specifics of the description recall Coole Park, and thus 'Coole Park and Ballylee, 1931'.[82] Illuminated by ghosts, the house recalls also 'The Curse of Cromwell', but without the bard; and instead of lords and ladies enjoying music and welcoming him there are only the spirits of the groom and the mother lost in her suffering. We feel contrast also with the lords and ladies gay of 'Under Ben Bulben', beaten into the clay but embodied in art that will strengthen a new generation. And the boy, sunk so far below his father, is one of those 'unremembering ... products of base beds'; he is also connected ironically with 'To a Shade', in which Yeats had written of how the Lane pictures might have given Irish children's children loftier thought, sweeter emotion, 'working in their veins / Like gentle blood'. Aristocrats who should have given 'the right twigs for an eagle's nest' had ignored the artist's admonishments to live up to the responsibilities of their class; now all that remains is 'a bit of an egg-shell thrown / Out of a jackdaw's nest' (*P* 192).

The goal of the artists was said in 'Under Ben Bulben' to be profane perfection of mankind; at the other end of the volume, in the final lines of *Purgatory*, 'Mankind can do no more' (*P* 199). Such an admission, coupled with the prayer to God, is particularly ominous as we approach an era in which the concept of reality as a congeries of beings will once more be dominant (see *OB* 25–7). When *On the Boiler* and *Last Poems and Two Plays* (both ending with *Purgatory*) are juxtaposed, they suggest two possible solutions, the eugenic and the artistic, to the same problem. Juxtaposed at the end of *Last Poems and Two Plays*, *The Death of Cuchulain* and *Purgatory* create an 'either-or' pattern in regard to the alternative of life changed by art. Had Yeats lived longer, both texts would have appeared as parts of other configurations, their implications altered thereby. Although he was not responsible for the posthumous placement of 'Under Ben Bulben' at the end of 'Last Poems' and *The Death of Cuchulain* at the end of *Collected Plays*, he might have welcomed the more positive emphasis such changes produced. He well knew, in any case, that the words of the dead man would be modified in the guts of the living.

5

Conclusion

Although W. H. Auden, writing just after Yeats's death, was attracted enough by the vision of 'Under Ben Bulben' so that his elegy for Yeats modulates into a similar voice and ends with an incantatory series of images of the poet's power, he himself was moving in an opposite direction, and 'In Memory of W.B. Yeats' has been remembered more for its counter-assertion, in a section added to the earliest version of the text, that 'poetry makes nothing happen'. In a contemporary essay, Auden made the dismissal even more categorical:

> Art is a product of history, not a cause. Unlike some other products, technical inventions for example, it does not re-enter history as an effective agent, so that the question whether art should or should not be propaganda is unreal. The case ... rests on the fallacious belief that art ever makes anything happen, whereas the honest truth ... is that, if not a poem had been written, not a picture painted, not a bar of music composed, the history of man would be materially unchanged.[1]

This attitude was a necessary step in the course of Auden's personal development; but it has been seen as emblematic of a larger-scale change as well. As Samuel Hynes has argued in *The Auden Generation*, 'in this change of heart, by the generation's greatest poet, we might say that the 'thirties really ended' (350). But Ireland's situation was predictably different, and there the faith that literature might make things happen survived the years when the intensity of the cause of national independence seemed to have abated. It did not, however, go unchallenged.

Today we are alert enough to the complex dynamics of literary influence, for the description of which such models as the burden of the past, Freudian rivalry, and seizure by eminent domain have all proved useful, not to be surprised that 'the example of Yeats' has often met with strong resistance. In the 1950s, Patrick Kavanagh was attacking Yeats's bardic posture and his conception of national literature.[2] More recently Michael Hartnett included strictures in his sequence *A Farewell to English* (1975). Occasionally the poem sounds Yeatsian:

> Poets with progress
> make no peace or pact:
> the act of poetry
> is a rebel act.[3]

Seanchan had similarly warned, 'When did the poets promise safety, King?' (*VPl* 306). But in the same section of Hartnett's poem Yeats was blamed for having 'forced us into exile / on islands of bad verse'. The description of Yeats's methods was not without a hint of admiration, but with a specific allusion to 'Under Ben Bulben' Hartnett left no doubt how he felt about the work of those who 'learn the trade' from the old master:

> Chef Yeats, that master of the use of herbs
> could raise mere stew to a glorious height,
> pinch of saga, soupçon of philosophy
> carefully stirred in to get the flavour right,
> and cook a poem around the basic verbs.
> Our commis-chefs attend and learn the trade,
> bemoan the scraps of Gaelic that they know:
> add to a simple Anglo-Saxon stock
> Cuchulainn's marrow-bones to marinate,
> a dash of O'Rathaille simmered slow,
> a glass of University hic-haec-hoc:
> sniff and stand back and proudly offer you
> the celebrated Anglo-Irish stew. (32)

Hartnett saw no access to the bardic tradition except through the medium of Gaelic, in which consequently he began to write.

Although the new outbreak of violence in the North in 1969 produced new pressures for an *engaged* Irish literature (*PW* 36), it also provided new causes for opposition to the Yeatsian 'demand' that poets cast their minds on other days.[4] As Seamus Heaney has described the situation, there was now

> a more than literary motive for ... castigation of the myth of Ireland as a spiritual entity, a mystical principle which could elicit

the religious devotion of not only the young Yeats but also of the executed poet and revolutionary, Patrick Pearse, martyr of Easter 1916 and sponsor of the blood-sacrific strain in Irish republicanism. With the outbreak of civic violence in Belfast and Derry, Irishism was perceived to be not only a manifestation of ethnic kitsch but potentially a code that spelled loyalty to the aims and (by extension) the methods of the IRA. Hence, as the seventies advanced, it became increasingly difficult to express fidelity to the ideals of the Irish Literary Revival, which were essentially born of a healthy desire to redress the impositions of cultural imperialism, without seeming to become allied with a terrorist campaign that justified itself by self-righteous rhetoric against British imperialism of the original, historically rejected and politically repugnant sort. (*PW* 38)

Heaney saw as an additional force at work the impact of recent trends in literary theory, 'a deconstructionist suspicion of the ideological depth-charges in all literature,' and 'doubts about the very possibility of justified language arts after Auschwitz'. It

all added up to a situation in which the literary intelligentsia of Britain and Ireland were anxious to confine the operations of imaginative writing to a sanitized realm that might include the ludic, the ironic, the parodic, the satiric, the pathetic, the domestic, the elegiac, and the self-inculpatory, but which would conscientiously exclude the visionary prophetic, the patriotic witness, the national epical. Because of their dangerous availability for co-option as generalized herd-emotion, and their bias towards inflation and slither, these latter modes are tacitly deemed to be obsolescent. (*PW* 38–9)

In support of this opposition, as Heaney noted, Auden himself has actually been resuscitated in a recent poem by Paul Muldoon, curtly answering 'Certainly not' to Yeats's anguished question in 'The Man and the Echo' about his possible responsibility for the Rising. Muldoon's own Introduction to *The Faber Book of Contemporary Irish Poetry* favours 'the sceptical over the committed, the cosmopolitan over the national, the lightness of detachment over the heaviness of attachment' (*PW* 41–3).

In at least a few cases, though, Yeats's conception of national literature has been viewed more sympathetically. From a relatively early point in his career Heaney himself was already enough of a 'strong poet' to be able to preserve his poetic integrity while absorbing elements of the work of others. In 1969, when he found that 'the problems of poetry moved from being simply a matter of achieving the satisfactory verbal icon to being a search for images and symbols adequate to our predicament', Yeats's stance provided an important model.[5] Heaney could not see himself writing 'public celebrations or execrations of resistance or atrocity', though 'Easter, 1916' had shown him that it was possible to do so without sacrificing literary merit. Heaney's own need, as he put it in 'Feeling into Words' (1974), was to 'discover a field of force in which, without abandoning fidelity to the processes and experience of poetry . . . , it would be possible to encompass the perspectives of a humane reason and at the same time to grant the religious intensity of the violence its deplorable authenticity and complexity'. '"How with this rage shall beauty hold a plea?"' was the question, and Heaney's answer, borrowed from Yeats, was 'by offering "befitting emblems of adversity"'. The essay makes clear that Heaney had in mind Yeats's bardic sense of the artist's role: 'I began by suggesting that my point of view involved poetry as divination, as a restoration of the culture to itself. In Ireland in this century it has involved for Yeats and many others an attempt to define and interpret the present by bringing it into significant relationship with the past, and I believe that effort in our present circumstances has to be urgently renewed' (60). The process of casting one's mind on other days would enable the poet not merely to understand the present violence but to discern values that would ultimately help restore the shattered nation.

Heaney found some 'emblems' relevant to the crisis in the North in P.V. Glob's *The Bog People*, in which the author argued that preserved bodies discovered in the bogs of Jutland, naked and strangled or with their throats cut, had been ritual sacrifices to the Mother Goddess, 'who needed new bridegrooms each winter to bed with her in her sacred place, in the bog, to ensure the renewal and fertility of the territory in the spring' (57). The illustrations showing the victims blended in Heaney's mind with 'photographs of atrocities, past and present, in the long rites of Irish political and religious struggles'; and he realised that 'the tradition of Irish political martyrdom for that cause whose icon is Kathleen Ni Houlihan' was part of 'an archetypal pattern' (57–8). Kathleen herself then became the Goddess, and by implication those who died in her service could perhaps be seen as themselves ritual sacrifices. In a comparable manner T.S.

Eliot, who had attributed to Yeats the adumbration of the modern 'mythic method', had claimed that it was a means of giving a shape and a significance to 'the immense panorama of futility and anarchy that is contemporary history';[6] and in a world haunted by the devastation of World War I and millions of corpses in the mud of European battlefields, he had seen in the fertility rites as interpreted by Frazer and Jessie Weston the hope of a final peace – Shantih shantih shantih. Perhaps the most pertinent of Yeats's own works is 'Parnell's Funeral'. As he had emphasised, the archetypal patterns offered a more attractive, and perhaps more effective, way of reaching an audience than political rhetoric. They spoke to what was common in the experience of all human beings; 'we move others . . . because all life has the same root', he had once written.[7] One might, by such means, feel that one's poetry was engaged, was 'doing something', without sacrificing one's artistic standards or putting party or expediency before vision.

But, as Heaney stressed at the end of 'Feeling into Words', he personally found carrying out such a task intimidating: 'To forge a poem is one thing, to forge the uncreated conscience of the race, as Stephen Dedalus put it, is quite another and places daunting pressures and responsibilities on anyone who would risk the name of poet' (60). He did in fact write a number of poems offering the 'emblems' drawn from Glob, including 'The Tollund Man', 'The Grauballe Man', and 'Punishment', yet he seems never to have been quite comfortable in the role. As early as 'Digging', which describes the pen resting 'snug as a gun' in his hand (*HP* 3), he had recognised the potentially dangerous power of language, and using his art as a weapon obviously did not come easily to him. 'Summer 1969' showed him in 'Joycean' detachment in Spain when the violence erupted in the North; when urged to 'Go back, . . . try to touch the people', he 'retreated to . . . the Prado', only to be confronted there by Goya's admonishing images of war (*HP* 224–5). 'The Unacknowledged Legislator's Dream' evoked Shelley's *Defence* ironically, for there the poet achieves only his own imprisonment,[8] though the phrase 'My wronged people' may have been intended to recall 'sang, to sweeten Ireland's wrong' from Yeats's 'Apologia . . .' (*HP* 211). In 'Whatever You Say Say Nothing' the poet appeared as Hamlet, aware that 'The times are out of joint' but feeling his responsibility to act as a heavy burden:

Christ, it's near time that some small leak was sprung

In the great dykes the Dutchman made
To dam the dangerous tide that followed Seamus.
Yet for all this art and sedentary trade
I am incapable. . . . (*HP* 212–15)

Although 'sedentary trade' was Yeats's term in 'The Tower' for the life of the artist, the context there had been one of poetic power to affect the future, and of course it was just for that purpose that he had urged his successors to learn their trade. A profound doubt about the efficacy of that process pervades Part VI of 'Kinship':

> And you, Tacitus,
> observe how I make my grove
> on an old crannog
> piled by the fearful dead:
>
> a desolate peace.
> Our mother ground
> is sour with the blood
> of her faithful,
>
> they lie gargling
> in her sacred heart
> as the legions stare
> from the ramparts.
>
> come back to this
> 'island of the ocean'
> where nothing will suffice.
> Read the inhumed faces
>
> of casualty and victim;
> report us fairly,
> how we slaughter
> for the common good
> and shave the heads
> of the notorious,
> how the goddess swallows
> our love and terror. (*HP* 200)

The key line is that describing Ireland as an island 'where nothing will suffice', which fuses a reference to Stevens's 'Of Modern

Poetry' ('The poem of the mind in the act of finding / What will suffice.'[9]) with 'O when will it suffice?' from 'Easter, 1916'. The first seems abstract and detached, while the second was part of a poem intended to affect the politics of that earlier troubled time, the repercussions of which were still being felt in 1969. There is a resonance also with 'Feeling into Words' suggesting that there *are* no 'images and symbols adequate to our predicament'. Thus the poem ends on a note of impotence. Although the poet has made a 'grove', built upon the past, as if he were a modern Druid or *file*, he seems unable to perform an efficacious ritual. It is perhaps significant that the related poem 'Ocean's Love to Ireland' describes Tudor troops beating 'the woods where her poets / Sink like Onan', their poetic seed shed barrenly. (*HP* 202). In the discouragement of 'Exposure' his mask is the more humble one of 'a wood-kerne / Escaped from the massacre' (*HP* 228).

The fugitive in the woods was to reappear in *Sweeney Astray* (1983), in which Heaney saw in the title character 'a figure of the artist, displaced, guilty, assuaging himself by his utterance,' but also suggested more positively that 'Sweeney's easy sense of cultural affinity with both western Scotland and southern Ireland' was 'exemplary for all men and women in contemporary Ulster....'[10] The use of paradigmatic myth in this text could be seen as a renewed effort in the Yeatsian mode; but in his unpublished earlier version of the story and in the 'Sweeney Redivivus' sequence the poet appears as 'alienated anti-hero, iconoclast, and critic of the tribe rather than mediator and healer';[11] and *Station Island*, though it contains passages involving feelings of guilt for inaction, also seems to move in the opposite direction, for in the final section the Joycean figure advises the poet 'to write / for the joy of it', to 'let others wear the sackcloth and the ashes', and, most importantly, to 'forget'.[12] Doing this last would of course reverse the process of casting one's mind on other days, and the ghostly mentor, mocking the poet's linguistic nationalism as 'raking at dead fires', does not urge him to provide sinews for an indomitable Irishry or to forge the uncreated conscience of his race but rather

> "... to swim
> out on your own and fill the element
> with signatures on your own frequency,
> echo soundings, searches, probes, allurements,
> elver-gleams in the dark of the whole sea."

Even such a move would not *necessarily* be inconsistent with the Yeatsian position, for as Sean Lucy has noted, the powers of the traditional bard 'came from complex disciplines of learning; but also, and often more so, from the practice of withdrawal and concentration, the deliberate cultivation of "otherness," and of communication with the unhuman presences which make up all of the worlds, including the everyday.'[13] Lucy was making this point in relation to John Montague, who has felt as deeply as Heaney the need to bring his art to bear upon the situation in Northern Ireland, and whom Lucy considers to be 'a file disguised by translation, a Shaman in search of natural magics and penetrating illusions, with which to heal and save himself and his people'; but it applies equally well to Heaney. Heaney's most recent attitude is difficult to determine. His statement in *The Government of the Tongue* that 'poetry is its own reality and no matter how much a poet may concede to the corrective pressures of social, moral, political and historical reality, the ultimate fidelity must be to the demands and promise of the artistic event' stressed artistic integrity but would still allow the finished work to affect the writer's world. The statement was offered as essentially Yeats's own view.[14] Later in the same lecture he added that 'in one sense the efficacy of poetry is nil – no lyric has ever stopped a tank. In another sense, it is unlimited. It is like the writing in the sand in the face of which accusers and accused are left speechless and renewed' (107). In *The Place of Writing* he surveyed at length the positions of those who have rejected the Yeatsian aesthetic but did not seem to identify himself with them. And in the poetry of *The Haw Lantern* there are numerous lines and images suggesting lingering remorse or regret for 'speechlessness'.[15] It remains possible that Heaney will once again clearly adopt a Yeatsian stance. But even if in the future he develops strictly along the lines called for by 'Joyce', it would still be arguable that his engagement with the Yeatsian aesthetic was a necessary stage in freeing him to do so.

If Heaney was correct in suggesting that deconstructive theory has been one of the forces working against an engaged national literature, the recent fading of its influence has important implications. Hillis Miller, writing sympathetically of Paul de Man's feeling that '*the* task of criticism in the coming years would be a kind of imperialistic appropriation of all literature by the method of rhetorical reading often called "deconstruction"', has noted ruefully that in the years since de Man made this prediction, there has actually been a massive shift of focus in literary study ... away from the 'intrinsic,' rhetorical study of literature toward study of the 'extrinsic' relations of literature, its placement within psychological, historical, or sociological contexts. To put this another way, there has been a shift away from an interest in 'reading,' which means a focus on language as such, its nature and powers, to various forms of hermeneutic interpretation, which means a focus on the relation of language to something else, God, nature, society, history, the self, something presumed to be outside language. There had been, by one of those (perhaps inexplicable, certainly 'overdetermined') displacements of interest, a tremendous increase in the appeal of psychologistic and sociological theories of literature such as Lacanian feminism, Marxism, Foucauldianism. This has been accompanied by a widespread return to old-fashioned biographical, thematic, and literary historical methods that antedate the New Criticism.[16]

But there is really nothing 'inexplicable' about these developments. On the contrary, in retrospect it seems surprising for anyone to have imagined that a theory that seemed to sever the connection between text and world could appeal to very many readers and writers for very long. Surely the vast majority of those who care for literature do so because of some perceived *connection* between it and the world in which they live. Martha Nussbaum has predicted 'a future in which our talk about literature will return, increasingly, to a concern with the practical – to the ethical and social questions that give literature its high importance in our lives.... In short: a future in which literary theory (while not forgetting its many other pursuits) will also join with ethical theory in pursuit of the question, "How should one live?"' (Cohen 58). And Heaney, in some comments on recent American poets, noted that 'it's the texture and the inner dynamics of a poem that interest them, and of course poems have to be able to live in that way. My impatience with a lot of American poetry is that that's the *only* way it can live. In one way, of course, that's all there is: there's just a form, and there's a form housing a set of harmonies and balances. But I think that in the culture and situation I come from, you want to punish the form with some relationship to the actual' (Corcoran 38). Furthermore, many of those attracted to 'theory' in the first place had been looking for an approach that would advance their own 'extrinsic' concerns, whether involving race, gender, or some other political or social agenda, and could accept deconstructive principles only so long as they did not seem to undermine such concerns. Thus, for example, near the end of an extended meditation on feminism and literature, Rachel Blau DuPlessis observed that 'we need a writer who would be for feminism what Brecht was for modernism – who understands, to put it a little crudely, that literature doesn't change things, people do. . . .' Then she went on to consider that literature itself *might* in fact 'change things': 'Our literature and thinking still seem quietistic to me, in that they require us to understand and respond, but not to act on our understanding, certainly not to act collectively. . . . I think we haven't even grasped the most radical implications of feminism for a theory which mediates back to practice. . . .' After this she quoted Sara Lennox: 'I've been angry recently that, while theory proliferates, we have given up on what was compelling about the late sixties and early seventies – that feeling of infinite possibility which challenged us to think and live differently.'[17] More recently, Elaine Showalter has argued that

> feminist criticism can't afford to settle for mimicry, or to give up the idea of female subjectivity, even if we accept it as a constructed or metaphysical one. . . . [W]e need . . . a 'strategic essentialism' to combat patriarchy. . . . Despite our awareness of diversity and deconstruction, feminist critics cannot depend on gynesic ruptures in discourse to bring about social change. During a period when many of the meager gains of the civil rights and women's movements are being threatened or undone by Reaganism and the New Right, when, indeed, there is a backlash against what the Bennetts and Blooms see as too *much* black and female power in the university, there is an urgent necessity to affirm the importance of black and female thinkers, speakers, readers, and writers. The Other Woman may be transparent or invisible to some; but she is still very vivid, important, and necessary to us. (Cohen 369)

Given this trend, it seems obvious that critical theory and practice of all types, from 'old-fashioned' to avant-garde, could re-establish or reaffirm as appropriate their 'relationship to the actual' by devoting themselves to the study of artistic power and the problems that inevitably accompany it.

One natural focus of such a study would be other writers' formulations of such an aesthetic and the manifestations of it in their work. Joyce, for example, was surely aware of Yeats's position and considered similar problems and solutions, while almost always signalling his divergence from the Yeatsian view. The aesthetic Stephen outlines in *A Portrait* calls for a 'static' art, which would be consistent with Yeats's concern that writers should not sacrifice artistic merit to serve propagandistic or didactic goals, but rejects as an 'improper' response the sort of 'desire' felt by the boys and girls who kiss the statue in Yeats's poem (*PA* 205). Stephen takes as his example of a 'kinetic' response of that sort his friend Lynch's confession that he had written his name 'on the backside of the Venus of Praxiteles in the Museum'; it is difficult not to see here a comic transformation of the Wildean image that was so important to Yeats (205–6). Stephen goes on to reject a Yeatsian definition of the *claritas* that beautiful objects embody: 'symbolism or idealism, the supreme quality of beauty being a light from some other world, the idea of which the matter is but the shadow, the reality of which it is but the symbol.... But that is literary talk' (212–13). His own villanelle, however, could pass for one of Yeats's early poems on the archetypal Goddess-Wisdom figure as femme fatale – 'The Rose of the World', for instance.[18] Stephen sees the disturbances at the inaugural performance of *The Countess Cathleen* (the protagonist of which herself reflects that archetype) as a sign of the inability of Irish audiences to appreciate real art (225–6); and a few pages later, contemplating in Kildare Street a hotel patronised by the Ascendancy, 'the patricians of Ireland', he ponders, 'how could he hit their conscience or how cast his shadow over the imaginations of their daughters, before their squires begat upon them, that they might breed a race less ignoble than their own?' (237–8). His dark vision here anticipates *Purgatory*, and the solution to his problem of bridging the gap between a static art and the desire to forge the conscience of his race could be the Yeatsian one that the work of art might plant in the imaginations of at least a few representatives of this class ideal images that would affect future generations, would 'breed the best'. In a diary entry Stephen rejects Yeats's lyric 'Michael Robartes remembers Forgotten Beauty' as merely nostalgic (251), though arguably the beloved there represents a *present* incarnation of a beauty otherwise 'long faded from the world' but which, presented in the poem as a model or 'type', could 'call up a new age'. If his final words in the novel reaffirm his commitment to developing an Irish conscience, his definition of Irish art as the cracked looking-glass of a servant in the opening episode of *Ulysses* suggests scepticism about similar efforts by others. Later Bloom re-enacts Lynch's kinetic response by visiting the statues of goddesses in the Museum only to ascertain whether they are 'anatomically correct', and Mulligan, who quotes Wilde and dresses the part, jestingly predicts during the episode in the maternity hospital that in the future 'plastercast reproductions of the classical statues such as Venus and Apollo ... would enable ladies who were in a particular condition to pass the intervening months in a most enjoyable manner' (*U* 8.920–32; 14.1251–6). 'Scylla and Charybdis' contains a reference to 'the Platonic dialogues Wilde wrote', placing Wilde along with Yeats at the 'Platonic' or idealist pole in the pattern of opposites that informs the structure of the episode, and also implying a challenge, for from that episode on, the increasingly self-referential narrative mode of the novel suggests that the paradox of life imitating art, still involving a mimetic process, was ultimately no more acceptable to Joyce than the realist aesthetic of holding 'the mirror up to nature' (*U* 9.1069; 15.3820). The novel does reincarnate an ancient Greek hero and heroine, and *Finnegans Wake* more daringly dramatises the archetypal figures, yet the essential comic aspects of those figures primarily create *contrast* with idealised models for imitation such as Cuchulain and the 'ancient queens'.

Stephen and his artistic tenets provide a link to another figure whose relation to the Yeatsian aesthetic would bear further investigation, Ezra Pound. As a young man he idolised Yeats and was steeped in his work, the romantic 'Celtic Twilight' aspects of which first attracted him, and the two poets worked closely together during the years when they were both developing their mature voices.[19] For Pound, the process of development involved a movement from aestheticism to an engaged art, one that could put 'ideas into action' and 'heal a sick world', a movement towards a poem like *The Cantos* in which history becomes 'a school book for princes' (Canto 54).[20] He dramatised that development in *Hugh Selwyn Mauberley* (1920). Mauberley resembles Stephen in a number of ways, and like him champions static art, 'the "sculpture" of rhyme', against the 'prose kinema'. (As late as 1918 Pound himself wrote 'art is a stasis'.[21]) James Longenbach has demonstrated that the geneology of Mauberley's tradition reflects Yeats's presentation of the *fin de siècle* in 'The Grey Rock' and other writings (*SC* 167ff). However, although the poem presents Mauberley sympathetically, it also presents him as ineffectual and quite unable to produce the poem that *The Cantos* had already begun to be.[22] It seems quite possible that Yeats played an important role in Pound's own movement

towards the aesthetic underlying *The Cantos*. In December 1912 or
January 1913 Pound read with great enthusiasm 'To a Wealthy Man
. . .' (*SC* 74–5). Longenbach notes that the poem 'remained a kind of
touchstone for Pound's sense of the Renaissance ideal of an aristocracy of the arts' and that both writers 'saw a return to certain
aspects of the quattrocento as a cure for modern culture's inadequacies.'
But the poem is also one Yeats's most memorable proclamations of
art's shaping power, which actually provides the *means* whereby
modern culture might be made to model itself after Italian Renaissance
values. Pound's recognition of this potential was crucial for his
later work. After 1917 the literary relationship of the two became
less close, and Yeats could make little sense of *The Cantos*; but with
the benefit of hindsight the poem's Yeatsian aspect becomes clear,
so that, for instance, Pound's expectations for Mussolini bear
comparison with the (similarly disappointed) ones Yeats held for
Kevin O'Higgins (*AV B* 4–5; Litz 129). In a section written after
Yeats's death Pound incorporated a tribute to 'William who dreamed
of nobility', a punning echo of 'Dream of the noble and the beggarman'
from 'The Municipal Gallery Re-visited', another of Yeats's major
poems about artistic power. It was a recognition of the importance
of those winters at Stone Cottage when he 'shared Yeats's heroic
dream' (Litz 145).

Instances such as these point also to another potentially fruitful
area of study, the possibility that the power of art to shape life
could be seen at work in the area of literary *influence*. In some
depersonalised theoretical models of 'intertextuality' there are *only*
texts, but 'life' returns as soon as we conceive of influence as the
preoccupation or even obsession of one writer with the work of
another. The way in which Yeats's valedictory prescription for
'Irish poets' has impinged upon the consciousness of later generations
itself exemplifies the process. The preoccupation can be unwilling
and the other's work quite threatening, as when T.S. Eliot, reading
Ulysses in manuscript in 1921, wrote Joyce 'I wish, for my own sake,
that I had not read it', and in his review of the published novel
termed it 'a book to which we are all indebted, and from which
none of us can escape.'[23] In the same review he confronted the issue
more generally, if not quite openly, asserting that 'the influence
which Mr Joyce's book may have is from my point of view an
irrelevance. A very great book may have a very bad influence
indeed; and a mediocre book may be in the event most salutary . . .'
(481). And, perhaps with an eye on Shelley's *Defence*, 'the question,

then, about Mr Joyce, is: how much living material does he deal with, and how does he deal with it: deal with, not as a legislator or exhorter, but as an artist?' (482). When instead of being contemporaries the writers are from different eras, the relationship involves, as in the Yeatsian aesthetic, the bringing to bear of the past upon the present. 'Swift haunts me', Yeats wrote (*WB* 7). Dante provided a paradigmatic instance of the process in his encounter in Canto XV of *The Inferno* with his dead master Brunetto Latini. The 'familiar compound ghost' of Eliot's 'Little Gidding' draws upon Dante's example, and both Dante and Eliot lie behind the scene in Heaney's *Station Island* in which the poet is upbraided by the spirit of Joyce. In such instances, although the junior writer's life and work may be much changed by the encounter, the text in which the incident is recorded may work as a counterforce, incorporating the senior figure into an alien context and thereby changing our perception of him and his work, a variation of the process described by Eliot in 'Tradition and the Individual Talent' in which 'the existing monuments [of the literary tradition] form an ideal order among themselves, which is modified by the introduction of the new (the really new) work of art among them.'[24]

While the question of the degree to which in specific instances works of art have precipitated social and political change will certainly remain highly controversial, exploration of the issue, especially if broadly interdisciplinary, would make our terms for describing such interactions more subtle, perhaps provide ways to gauge effects more confidently. Psychoanalytic and mythic approaches, studies of reader response, and analyses of 'popular culture' could all throw light on possible processes of transmission. And literary and ethical theory might join forces, as Nussbaum urged, in the evaluation of the problems concomitant with the exercise of such power. Those problems, most of which have been noted in preceding chapters, all involve the recognition that if literature *can* change our world, then creating and publishing it involves a heavy burden of *responsibility*. 'Literature must take the responsibility of its power', as Yeats himself warned. Writing becomes as fraught with risk as handling a loaded weapon, Heaney's pen snug as a gun in his hand. Although Yeats, in contrast to many contemporary theorists, assumed 'transcendental foundations of knowledge' and a visionary gift that gave the writer privileged status, he still had to recognise that art sometimes has effects quite at odds with the intentions of its creator – effects that were particularly troubling when they

involved violence and death.[25] Even if one's play sent certain men
out to die in a just cause, one might question the *necessity* of the
deaths and feel remorse.

Declan Kiberd has noted the irony in the appropriation of Cuchulain,
intended by O'Grady as a model for an aristocracy in decline, by
'lower-middle-class clerks and schoolmasters who wanted nothing
more than to erase that aristocracy,' and the recent compounding of
that irony in the adoption of the hero as a role model by a Northern
Irish Protestant paramilitary organisation, the Ulster Defence
Association.[26] The metaphor that comes to mind here would be an
undefusable bomb that will go off at some unpredictable time in
the future, its victims perhaps not those for whom it was intended –
perhaps including even some of those who had made it in the first
place. For Yeats, who eventually took up O'Grady's efforts to
revitalise the Ascendancy, Pearse's emulation of Cuchulain had
been justified if at all by the 'heroism' it produced (*VP* 820).
Presumably he did not *intend* for *The Death of Cuchulain* to increase
sectarian violence in the North, and would have lamented such an
effect; but although he had claimed Ferguson as a Nationalist
malgré lui and in defending his personal interpretation of Alice
Milligan's *The Last Feast of the Fianna* had once written that 'the
emotion which a work of art awakens in an onlooker has
commonly little to do with the deliberate purpose of its maker,'
such a position was not typical of him,[27] and we must ask whether,
given the potency art can have, the artist should be held
responsible when the forces he or she unleashes prove undesirable.
The recent trial of the English heavy-metal rock group Judas Priest
for allegedly encoding their music with subliminal messages that
led two troubled youths to take their own lives raised some of the
same issues; but we are too well aware of ambiguities and of those
'ideological depth-charges' to dismiss UDA emulation of the Hound
of the North as perverse 'misreading'. Violence was endemic to the
world in which Cuchulain's exploits took place, and one of the
most famous of those exploits involved his indomitable resistance
to opposing forces in a divided land. In the speech in which Yeats
confronted this problem directly in regard to men who had
drowned themselves after (and perhaps because of) reading *Riders
to the Sea* or *Werther*, he said, 'we comfort ourselves in the way
Goethe comforted himself, that there must have been other men
saved from suicide by having read "Werther."' Certainly he was
right in advising his colleagues in the Senate to 'leave the arts . . . to

the general conscience of mankind' rather than attempting to control potential negative ramifications through censorship, since to suppress every text that could *potentially* produce such ramifications would be to suppress them all. But those of us who write about and teach literature as a profession might assume some of the responsibility of informing that general conscience.

Even a writer as well aware as Yeats was of the potential for abuse of literary power was capable of succumbing to the temptation. The ballads he wrote about Roger Casement provide a graphic example, not because they produced effects other than those he had intended but because in writing and publishing them he violated principles he himself had formulated in order to ensure that momentary passions would never lead him to sacrifice his integrity as an artist.

On 16 November 1936 Yeats wrote Ethel Mannin that he was 'in a rage' from reading Dr. William J. Maloney's *The Forged Casement Diaries*:

> He has proved that the diaries, supposed to proved Casement 'a Degenerate' and successfully used to prevent an agitation for his reprieve, were forged. Casement was not a very able man but he was gallant and unselfish, and had surely his right to leave what he would have considered an unsullied name. I long to break my rule against politics and call these men criminals but I must not. Perhaps a verse may come to me, now or a year hence. I have lately written a song in defence of Parnell (about love and marriage less foul lies were circulated), a drinking song to a popular tune and will have it sung from the Abbey stage at Xmas. All my life it has been hard to keep from action, as I wrote when a boy, – 'to be not of the things I dream.' (*L* 867–8)

The 'rule against politics' was, of course, a rule against writing in the heat of political passion in order to have an immediate influence upon public opinion (*Mem* 84), writing as the Young Irelanders had often done, as Yeats himself had done in 'Mourn – And Then Onward!' Earlier in the same year, when Mannin was pressing him to act on behalf of Ossietsky, he had told her 'it takes fifty years for a poet's weapons to influence the issue' (*L* 850–1). If a verse 'came to' him, as the idea for *Cathleen ni Houlihan* had come to him in a dream, then he could produce a poem without fear that vision or formal perfection would be sacrificed to expediency. The allusion to 'Fergus and the Druid' suggests the frustration of one with 'wisdom' who can never have 'power', though ironically the poem as a whole dramatises the folly of sacrificing power in the pursuit of wisdom (see also *Mem* 161). In fact, the Parnell ballad had been written at the request of the author of a book defending his behaviour in the O'Shea affair (*LDW* 92–3, *E&I* 486). And less than two weeks after the letter to Mannin Yeats did write about Casement; as he informed Dorothy Wellesley, he had 'sent off a ferocious ballad written to a popular tune, to a newspaper' (*LDW* 107–8). In the absence of statements such as those he had made about the dream origin of the play, it seems fair to assume that he had been unable to resist breaking his rule. His choice of the ballad form and newspaper publication indicates a concern for popular impact, though in a postscript he added comments about the formal challenge involved: 'You will not find the four line stanza "too easy" if you struggle to make your spirit at once natural & imaginative. My "Casement" is better written than my "Parnell" because I passed things when I had to find three rhymes & did not pass when I had to find two.' He was perhaps surprised when Dorothy Wellesley urged him not to insist on the 'savage attack' until he had found out the facts, but he responded impenitently, 'I could not stop that ballad if I would, people have copies, & I don't want to. . .' (*LDW* 108). On 7 December, however, he acknowledged that she had been 'quite right' and that he was 'upset & full of remorse': 'I have wronged [Alfred Noyes], though not [Cecil Spring-Rice], I got in a blind rage & only half read the passage that excited it. . . . All my life I have been subject to these fits of rage though thank God seldom if ever about any matter that effects [*sic*] myself. In this case I lost the book & trusted to memory. I am full of shame' (*LDW* 110). Shortly afterwards he received a letter from Mannin, to whom he had sent a copy of the ballad, approving of what she took to be a 'hatred of England' in it that he was at pains to deny, stressing that his debt to English literature made it impossible for him to hate 'the people of England', though he did admit to hating 'certain characteristics of modern England', probably meaning imperialism. He added that he hated more than she did because his hatred could 'have no expression in action' (*L* 872–3; *LDW* 111; Krimm 231). Dorothy Wellesley herself, though willing to exonerate him on the score of hating England, made the yet more damaging criticism that he did not 'hate hate, and love love' as she did, a failure of great magnitude because 'if hatred grows as it seems to be doing all European culture may be destroyed, and all of us reduced to brutes' (*LDW* 112). Her forebodings anticipated Auden's lines 'In the nightmare of the dark / All the dogs of Europe bark. / And the living nations wait, / Each sequestered in its hate' – ironically, lines occurring in the most 'Yeatsian' section of the poem and even moving towards his own view of the power of art to change things for the better, to 'Make a vineyard of the curse.'[28]

Though Yeats 'had a black fortnight' as a 'result of nervous strain' from writing this and the second Casement ballad, his determination persisted. He even claimed he was fighting in those ballads for something he had been fighting for all his life – 'It is our Irish fight though it has nothing to do with this or that country. Bernard Shaw fights with the same object' and so had Swift:

> I said when I started my movement in my 25th or 26th year 'I am going to stiffen the back-bone'. Bernard Shaw may have said the same in his youth; it has been stiffened in Ireland with results. I am an old man now & month by month my capacity & energy must slip away, so what is the use of saying that both in England & Ireland I want to stiffen the back bone of the high hearted & high-minded & the sweet hearted & sweet-minded, so that they may no longer shrink & hedge, when they face rag merchants like ──. Indeed before all I want to strengthen myself. It is not our business to reply to this & that, but to set up our love and indignation against their pity & hate – but how I run on – Forgive me. (*LDW* 113–15)

Apparently his continued conviction of the general validity of Maloney's case and his sense that the ballads were part of a greater fight to strengthen the good against the evil overcame his troubled feelings at the discovery of the error caused by his rage. By identifying his feeling with Swiftian 'indignation' ('a kind of joy') he could shift the onus of perpetuating hatred onto his opponents. And by treating the ballads as an episode in a lifelong campaign he convinced himself that he was not merely replying 'to this & that' and thus was in less danger of sacrificing artistic integrity in the interest of impact on the moment.

Impact enough there soon was. On the night of 1 February 1937 he broadcast the poem from the Abbey stage as part of a programme intended for relay on the BBC, from which it would go out to over eight million people: a bold effort to reach the broadest possible audience directly (McCartan 386–7, Krimm 232). The next day the poem appeared in de Valera's paper, *The Irish Press*, and Yeats wrote approvingly of the result:

> On Feb. 2 my wife went to Dublin shopping & was surprised at the defference [*sic*] everybody showed her in buses & shop. Then she found what it was – the Casement poem was in the morning paper. Next day I was publicly thanked by the vice-president of the Executive Counsil [*sic*], by De Valera's political secretary, by our chief antiquarian & an old revolutionist, Count Plunket, who calls my poem 'a ballad the people much needed'. De Valera's newspaper gave me a long leader saying that for generations to come my poem will pour scorn on the forgers & their backers. The only English comment is in *The Evening Standard* which points out my bad rhymes & says that after so many years it is impossible to discuss the authenticity of the diaries. (The British Government has hidden them for years). (*LDW* 126)

If the process of artistic influence figured by the image of the Greek statues affecting the children through their mothers was so slow and intangible as to be difficult to demonstrate, in this case there was no room for doubt. The popular success of the ballad was attested to by the response of ordinary readers in buses and shop. Yeats had originally sent the poem to *The Irish Times*, but clearly found it gratifying to receive such a response from a de Valera Government with which he was by this point generally so much at odds (*L* 869).[29] The approbation of Count Plunkett and de Valera seemed to provide the sanction of the Nationalist tradition past and present. But Dorothy Wellesley, still troubled, could not share the enthusiasm of *The Irish Press* at the thought that the poem would continue to have an effect 'for generations to come': writing of the Parnell ballad she remonstrated that it 'will be sung for ever in Ireland spreading yet more hatred for many centuries. Meanwhile I think of Europe.... Also the Casement ballad' (*LDW* 127). Before receiving this letter Yeats had sent further news of the response to the Casement poem, saying it 'has stirred up no end of a commotion.' Shaw, whose fight Yeats had claimed was his own, had in fact 'written a long, rambling, vegetarian, sexless letter, disturbed by my causing "bad-blood" between the nations ....' and 'strange to say', Noyes had done what Yeats had asked and responded with a 'noble letter' of explanation, receiving Yeats's commendation though he took advantage of the occasion to assert anew the turpitude of Spring-Rice (*VP* 838; McCartan 392). This must have seemed an instance of art affecting life in the most dramatic of ways, as if Lord Ardilaun upon reading 'To a Wealthy Man . . .' had decided to put up all the funds necessary for the new gallery. And a further practical development was the growing 'demand for a production of the documents & their submission to some impartial tribunal.' To this information Yeats added that he would be relieved 'if they were so submitted & proved genuine. If Casement were a homo-sexual what matter! But if the British Government can with impunity forge evidence to prove him so no unpopular man with a cause will ever be safe' (*LDW* 128). What Yeats seems not to have considered is that if (as is now generally considered to be the case) the diaries were genuine the impetus for the rage behind his composition of the Casement ballads would no longer have *any* significant foundation, leaving only the perpetuated ill-feeling attested to in various ways by three people he knew.

When he did receive Dorothy Wellesley's second letter on the subject, his response was to claim that 'the Parnell Ballad is on a theme which is here looked upon as ancient history. It no more rouses anti-English feelings than a poem upon the battle of Trafalgar rouses anti-French feelings. . . . The Irish reader of the *Broadsides* would [not] consider the Parnell ballad political. It is a song about a personality far removed from politics of the day' (*LDW* 130). This response seems disingenuous, not only because the French parallel ignores the continuing English presence in the North but also because, as the Casement controversy illustrated, it took only one spark to turn 'ancient history' into contemporary hostility and bitterness. And one has to wonder whether Yeats failed to respond to the charge as applied to the Casement ballad because in fact he had no answer to give.

Virtually from the beginning of his career he had shown so clear an understanding of the major issues involved and had so seldom broken his 'rule' in such a manner that his doing so in this instance comes as a surprise and suggests how really difficult it *had* been, as he had written to Mannin, 'to keep from action'. It should be recalled that the period during which Yeats read Maloney's book was one in which he felt cut off from meaningful direct involvement in Irish politics, disillusioned with the country Ireland had become during the Free State era, and extremely discouraged about the possibility that through his art he could refashion it. Although

Yeats did not mention the fact in his correspondence during the controversy, he and Patrick McCartan had been instrumental in getting Maloney's book published and McCartan himself had come to Dublin in connection with its appearance, his conversations about it with Yeats helping to stir up the latter's rage. McCartan, as we have already seen, was to play a crucial role in re-establishing Yeats's sense that he had always been and was still a central force in the Irish revolutionary movement. The result in regard to the Casement ballads seems less felicitous than with 'The Municipal Gallery Re-visited'. In the one case he had brought into play the poet's bardic role as celebrator of great persons and events while in the other it was the role of bardic satirist that he encouraged (McCartan 370, 385–7; L 881–2). Both modes are subject to abuse, and a poet who praised an incompetent leader for personal gain, made a poorer song that he might have a heavier purse, would be every bit as culpable as one who had unjustly attacked an enemy. There may be readers who would deny that Lady Gregory constituted an appropriate 'type' upon which to model a future Ireland, but it is hard to imagine anyone justifying the risk of blackening a man's character though carelessness; unjust sullying of Casement's character, after all, was just what was at stake in the situation that had stimulated Yeats's indignation in the first place. He had by his own admission 'got in a blind rage & only half read the passage that excited it' instead of waiting for a verse to come to him through the 'visionary' process that evidenced origin in the realm of 'truth' (L 922). And although there might be numerous valid reasons to attack the English Government's handling of the Casement affair, Yeats's first poem had as its foundation what is now believed to be an invalid one, the forging of evidence. Despite his statements of satisfaction about the widespread and immediate effects of the ballad, he may have been at least unconsciously troubled, for the 'success' (L 881) they achieved did not save him from the feelings that he had 'no nation' and that there was little prospect of changing Ireland through his art that lay behind 'The Curse of Cromwell', which he began shortly after he completed the ballads (LDW 116). After all, much of the approbation had a false basis; and in the area of domestic policy de Valera's Government was working against most of the values Yeats would have wished to see encouraged. Later in 1937 he included in the 'General Introduction' a more profound confrontation with the potential in his aesthetic for the perpetuation and spread of hatred by keeping alive bitter memories of the past, his anguished description of how 'my hatred tortures me with love, my love with hate' possibly a conscious echo of the letter in which Dorothy Wellesley had chided him because he, unlike her, did not hate hate and love love, possibly a tacit recognition of the validity of her point.

For theorists and other literary scholars of all persuasions, making judgments about the abuses of artistic power will undoubtedly sometimes seem burdensome, but in compensation will help justify pursuits that have frequently been accused of having little to do with answering the question of how one should live. As 'Whatever You Say Say Nothing' suggests, some of Heaney's discomfort with the Yeatsian aesthetic may have arisen from a recognition that the burden of responsibility accompanying it might be at least as difficult to bear as the opprobrium arising from *not* wielding his art as a weapon in the war-torn streets and ghettos of the North. In any event, his poem 'The Harvest Bow', from *Field Work* (1979), contains an image that memorably focusses the problem and the opportunity. The final stanza describes the bow itself, a small relic of the fertility rituals in which he had attempted to find befitting emblems of adversity:

> *The end of art is peace*
> Could be the motto of this frail device
> That I have pinned up on our deal dresser –
> Like a drawn snare
> Slipped lately by the spirit of corn
> Yet burnished by its passage, and still warm.[30]

The first line was borrowed by Yeats from Coventry Patmore and used in 'To Wealthy Man...' to describe the impact of Classical civilisation upon the Renaissance and the comparably nourishing effect the Lane pictures might have upon a future Ireland.[31] 'The spirit of the corn' from *The Golden Bough* likewise promises rebirth and regeneration. The intricate bow itself would then be a figure for the work of art. Its resemblance to 'a drawn snare' suggests the potential for harm or abuse; but having been made by the poet's father it brings the past into the present, and 'frail' as it is, its continued warmth offers hope.[32] Although Yeats might in a moment of defiance echo his Seanchan's 'When did the poets promise safety, King?' 'The end of art is peace' could be the motto of his own art, too.

Notes

1 INTRODUCTION: CAST YOUR MIND ON OTHER DAYS

1. Tom Stoppard, *Travesties* (New York: Grove Press, 1975) pp. 64–5.
2. See, e.g., Paul Fussell, *The Great War and Modern Memory* (New York and London: Oxford University Press, 1975) and Robert Giddings, *The War Poets* (New York: Orion Books, 1988).
3. Quoted by Hans Richter, *Dada: Art and Anti-Art* (1965; reprinted London: Thames and Hudson, 1978) p. 25.
4. Seamus Heaney, *Poems 1965–1975* (1980; reprinted New York: Noonday Press, 1988) p. 224; hereafter cited as *HP*. See also Chapter 5, pp. 216–21.
5. On Yeats's early criticism of Young Ireland literature, see *YBIR* 8–12.
6. My use of 'aesthetic' follows the definition of Edward Engelberg, *The Vast Design: Patterns in W. B. Yeats's Aesthetic* (Toronto: University of Toronto Press, 1964) p. xiv: 'his conceptions of what art is and how it affects us.' See *UP2* 263–4 for Yeats himself using 'aesthetics' in relation to the issues dealt with in this study.
7. *Last Poems and Two Plays* (Dublin: Cuala Press, 1939) p. 44; hereafter cited as *LPTP*. Yeats died before this or any other version of 'Under Ben Bulben' appeared in print or even in proof, and the extant typescripts do not yield a copy text that can be used with confidence. However, there are no significant textual problems in this section of the poem. The phrase 'coming times' appears also in a manuscript of 'The Fish' now in the Berg Collection of the New York Public Library; published versions were revised to 'coming days'. The manuscript is connected by its title, 'The Fisher Aodh', and by its concern with the subject of the poet's verse shaping future perceptions of the beloved, with 'Aodh thinks of those who have Spoken Evil of his Beloved', discussed in Chapter 2, p. 53.
8. See also *UP2* 306–8, where Yeats refers to the politician 'who would reject every idea which is not of immediate service to his cause.'
9. Frank O'Connor, *The Wild Bird's Nest: Poems from the Irish* (Dublin: Cuala Press, 1932) p. 24; hereafter cited as *WBN*.
10. Patrick S. Dinneen and Tadgh O'Donoghue (eds), *Dánta Aodhagáin Uí Rathaille: The Poems of Egan O'Rahilly*, 2nd edn (London: Irish Texts Society, 1911) p. 114; hereafter cited as *DUR*; Seán O'Tuama and Thomas Kinsella (eds), *An Duanaire: An Irish Anthology* (Philadelphia: University of Pennsylvania Press, 1981) pp. 164–7; hereafter cited as *AD*.
11. The relationship between Yeats's work and the formal aspects of bardic literature has been examined by Sheila Deane, *Bardic Style in the Poetry of Gerard Manley Hopkins, W. B. Yeats and Dylan Thomas* (Ann Arbor, Mich. and London: UMI Research Press, 1989), especially pp. 101–31.
12. Eleanor Knott, *Irish Classical Poetry* (Dublin: Colm O'Lochlainn, 1957) p. 7; hereafter cited as Knott.

13. Ann Ross, *Everyday Life of the Pagan Celts* (1970), quoted in Joseph Falaky Nagy, *The Wisdom of the Outlaw: The Boyhood Deeds of Finn in Gaelic Narrative Tradition* (Berkeley, Los Angeles and London: University of California Press, 1985) p. 237; hereafter cited as Nagy.

14. 'Medieval Irish Lyrics' with 'The Irish Bardic Poet' (1967; reprinted Dublin: Dolmen Press, 1985) pp. 107–8; hereafter cited as Carney.

15. Patrick S. Dinneen (ed.), Geoffrey Keating, *Foras Feasa ar Éirinn: The History of Ireland*, Vol. II (London: Irish Texts Society, 1908) 366–7.

16. Robert Graves, *The White Goddess: A Historical Grammar of Poetic Myth*, amended and enlarged edn (New York: Farrar, Straus and Giroux, 1966) p. 92 *et passim*; hereafter cited as *WG*. Graves's scholarship has been questioned, but I have used him extensively, for although his work was published too late to have been one of Yeats's sources and he does not mention Yeats he is the most 'Yeatsian' of interpreters of early Irish culture and his interpretations often struck a chord with those Yeats made or suggest how he might have seen similar material. See also Mary Condren, *The Serpent and the Goddess: Women, Religion, and Power in Celtic Ireland* (San Francisco: Harper and Row, 1989) p. 57, for a passage from *Cormac's Glossary* in which there is a reference to 'Brigit a Goddess whom poets worshipped.'

17. Alwyn Rees and Brinley Rees, *Celtic Heritage: Ancient Tradition in Ireland and Wales* (1961; reprinted London: Thames and Hudson, 1989) p. 211; hereafter cited as Rees. See also Morton W. Bloomfield and Charles W. Dunn, *The Role of the Poet in Early Societies* (Cambridge: D. S. Brewer, 1989) p. 47: 'The deeply rooted belief that poetry ... is divinely inspired is reflected in the most ancient survivals of Irish mythology.... Irish mythographers refer to the three gods who preside over craftsmanship and are the begetters of esoteric Wisdom (*ecna*) and whose mother is the goddess Brigit the poet-seer'; and p. 31: 'In function, generally speaking, utterances pertaining to the past are exemplary.' This volume (hereafter cited as *RPES*), which provides a comprehensive survey of the functions of the poet, uses the Irish instance as paradigmatic (30–55).

18. Carney 111–12; see also Fergus Kelly (ed.), *Audacht Morainn* (Dublin: Dublin Institute for Advanced Studies, 1976), especially pp. xviii, 23.

19. Kenneth Hurlstone Jackson, *The Oldest Irish Tradition: A Window on the Iron Age* (Cambridge: Cambridge University Press, 1964) pp. 24–6; Osborn Bergin, 'Bardic Poetry', *Journal of the Ivernian Society*, V (April–July 1913) 153–66, 203–19; Knott 9ff; Robin Flower, *The Irish Tradition* (1947; reprinted Oxford: Clarendon Press, 1963) pp. 95–8; hereafter cited as Flower; *YBIR* 210–11.

20. Flower 99.

21. The fullest dramatisation of bardic excesses is that in Yeats's ultimate source for *The King's Threshold*, Owen Connellan (ed.), *Imtheacht na Tromdhaimhe, The Proceedings of the Great Bardic Institution*, Transactions of the Ossianic Society, Vol. V (Dublin: John O'Daly, 1860); hereafter cited as Connellan; Roy Foster, *Modern Ireland 1600–1972* (London: Allen Lane: Penguin, 1988) p. 28, notes seventeenth-century bards prepared to write *against* the native Irish. See also Declan Kiberd, 'Irish Literature

and Irish History', in Roy Foster (ed.), *The Oxford Illustrated History of Ireland* (Oxford and New York: Oxford University Press, 1989) pp. 281–2.

22. See Patrick S. Dinneen (ed.), Geoffrey Keating, *Foras Feasa ar Éirinn: The History of Ireland*, Vol. III (London: Irish Texts Society, 1908) 78–83.

23. On the impact of Christianity, see Flower *passim*, and, for a much more negative view, Condren, *The Serpent and the Goddess*, pp. 65ff.

24. Yeats's earliest sources of information about the bardic tradition included the various volumes of the Transactions of the Ossianic Society and the work of Ferguson and O'Grady. Over the years these were supplemented by other sources such as the *Memoirs* of the Marquis of Clanricarde, in which he 'found a wonderful account of the old bardic colleges' (*CL1* 133), Lady Wilde, Sophie Bryant's *Celtic Ireland*, and Douglas Hyde. He drew from them a sense of the tradition very much like that synthesised primarily from more recent sources in this chapter. Further information about his specific sources is given in succeeding chapters. For an extended but quirky consideration of Yeats's interest in Druidism, see Virginia Moore, *The Unicorn: William Butler Yeats' Search for Reality* (London: Macmillan, 1954) pp. 46–57.

25. D. Ellis Evans, John G. Griffith and E. M. Jope (eds), *Proceedings of the Seventh International Congress of Celtic Studies* (Oxford: Oxbow Books, 1986) p. 153; *Ireland Since 1800: Conflict and Conformity* (London and New York: Longman, 1989) p. 1. See also Audrey S. Eyler and Robert F. Garratt (eds), *The Uses of the Past: Essays on Irish Culture* (Newark: University of Delaware Press, London and Toronto: Associated University Presses, 1988) p. 7 *et passim*.

26. The latter suggestion is Roy Foster's in *The Oxford Illustrated History*, p. 190.

27. 'The Necessity for De-Anglicising Ireland', in *The Revival of Irish Literature* (London: T. Fisher Unwin, 1894) p. 126.

28. Michel Foucault, *Power / Knowledge: Selected Interviews and Other Writings, 1972–1977*, ed. Colin Gordon (New York: Random House, 1977) p. 39.

29. *Ideas of Good and Evil* (London: A. H. Bullen, 1903) pp. 244–5; hereafter cited as *IGE*.

30. Cecile O'Rahilly (ed.), *Táin Bó Cúalnge* (Dublin: Dublin Institute for Advanced Studies, 1967) pp. 72, 211; Carney 112. Yeats's observations were part of his 1890 review of Sophie Bryant's *Celtic Ireland* (*UP1* 163–4); on the fear of bardic satire surviving well into the twentieth century, see Jackson 27. A full account of Irish satire can be found in Vivian Mercier, *The Irish Comic Tradition* (Oxford: Clarendon Press, 1962) pp. 105–81.

31. *A Book of Irish Verse: Selected from Irish Writers* (London: Methuen, 1895) p. xii; for date see p. xxvii; hereafter cited parenthetically in the text.

32. See also *SS* 75.

33. *Samhain*, October 1902, p. 12n.

34. Thomas Smyth, quoted by E. C. Quiggin, *Prolegomena to the Study of the Later Irish Bards 1200–1500* (Oxford: Proceedings of the British Academy, 1911) pp. 20–1. Cf. also the rhymed account of the bards in Derricke's *Image of Irelande* (1581): 'And more to stirre [the rebels] up, to pro-

secute their ill: / What greate renowne their fathers gotte, thei shewe by Rimyng skill' (quoted by Quiggin, p. 21).
35. W. L. Renwick (ed.), *A View of the Present State of Ireland* (London: E. Partridge, 1934) pp. 95–6.
36. N. J. A. Williams (ed.), *The Poems of Giolla Brighde Mac Con Midhe* (Dublin: Irish Texts Society, 1980) pp. 60–1. See also Mac Con Midhe's *'Iongnadh mh'aisling in Eamhain . . .'* ('Wondrous my vision in Eamhain . . .'), a vision poem in which the Red Branch heroes are evoked to sanction the monarchic aspirations of a contemporary nobleman; in the poem the bards themselves are called 'fir do Thuathaibh Dé Danann', men of the Tribes of Dana the mother goddess (pp. 170–83).

2 THE EARLY WORK

1. An earlier version of some of the material in this chapter appeared as a 'Preface to the New Edition' in the second edition of my *Yeats and the Beginning of the Irish Renaissance* (Syracuse: Syracuse University Press, 1987) pp. xi–xxxvi.
2. Lady Mary Ferguson, *Sir Samuel Ferguson in the Ireland of His Day* (Edinburgh and London: W. Backwood, 1896), II, 249; Ferguson's statement was made in a letter of 18 March 1886, shortly before his death and Yeats's essays about him. See also Robert O'Driscoll, 'Two Voices: One Beginning', *University Review*, III (n.d.), 88–100.
3. 'John Eglinton and Spiritual Art', *UP2* 131; later included in *Literary Ideals in Ireland* (London: T. Fisher Unwin, and Dublin: at the *Daily Express* Office, 1899) p. 36. The quotation is from Blake: see pp. 30–1 of this study.
4. *E&I* 518. See *Au* 190: 'My father, from whom I had learned the term [Unity of Being], preferred a comparison to a musical instrument so strung that if we touch a string all the strings murmur faintly.' See also *LTWBY* 217.
5. For the Irish legends used in a modern literature leading to Unity of Culture, see *Au* 193–4.
6. Stephen Halliwell (ed.), *The "Poetics" of Aristotle* (Chapel Hill: University of North Carolina Press, 1987) p. 41; hereafter cited as Halliwell.
7. Quoted by M. H. Abrams, *The Mirror and the Lamp: Romantic Theory and the Critical Tradition* (1953; reprinted New York: W W. Norton, 1958) p. 43; hereafter cited as Abrams.
8. Plotinus, *The Divine Mind, Being the Treatises of the Fifth Ennead*, trans. Stephen MacKenna (London: Medici Society, 1926) p. 74. This passage was from a section (V, vii, 1) not included in Thomas Taylor's *Select Works of Plotinus* (1817 and new edition, ed. G.R.S. Mead), copies of which were owned by George Yeats (*YL* 1595).
9. Sir Philip Sidney, *An Apology for Poetry*, ed. Forrest G. Robinson (1970; reprinted Indianapolis: Bobbs-Merrill, 1983) p. 16; hereafter cited parenthetically in the text.
10. *UP1* 277; see also *UP2* 263 and *IGE* 93, where Yeats calls the *Defence* 'the profoundest essay on the foundation of poetry in English.' For a

critical discussion of Yeats's debt, see George Bornstein, *Yeats and Shelley* (Chicago: University of Chicago Press, 1970) pp. 60–6.

11. Quoted by Abrams, p. 127.

12. Harry Buxton Forman (ed.), *The Works of Percy Bysshe Shelley in Verse and Prose*, 8 vols (London: Reeves and Turner, 1880), VII, 104, 108; hereafter cited parenthetically in the text. Yeats owned and annotated Ernest Rhys's edition of Shelley's *Essays and Letters*, The Camelot Classics (London: Walter Scott, 1886); see *YL* 1902. When Yeats read this volume is unknown, and he may already have encountered the *Defence* elsewhere. In all the passages cited in this study, Rhys's text and Forman's are virtually identical.

13. *Yeats and Shelley*, p. 61.

14. *Samhain*, October 1902, p. 12n; see also *Mem* 59.

15. *History of Ireland*, 2 vols, Vol. I, *History of Ireland: The Heroic Period* (London: Sampson Low, Searle, Marston and Rivington, and Dublin: E. Ponsonby, 1878); Vol. II, *History of Ireland: Cuculain and his Contemporaries* (London: Sampson, Low, Searle, Marston and Rivington, Dublin: E. Ponsonby, 1880); I, 22–3; hereafter cited parenthetically in the text.

16. 'Aesthete among the Athletes: Yeats's Contributions to *The Gael*', in Richard J. Finneran (ed.), *Yeats: An Annual of Critical and Textual Studies*, Vol. II (Ithaca, NY and London: Cornell University Press, 1984) p. 91.

17. *History of Ireland: Critical and Philosophical*, Vol. I (London: Sampson Low, and Dublin: E. Ponsonby, 1881) p. 58; hereafter cited as *HCP*.

18. Kelly, 'Aesthete among the Athletes', p. 91.

19. *On the Boiler* (Dublin: Cuala Press, 1939) p. 37; hereafter cited as *OB*.

20. See C. G. Jung, *The Archetypes and the Collective Unconscious*, 2nd edn, trans. R.F.C. Hull (1968; reprinted Princeton: Princeton University Press, 1971) p. 4.

21. *Wheels and Butterflies* (London: Macmillan, 1934) p. 70; hereafter cited as *WB*. In O'Grady's *The Flight of the Eagle* there was a description of a 'youth ... rapt with visions' who was inspired by Celtic goddess-Muses so that 'the word out of his mouth becomes a sword wherewith he shears through mountains; with his right hand, he upholds the weak, and with the left prostrates powers, and tyrants tremble before the light of his mild eyes' (London: Lawrence and Bullen, 1897, pp. 255–6); Yeats believed that this Shelleyan image of artistic power referred specifically to him (*Mem* 59).

22. Rupert Hart-Davis (ed.), *The Letters of Oscar Wilde* (New York: Harcourt, Brace and World, 1962) p. 236.

23. Richard Ellmann, *Oscar Wilde* (New York: Alfred A. Knopf, 1988) p. 304. See also Ellmann's *Eminent Domain* (New York: Oxford University Press, 1967) pp. 9–27.

24. Ellmann, *Wilde*, p. 165.

25. Richard Ellmann (ed.), *The Critic as Artist: Critical Writings of Oscar Wilde* (1969; reprinted New York: Vintage Books, 1970) p. 306; hereafter cited parenthetically in the text.

26. Donald L. Hill (ed.), *The Renaissance: Studies in Art and Poetry* (Berkeley, Los Angeles, and London: University of California Press, 1980) p. 166; hereafter cited as *Renaissance*.

27. See Paul Scott Stanfield, *Yeats and Politics in the 1930s* (New York: St. Martin's Press, 1988) pp. 158–83.
28. Yeats's 1898 reference to the renewal of belief liberating the arts from their age and from life and leaving them free to lose themselves in beauty and in 'old faiths, myths, dreams' (*UP2* 131) may echo the description of Renaissance drama in 'The Decay of Lying': 'Old myth and legend and dream took shape and substance. History was entirely re-written, and there was hardly one of the dramatists who did not recognize that the object of Art is not simple truth but complex beauty' (302).
29. Edwin J. Ellis and W. B. Yeats (eds), *The Works of William Blake: Poetic, Symbolic, and Critical*, 3 vols. (London: Bernard Quaritch, 1893), III, *Milton*, plate 11, l.51; hereafter cited parenthetically in the text. Of Blake's bardic role, Graves wrote 'the only poet, as far as I know, who ever seriously tried to institute bardism in England was William Blake: he intended his Prophetic Books as a complete corpus of poetic reference, but for want of intelligent colleagues was obliged to become a whole Bardic college in himself, without even an initiate to carry on the tradition after his death' (*WG* 460).
30. II, 397; see also *IGE* 177–8.
31. See also 'Vision, or imagination, is a representation of what actually exists, really, and unchangeably' (II, 393; *IGE* 176).
32. II, 393; modern editions read 'Imaginative'. See also 'The Theatre', *Beltaine*, No. 1 (May 1899) p. 21; *IGE* 212–13; and Stuart Piggott, *The Druids* (1968; reprinted London: Thames and Hudson, 1985) pp. 130ff.
33. See pp. 199–200.
34. Justin McCarthy (ed.), *Irish Literature*, 10 vols. (Chicago: DeBower-Elliott, 1904), VII, 2842; *DNB*; *Au* 155–9.
35. In 1930 Yeats quoted O'Shaughnessy again; see *Pages from a Diary Written in Nineteen Hundred and Thirty* (Dublin: Cuala Press, 1944) p. 54; hereafter cited as *D*.
36. Arthur O'Shaughnessy, *Music and Moonlight: Poems and Songs* (London: Chatto and Windus, 1874) pp. 1–5.
37. See also Hugh Kenner, *A Colder Eye: The Modern Irish Writers* (New York: Alfred A. Knopf, 1983) p. 81n.
38. See also *Au* 151: 'Elaborate modern psychology sounds egotistical, I thought, when it speaks in the first person, but not those simple emotions which resemble the more, the more powerful they are, everybody's emotion, and I was soon to write many poems where an always personal emotion was woven into a general pattern of myth and symbol.'
39. I am indebted here and throughout my discussion of the play to Michael J. Sidnell, 'Yeats's First Work for the Stage: The Earliest Versions of "The Countess Kathleen"', in D. E. S. Maxwell and S. B. Bushrui (eds), *W. B. Yeats: Centenary Essays on the Art of W. B. Yeats* (Ibadan: Ibadan University Press, 1965) p. 183; hereafter cited as Sidnell.
40. Yeats first thought of a seventeenth-century date for the action (Sidnell 172); later he asserted that he had meant that less specific period 'in which the events in the folk-tales have happened' (*UP2* 160–1). It was

a common bardic convention to depict patron and poet as husband and wife (Carney 112–13).

41. I, 238–45; II, 383. Yeats's poem 'The Moods' was first published in 1893, and in the same year was linked with Irish traditional material through its use as a proem to *The Celtic Twilight*; see also *VSR* 31.

42. It may be significant that Lionel Johnson had emphasised the Irish bardic 'passion for perfection' in his 1894 lecture 'Poetry and Patriotism in Ireland'; see *YBIR* 169–71.

43. II, 393; see p. 31 of this study, and also *UP1* 407, where Yeats quotes the passage in 'The New Irish Library' (June 1896).

44. Alan Denson (ed.), *Letters from Æ* (London, New York, Toronto: Abelard-Schuman, 1961) pp. 17–18.

45. *Some Passages from the Letters of Æ to W. B. Yeats* (Dublin: Cuala Press, 1936) pp. 1–9; *YBIR* 121–9.

46. *Literary Ideals*, pp. 84–6; see also *YBIR* 194–5; and, for a different emphasis, Peter Kuch, *Yeats and A. E.: 'The antagonism that unites dear friends'* (Gerrards Cross: Colin Smythe, and Totowa, New Jersey: Barnes and Noble Books, 1986) pp. 110–12, 163–8.

47. See *Au* 358, *AV A* 94, *Ex* 332–3, *E&I* 404–5, *WB* 72–3, and the unpublished 1936 radio broadcast quoted by Donald T. Torchiana, *W. B. Yeats and Georgian Ireland* (Evanston: Northwestern University Press, 1966) p. 244; hereafter cited as Torchiana. See also *IGE* 152: ' "Art is art, because it is not nature!" It brings us near to the archetypal ideas themselves, and away from nature, which is but their looking-glass.'

48. Richard Ellmann (ed.), *A Portrait of the Artist as a Young Man*, the definitive text (1916; reprinted New York: Viking Press, 1964) pp. 225–6; hereafter cited as *PA*; Hans Walter Gabler (ed.), *Ulysses*, the Corrected Text (1922; reprinted New York: Vintage, 1986) 1.146; hereafter cited as *U*; Wilde, *The Critic as Artist*, p. 235. In Max Beerbohm's drawing of 'Mr W. B. Yeats presenting Mr George Moore to the Queen of the Fairies' there is a shelf of books including *Realism: Its Cause & Cure*; see Micheál Mac Liammóir and Eavan Boland, *The World of W. B. Yeats* (London: Thames and Hudson, 1971) p. 65.

49. Michael J. Sidnell, George P. Mayhew, and David R. Clark (eds), *Druid Craft: The Writing of "The Shadowy Waters"* (Amherst: University of Massachusetts Press, 1971) pp. 38–9; hereafter cited as *DC*. My own discussion draws heavily upon this edition.

50. See also *Beltaine*, No. 2 (February 1900) p. 21n: 'that contrast between immortal beauty and the ignominy and mortality of life, which is the central theme of ancient art'; and *UP2* 200: 'This thought of the war of immortal upon mortal life has been the moving thought of much Irish poetry, and may yet, so moving and necessary a thought it is, inspire many plays....'

51. See Phillip L. Marcus, 'Yeats and the Image of the Singing Head', *Éire-Ireland*, IX (1974) 86–93.

52. Yeats's debt to Frazer has been explored by John B. Vickery, *The Literary Impact of 'The Golden Bough'* (Princeton: Princeton University Press, 1973) pp. 179–232; and Warwick Gould, 'Frazer, Yeats and the Reconsecration of Folklore', in Robert Fraser (ed.), *Sir James Frazer and*

the Literary Imagination (London: Macmillan, 1990) pp. 121–53. When Yeats first read *The Golden Bough* is uncertain; the notes to *The Wind Among the Reeds* (1899) contain specific citations (*VP* 809), but much else in his work from 1890 onward *could* have been derived from it. During that period he was also finding very similar materials in other sources dealing with myth and legend, folklore and the occult.

53. On the Wisdom figure, see Allen R. Grossman, *Poetic Knowledge in the Early Yeats* (Charlottesville: University Press of Virginia, 1969).

54. Yeats returned to these considerations in his late plays *The King of the Great Clock Tower* and *A Full Moon in March* as well as in *The Death of Cuchulain*, discussed in detail on pp. 201–11. A study of some of the same materials with more emphasis on their negative aspects is Patrick J. Keane's *Terrible Beauty: Yeats, Joyce, Ireland, and the Myth of the Devouring Female* (Columbia: University of Missouri Press, 1988); he notes that 'there is much to be said about the *positive* treatment of the Female' in Yeats (p. xv).

55. The Bard was Cir; see Keating, *History*, II, 102–3.

56. For the rose as both 'a symbol of woman's beauty' and 'a symbol of Ireland', see *VP* 811–12; see also *Au* 254 for a comparable strategy.

57. Yeats quoted a stanza from this poem as an epigraph to *Cathleen ni Hoolihan* (London, 1902); see *VPl* 214. His source may have been H. Haliday Sparling (ed.), *Irish Minstrelsy* (London: Walter Scott, 1888) pp. 141–2 (*YL* 1967).

58. James Kilroy, *The "Playboy" Riots* (Dublin: Dolmen Press, 1971) p. 16.

59. *The Spirit of the Nation* (Dublin: James Duffy, 1845) pp. 72–3.

60. See *VSR* 269–70.

61. *VSR* 133. See *IGE* 246–7: 'Solitary men in moments of contemplation receive ... the creative impulse from the lowest of the Nine Hierarchies, and so make and unmake mankind, and even the world itself....'

62. See also *Au* 254, where Yeats suggests that the order might have 'mysteries like those of Eleusis and Samothrace'; and *Mem* 123–4.

63. Quoted by William H. O'Donnell, *A Guide to the Prose Fiction of W.B. Yeats* (Ann Arbor, Mich.: UMI Research Press, 1983) p. 136.

3 1899–1917

1. Earlier versions of some of the material in this chapter appeared as 'Artificers of the Great Moment: An Essay on Yeats and National Literature', *CLQ*, XV (1979) 71–92, and 'Incarnation in "Middle Yeats"', in Richard J. Finneran (ed.), *Yeats Annual* No. 1 (London: Macmillan, 1982) pp. 68–81.

2. I have corrected Wade's transcriptions from those of Ronald Schuchard for the forthcoaming Volume III of the *Collected Letters*. In Yeats's Preface to Lady Gregory's *Gods and Fighting Men* (London: John Murray, 1904) p. xix (hereafter cited as *GFM*) he described the process in terms of power, with reference to the way in which Christianity had supplanted the era of Finn, Oisin and the Fianna: 'It sometimes seems to one as if

there is a kind of day and night of religion, and that a period when the influences are those that shape the world is followed by a period when the greater power is in influences that would lure the soul out of the world, out of the body'; see also *D* 18–19.

3. See also *Mem* 210: 'Man clothes himself to descend, unclothes himself to ascend'.

4. Quoted by Lady Gregory, *Our Irish Theatre* (1914; reprinted New York: Capricorn Books, 1965) pp. 8–9; see also *YBIR* 276–81.

5. *Our Irish Theatre*, p. 2; *UP2* 138, 160.

6. 'The Play, the Player, and the Scene', *Samhain*, December 1904, pp. 27–8; text reads 'shadow or declining'. The choice of *Beltaine* and *Samhain* as titles for the Theatre's publication links the drama with key points in the ritual cycle of the seasons in pre-Christian Irish religion. Unpublished lecture, New York Public Library, p. [1].

7. 'The Theatre, the Pulpit, and the Newspapers', *United Irishman*, 17 October 1903, p. 2.

8. In fact, there was criticism of the 'morality' of Yeats's and George Moore's *Diarmuid and Grania*; see *L* 356, and Robert Hogan and James Kilroy, *The Irish Literary Theatre 1899–1901*, *The Modern Irish Drama*, Vol. I (Dublin: Dolmen Press, 1975) 101–17.

9. See *Beltaine*, No. 1 (May 1899) p. 4.

10. 'The Theatre', *Beltaine*, No. 1 (May 1899) pp. 20–1.

11. *IGE* 152; quoted also in 'Notes', *Samhain*, October 1902, p. 4, and *Au* 279.

12. 'The Theatre', pp. 21–2.

13. Ellsworth Mason and Richard Ellmann (eds), *The Critical Writings of James Joyce* (New York: Viking Press, 1959) pp. 68–72; *PA* 226.

14. Quoted by Colin Meir, *The Ballads and Songs of W. B. Yeats* (New York: Barnes and Noble, 1974) p. 29.

15. Cf. 'that great Queen, that rose out of the spray' in 'A Prayer for my Daughter' (*VP* 404); and 'the drunken woman of *The Tinker's Wedding* is but the more drunken and the more thieving because she can remember great queens,' *The Cutting of an Agate* (New York: Macmillan, 1912) pp. 143–4; hereafter cited as *CA*. See also the reference to 'our ancient queens' in 'A General Introduction for my Work' (*E&I* 516). In *Au* 364 Yeats thus described Maud Gonne as she was in the late 1890s: 'There was an element in her beauty that moved minds full of old Gaelic stories and poems, for she looked as though she lived in an ancient civilization where all superiorities whether of the mind or the body were a part of public ceremonial.'

16. Unpublished letter, datable late December 1903.

17. Unpublished letter to Lady Gregory, 8 May 1903.

18. 'Literature and the Living Voice', *Samhain*, December 1906, p. 10.

19. Ronald Schuchard, 'The Minstrel in the Theatre: Arnold, Chaucer, and Yeats's New Spiritual Democracy', in Richard J. Finneran (ed.), *Yeats Annual* No. 2 (London: Macmillan, 1983) pp. 3–24.

20. See also Ronald Schuchard, 'An Attendant Lord: H. W. Nevinson's Friendship with W. B. Yeats', in Warwick Gould (ed.), *Yeats Annual* No. 7 (London: Macmillan, 1990) p. 96.

21. Unpublished letter to Lady Gregory, 23 August 1901.
22. '"Dust Hath Closed Helen's Eye"', *The Celtic Twilight* (London: A. H. Bullen, 1902) p. 38; see also 'Literature and the Living Voice', *Samhain*, December 1906, p. 4.
23. *The Celtic Twilight*, p. 37.
24. Lady Gregory, *Poets and Dreamers: Studies and Translations from the Irish* (Dublin: Hodges, Figgis, and London: John Murray, 1903) pp. 3–10.
25. Schuchard, 'An Attendant Lord', pp. 100, 106, 128.
26. Schuchard, 'The Minstrel in the Theatre', pp. 14–15, 21–2.
27. Unpublished lecture, New York Public Library, pp. 7–8. Unpublished letter to John Quinn, 20 March 1903. See also 'Windlestraws', *Samhain*, October 1901, p. 6: 'I hope to get our heroic age into verse'; *Ex* 228: 'Manhood is all, and the root of manhood is courage and courtesy'; *LTSM* 2; *L* 353–4. For Yeats's concern with the 'heroical ideal' see Alex Zwerdling, *Yeats and the Heroic Ideal* (New York: New York University Press, 1965); the relevance of Nietzsche is discussed on pp. 20–2.
28. Schuchard, 'An Attendant Lord', pp. 105–6. Yeats also quoted *The Dawn of Day* on the 'four essential virtues' (attributing the thought to 'the Japanese') in the Preface to *GFM*, p. xvi. In 'The Phases of the Moon' he placed Nietzsche at Phase 12, 'the hero's crescent' (*VP* 374).
29. See AE, 'The Dramatic Treatment of Heroic Literature', *Samhain*, October 1902, p. 11.
30. Schuchard, 'The Minstrel in the Theatre', p. 6. In 1903 Yeats wrote in regard to her *Poets and Dreamers* of 'a past of great passions which can still waken the heart to imaginative action': 'The Galway Plains', *IGE* 337. See also AE's 1902 essay on *Cuchulain of Muirthemne*, 'The Character of Heroic Literature', in *Imaginations and Reveries* (New York: Macmillan [1915]) pp. 1–6, especially p. 6, where he treats the legends as examples of literature that has 'some image of the Golden Life lurking within it' and says 'we are indebted to her for this labour as much as to any of those "who sang to sweeten Ireland's wrong"'.
31. See also Virginia Rohan, 'Yeats and *Deirdre*: from Story to Fable', in Warwick Gould (ed.), *Yeats Annual* No. 6 (London: Macmillan, 1988) p. 33; hereafter cited as Rohan.
32. Lady Gregory, *Cuchulain of Muirthemne* (London: John Murray, 1902) p. xvii; hereafter cited as *CM*. See also *VP* 843, where Yeats says of Lady Gregory's books that he would 'give them before all other books to Irish boys and girls' (cf. 'The Statues', 1.4); *Mem* 88, 123 and *Au* 380.
33. See James Pethica, '"Our Kathleen": Yeats's Collaboration with Lady Gregory in the Writing of *Cathleen ni Houlihan*', in Warwick Gould (ed.), *Yeats Annual* No. 6 (London: Macmillan, 1988) p. 7.
34. When first published as a separate volume in 1902 the play bore a dedication 'To the Memory of William Rooney', the recently deceased ardent Nationalist and close friend of Arthur Griffith (*VPl* 214). For the impact of the play, see p. 122 of this study.
35. 'First Principles', *Samhain*, November 1908, p. 10.
36. See p. 57 of this study. See also Ronald Schuchard, 'The Lady Gregory-Yeats Collection at Emory University', in Warwick Gould (ed.) *Yeats*

Annual No. 3 (London: Macmillan, 1985) p. 159, for Yeats's unpublished 'The Song of Heffernan the Blind: a translation'.

37. On Irish versions of the myth, see Condren, *The Serpent and the Goddess*, pp. 23–4, 221; also Proinsias Mac Cana, *Celtic Mythology*, revised ed. (Feltham, Middlesex: Newnes, 1983) p. 92: 'And where the kingdom was conceived anthropomorphically as a goddess, the latter then symbolised not merely the soil and substance of its territory, but also the spiritual and legal dominion which the king exercised over it, in other words his sovereignty. Nowhere was this divine image of sovereignty visualised so clearly as among the Celts, and more especially in Ireland, where it remained a remarkably evocative and compelling concept for as long as native tradition lasted.'

38. 'An Irish National Theatre', *United Irishman*, 10 October 1903, p. 2. On the dream origin of the play see also *VPl* 232 and Daniel J. Murphy (ed.), *Lady Gregory's Journals*, Vol. 2 (New York: Oxford University Press, 1987) 13; hereafter cited as *J*. In an unpublished letter to Horace Plunkett written in July 1904 Yeats denied any propagandist intent: 'I have never written a play to advocate any kind of opinion and I think that such a play would be necessarily bad art.' See also 'Notes and Opinions', *Samhain*, November 1905, pp. 12–13; and Robin Skelton and David R. Clark (eds), *Irish Renaissance* (Dublin: Dolmen Press, 1965) p. 18; hereafter cited as *IR*. Yeats told Patrick McCartan 'my Cathleen Ni Houlihan was propaganda but I was not conscious of it at the time': John Unterecker (ed.), *Yeats and Patrick McCartan: A Fenian Friendship* (Dublin: Dolmen Press, 1967) p. 430; hereafter cited as McCartan.

39. Robert O'Driscoll (ed.), 'Letters and Lectures of W. B. Yeats', *University Review*, III (n. d.), 46; see also pp. 43, 45 and *IGE* 88. For a general study of ways in which immersion in the Irish theatre movement sometimes diverted the natural course of Yeats's own development as a dramatist, see James W. Flannery, *W. B. Yeats and the Idea of a Theatre: The Early Abbey Theatre in Theory and Practice* (New Haven and London: Yale University Press, 1976).

40. Stephen Gwynn, *Irish Literature and Drama in the English Language* (London: Nelson, 1936) pp. 158–9.

41. Robert Hogan and James Kilroy, *Laying the Foundations: 1902–1904, The Modern Irish Drama*, Vol. II (Dublin: Dolmen Press, 1976) 48–51, 70.

42. David H. Greene and Edward M. Stephens, *J. M. Synge: 1871–1909* (1959; reprinted New York: Collier, 1961) p. 141; Gerard Fay, *The Abbey Theatre: Cradle of Genius* (New York: Macmillan, 1958) pp. 59–60; Máire nic Shiublaigh, *The Splendid Years* (Dublin: James Duffy, 1955) p. 42; Samuel Levenson, *Maud Gonne* (New York: Reader's Digest Press, 1976) p. 202.

43. G. Fay, *The Abbey Theatre*, pp. 62–3.

44. 'Notes', *Samhain*, September 1903, p. 4; 'The Reform of the Theatre', *Samhain*, September 1903, p. 9.

45. Unpublished letters to A. B. Walkley, 28 June 1903, and to E. Craig and Frank Fay, 14 August 1903.

46. Harold Bloom, *Yeats* (New York: Oxford University Press, 1970) p. 149; see also Barton R. Friedman, 'Under a Leprous Moon: Action

and Image in *The King's Threshold'*, *Arizona Quarterly*, XXVI (1970) 39–53.

47. See George Bornstein, 'A Borrowing from Wilde in Yeats's "The King's Threshold"', *NQ*, November 1971, pp. 421–2.
48. Schuchard, 'An Attendant Lord', p. 109.
49. S. B. Bushrui, *Yeats's Verse Plays: The Revisions 1900–1910* (Oxford: Clarendon Press, 1965) p. 74. See also Bushrui's more general analysis of the play, *'The King's Threshold*: A Defence of Poetry', *REL*, IV (1963) 81–94.
50. In an unpublished letter of 6 January 1904 Yeats wrote Lady Gregory that 'John Devoy, the fenian brought a deputation of Clan-na-Gael men to see me after my big New York lecture & he said I had "got at people here in America no Irish man had ever got at before."' See also McCartan 427–8.
51. 'First Principles', *Samhain*, December 1904, pp. 23, 21. Bushrui (103–8) shows that Yeats's revisions of *The King's Threshold* between 1903 and 1905 were partly for the purpose of giving greater emphasis to the sacredness of poetry and of the poet's position in society.
52. See Greene and Stephens, *Synge*, pp. 181–4.
53. Unpublished letter, 24 January 1905.
54. See Robert Hogan and Michael J. O'Neill (eds), *Joseph Holloway's Abbey Theatre* (Carbondale and Edwardsville: Southern Illinois University Press, 1967) p. 62; *L* 461–3; Greene and Stephens, *Synge*, pp. 196–202; Robin Skelton and Ann Saddlemyer (eds), *The World of W. B. Yeats*, revised edn (Seattle: University of Washington Press, 1967) p. 86. A more negative assessment of Yeats's role in the theatre movement is offered by Adrian Frazier, *Behind the Scenes: Yeats, Horniman, and the Struggle for the Abbey Theatre* (Berkeley, Los Angeles, and London: University of California Press, 1990).
55. Unpublished letter to AE, 7 August 1905.
56. 'Notes and Opinions', *Samhain*, November 1905, pp. 12–13.
57. Greene and Stephens, *Synge*, pp. 201–2.
58. 'Literature and the Living Voice', *Samhain*, December 1906, pp. 7–8.
59. See *Au* 295.
60. F. S. L. Lyons, *Ireland Since the Famine*, revised edn (London: Fontana, 1973) p. 243.
61. Kilroy, *The "Playboy" Riots*, p. 32.
62. See 'Discoveries: Second Series', *IR* 88; and Daniel A. Harris, *Yeats: Coole Park and Ballylee* (Baltimore and London: Johns Hopkins University Press, 1974) p. 5n; hereafter cited as Harris.
63. See also *L* 534: 'It is in practice a summary of the last fifty years in Ireland'.
64. This subject has been explored by Barton R. Friedman, *Adventures in the Deeps of the Mind: The Cuchulain Cycle of W. B. Yeats* (Princeton: Princeton University Press, 1977).
65. See *Our Irish Theatre*, p. 3: '[Yeats] believes there will be a reaction after the realism of Ibsen, and romance will have its turn.' A full account of Realism at the Abbey can be found in Robert Hogan, Richard Burnham

and Daniel P. Poteet (eds), *The Rise of the Realists: 1910–1915*, *The Modern Irish Drama*, Vol. IV (Dublin: Dolmen Press, 1979).

66. Lennox Robinson, *Ireland's Abbey Theatre: A History 1899–1951* (London: Sidgwick and Jackson, 1951) p. 84.
67. Stuart Gilbert (ed.), *The Letters of James Joyce* (New York: Viking Press, 1957) p. 64.
68. See, e.g., 'The Play, the Player, and the Scene', *Samhain*, December 1904, pp. 25–8. Unpublished lecture, New York Public Library, p. 4.
69. Curtis Baker Bradford (ed.), *W. B. Yeats: The Writing of "The Player Queen"* (De Kalb: Northern Illinois University Press, 1977) p. 48; hereafter cited parenthetically in the text.
70. See also 'Upon a House shaken by the Land Agitation': 'To breed the lidless eye that loves the sun? / And the sweet laughing eagle thoughts that grow / Where wings have memory of wings, and all / That comes of the best knit to the best?' (*VP* 264); and Bradford, *Player Queen*, p. 66.
71. Its first performance at the Abbey, in 1919, was not a success with the critics; see Bradford, *Player Queen*, pp. 413ff.
72. See David R. Clark, *Yeats at Songs and Choruses* (Amherst: University of Massachusetts Press, 1983) pp. 90ff. Yeats's unpublished poem 'Art without Imitation' seems implicitly to espouse the conventional conception of art as imitation of nature, but, as the reference to 'Mathematics' suggests, the real target of his satire here was *abstract* art with *no* relationship to life; see *CA* 106–7 and Richard Ellmann, *The Identity of Yeats*, 2nd edn (New York: Oxford University Press, 1964) p. 243.
73. See Lady Gregory, *J*, II, 76: 'I told them of Hugh wanting his gallery built on the bridge because it was the workers' highway and saying he "would be quite satisfied if they went in to rest and warm themselves"'. Yeats had liked the projected location in Earlsfort Terrace because it could put the pictures 'into the midst of the students of the new University', and liked the bridge site even more because it would bring the pictures close to the working classes and 'to the doors of many business men and women' (*L* 579–80).
74. Levenson, *Maud Gonne*, pp. 280–1 (4 September 1914). For other aspects of the opposition, see *VP* 819 and Donald T. Torchiana and Glenn O'Malley, 'Some New Letters from W. B. Yeats to Lady Gregory', *REL*, IV (1963) 9–47, especially 25–9. Yeats refers to Lady Alix Egerton's response in the letter given on p. 19 of 'Some New Letters ...'; the passages cited from the interview and from a contemporary speech in London appear on pp. 12, 34–5.
75. The date of completion is indicated in an unpublished letter from Yeats to John Quinn, ca 6 July 1904.
76. Ann Saddlemyer (ed.), *The Collected Letters of John Millington Synge*, Vol. I, 1871–1907 (Oxford: Clarendon Press, 1983) 93–6; for the actors' enthusiasm see also Yeats's unpublished letter to John Quinn, 13 July 1904.
77. Ann Saddlemyer (ed.), *The Tragedies and Tragi-Comedies of Lady Gregory* (Gerrards Cross, Buckinghamshire: Colin Smythe, 1970) pp. 316 (emphasis added) 350–1.
78. *L* 448. In *Our Irish Theatre*, p. 92, Lady Gregory indicates that at an early stage in the composition of the play, Yeats had advised her to give it up.

79. *Holloway's Abbey Theatre*, p. 58.

80. The phrase comes from Blake's 'Public Address'; see also *Mem* 191–2, where Yeats quotes it again, in relation to Maud Gonne's political activities.

81. On this aspect of 'The Dolls' see Marcus, 'Incarnation', pp. 74–5.

82. A. Norman Jeffares (ed.), *Yeats's Poems* (London: Macmillan, 1989) p. 559.

83. Phillip L. Marcus (ed.), *"The Death of Cuchulain": Manuscript Materials including the Author's Final Text* (Ithaca, NY and London: Cornell University Press, 1982) p. 180; hereafter cited as *DCU*.

84. Yeats quoted Finn's phrase in his Preface to *GFM*, p. xx. In *Au* he tells how in the later 1890s he himself wore 'Connemara cloth' because he thought it politically unimpeachable until he learned from his tailor that it had to be imported from Scotland (361).

85. George Mills Harper (ed.), *Yeats and the Occult* (Toronto: Macmillan of Canada/ MacLean-Hunter Press, 1975) p. 172ff.

86. Harper, *Yeats and the Occult*, p. 187; cf. 'Ego Dominus Tuus' (*VP* 367). For 'cold' and 'passionate' see *E&I* 522–3, *Au* 74, *Renaissance* 183.

87. See Harris 194.

88. A. E., *The National Being* (New York: Macmillan, 1916) pp. 130, 4; hereafter cited parenthetically in the text. The book was apparently published in September 1916, but the royalty agreement signed on 25 January 1916 indicates that the manuscript was to be in the publisher's hands only five days later, so presumably it was virtually complete at that point; see Alan Denson, *Printed Writings by George W. Russell (AE): A Bibliography* (Evanston: Northwestern University Press, 1961) pp. 77–8.

89. Ruth Dudley Edwards, *Patrick Pearse: The Triumph of Failure* (New York: Taplinger, 1978) p. 38; hereafter cited parenthetically in the text.

90. See Raymond J. Porter, 'Language and Literature in Revival Ireland: The Views of P. H. Pearse', in Raymond J. Porter and James D. Brophy (eds), *Modern Irish Literature: Essays in Honor of William York Tindall* (New York: Iona College Press, 1972) pp. 195-214, especially p. 209. In 1905 Pearse called *Cathleen ni Houlihan* 'the most beautiful play that has been written in Ireland in our time'.

91. Padraic H. Pearse, *Collected Works of Padraic H. Pearse: Plays / Stories / Poems* (1917; reprinted Dublin and London: Maunsel and Roberts 1922) p. 333.

92. There is at least a suggestion of such an aesthetic in MacDonagh's 'Of a Poet Patriot', *The Poetical Works of Thomas MacDonagh* (London: T. Fisher Unwin, 1916) p. 91.

93. See, e.g., George P. Mayhew, 'A Corrected Typescript of Yeats' "Easter 1916"', *Huntington Library Quarterly*, XXVII (1963) 53–71.

94. *Modern Ireland*, p. 479.

95. Helen Hennessy Vendler, *Yeats's "Vision" and the Later Plays* (Cambridge: Harvard University Press, 1963) p. 187; hereafter cited as Vendler.

96. David R. Clark, 'Yeats, Theatre, and Nationalism', in Robert O'Driscoll (ed.), *Theatre and Nationalism in Twentieth-Century Ireland* (Toronto: University of Toronto Press, 1971) p. 150; *L* 629.

97. *L* 665; see also *LTWBY* 373–5. On the contemporary relevance of *The Trembling of the Veil* see Bernard J. Krimm, *W. B. Yeats and the Emergence of*

the Irish Free State 1918–1939: Living in the Explosion (Troy, NY: Whitston, 1981) pp. 84–91; hereafter cited as Krimm.

4 THE TWENTIES AND THIRTIES

1. Richard Ellmann, *Yeats: The Man and the Masks* (1948; reprinted New York and London: W. W. Norton, 1978) pp. xii–xiii; George Mills Harper, *The Making of Yeats's "A Vision": A Study of the Automatic Script*, 2 vols (Carbondale and Edwardsville: Southern Illinois University Press, 1987) I, 3–5; hereafter cited parenthetically in the text. See also Phillip L. Marcus, 'The Authors Were in Eternity – or Oxford: George Yeats, George Harper, and the Making of *A Vision*', in Richard J. Finneran (ed.), *Yeats: An Annual of Critical and Textual Studies*, Vol. VI (1988) pp. 233–44. I have drawn upon this review essay throughout the discussion here of Mrs Yeats and *A Vision*. Alex Owen's *The Darkened Room: Women, Power and Spiritualism in Late Victorian England* (Philadelphia: University of Pennsylvania Press, 1990) provides a valuable background for the Yeatses' experiments with automatic writing.
2. Ellmann, *Man and Masks*, p. 266.
3. Yeats completed a draft of the entire poem on 7 October 1925; see Curtis Bradford, *Yeats at Work* (Carbondale and Edwardsville: Southern Illinois University Press, 1965) p. 81; hereafter cited as YW. See also Lady Gregory, *J.* II, 9 (23 April 1925): 'Yeats wrote ... "Yesterday I finished my book"'.
4. David Fitzpatrick, 'W. B. Yeats in Seanad Éireann', in Robert O'Driscoll and Lorna Reynolds (eds), *Yeats and the Theatre* (Toronto: Macmillan of Canada / MacLean-Hunter Press, 1975) pp. 160–1.
5. Foster, *Modern Ireland*, p. 518.
6. I have offered my own interpretation along these lines in '"I declare my faith": Eliot's "Gerontion" and Yeats's "The Tower"', *PLL*, XIV (1978) 74–82.
7. George Bornstein, *Poetic Remaking: The Art of Browning, Yeats, and Pound* (University Park and London: Pennsylvania State University Press, 1988) pp. 57ff.
8. Thomas R. Whitaker, *Swan and Shadow: Yeats's Dialogue with History* (Chapel Hill: University of North Carolina Press, 1964) p. 196; hereafter cited as Whitaker.
9. *The Celtic Twilight*, p. 41.
10. Cf. C. G. Jung, *Mysterium Coniunctionis: An Inquiry into the Separation and Synthesis of Psychic Opposites in Alchemy*, 2nd edn, trans. R. F. C. Hull (Princeton: Princeton University Press, 1974) p. 97 *et passim*.
11. *YW* 86–7. The order of composition is uncertain.
12. See Lady Gregory, *J.* II, 101 for a passage of 28 May 1926 indicating that Yeats had already conceived the idea for what are now the first two parts of the poem, which would contain 'all his ideas about Burke and Berkeley and Swift, and now Goldsmith'.

13. In June 1923, expecting a visit from Joyce, Yeats told Olivia Shakespear that he would have to 'use the utmost ingenuity' to hide the fact that he had 'never finished *Ulysses*' (*L* 698).
14. Warren Roberts and Harry T. Moore (eds), *Phoenix II: Uncollected, Unpublished, and Other Prose Works by D. H. Lawrence* (New York: Viking Press, 1970) p. 436; hereafter cited parenthetically in the text. For a more extensive examination of similarities between Yeats and Lawrence, see my 'Lawrence, Yeats, and "the Resurrection of the Body"', in Peter Balbert and Phillip L. Marcus (eds), *D. H. Lawrence: A Centenary Consideration* (Ithaca, NY: Cornell University Press, 1985) pp. 210–36.
15. Daniel Corkery, *The Hidden Ireland: A Study of Gaelic Munster in the Eighteenth Century* (1925; reprinted Dublin: M. H. Gill, 1941) p. vii; hereafter cited parenthetically in the text.
16. W. E. H. Lecky, *A History of Ireland in the Eighteenth Century*, new ed., 5 vols. (1892; reprinted New York: AMS Press, 1969) I, 277.
17. Cf. also *Au* 295: 'This much at any rate is certain – the dream of my early manhood, that a modern nation can return to Unity of Culture, is false; though it may be we can achieve it for some small circle of men and women, and there leave it till the moon bring round its century'; also *Au* 355.
18. Unpublished manuscript related to *A Vision*, quoted in Hazard Adams, *Blake and Yeats: The Contrary Vision* (Ithaca, NY: Cornell University Press, 1955) p. 301.
19. See also Lady Gregory, *J.*, II, 552.
20. Plotinus, *Plotinus: The Ethical Treatises, Being the Treatises of the First Ennead*, trans. Stephen MacKenna (London: Philip Lee Warner for the Medici Society, 1917) I. 6. 8, p. 87.
21. Porphyry, *De Antro Nympharum*, trans. Thomas Taylor, in Kathleen Raine and George Mills Harper (eds), *Thomas Taylor the Platonist: Selected Writings* (Princeton: Princeton University Press, 1969) pp. 321–2; for Yeats's familiarity with this essay, see *IGE* 118ff. Neoplatonic allegorising of Homer by Plotinus and Porphyry is discussed in detail by Robert Lamberton, *Homer the Theologian: Neoplatonist Allegorical Reading and the Growth of the Epic Tradition* (1986; reprinted Berkeley, Los Angeles and London: University of California Press, 1989) pp. 106–33.
22. *L* 812; Connie K. Hood, 'The Remaking of *A Vision*', in Richard J. Finneran (ed.), *Yeats: An Annual of Critical and Textual Studies*, Vol. I (Ithaca, NY and London: Cornell University Press, 1983) p. 51.
23. Cf. Whitaker (221), who sees some hope; and Harris (234), who does not.
24. See *E&I* 514 for a 1937 example of Yeats interpreting history by way of *The Golden Bough*.
25. *IR* 22; see also *VP* 608 for the same phrase, and Colin Smythe (ed.), *Seventy Years: Being the Autobiography of Lady Gregory* (Gerrards Cross: Colin Smythe Ltd., 1974) p. 549, where Yeats has told her 'I remember saying "Pearse is a dangerous man; he has the vertigo of self-sacrifice"'.
26. The bardic element has been noted by Krimm (169).

27. See, e.g., Anne Ross and Don Robins, *The Life and Death of a Druid Prince: The Story of Lindow Man, An Archaeological Sensation* (New York: Summit Books, 1989) pp. 99, 131–2.
28. See also *E&I* 519 and Robert Fraser, 'The Face beneath the Text: Sir James Frazer in his Time', in *Sir James Frazer and the Literary Imagination*, p. 15: 'We also seem to understand why in perusing Frazer's disquisition we experience a sensation at once so familiar and so strange. I said that each of us feels that he is remembering something. What we seem to be remembering is not merely that each of us somewhere sometime killed a god, but that we were the god we killed.'
29. See Edward O'Shea, ' "An Old Bullet Imbedded in the Flesh": The Migration of Yeats's "Three Songs to the Same Tune" ', in Richard J. Finneran (ed.), *Yeats: An Annual of Critical and Textual Studies*, Vol. IV (Ann Arbor, Mich.: UMI Research Press, 1986) 121–42.
30. On the chronology of composition, see Patrick Holland, 'From Parnell to O'Duffy: The Composition of Yeats's "Parnell's Funeral" ', *Canadian Journal of Irish Studies*, II (1976) 15–20.
31. Unpublished letter to Ethel Mannin, February 1935 (datable from internal evidence).
32. James Matthews, *Voices: A Life of Frank O'Connor* (New York: Atheneum, 1983) p. 98.
33. Frank O'Connor, *Kings, Lords, and Commons: an Anthology from the Irish* (New York: Alfred A. Knopf, 1959) p. 100; hereafter cited as *KLC*.
34. McCarthy, *Irish Literature*, V, 1741. There *are* bardic poems about the impact of Cromwell; see, e.g., *AD* 102–9, and *DUR* v–vi, 176–7.
35. *New English Weekly*, X, No. 13, 7 January 1937, pp. 252–3. There is no comparable article in *The English Review*; and see *LDW* 120, where Yeats indicates that the article he has in mind begins, as Porteus's does, on p. 252.
36. In 'A General Introduction for my Work' Yeats writes of Shakespearian tragic heroes and heroines that in 'their ecstasy at the approach of death … [t]hey have become God or Mother Goddess' (*E&I* 522–3), providing an implicit link between 'Lapis Lazuli' and poems such as 'Parnell's Funeral'.
37. Jeffares, *Yeats's Poems*, p. 621; *YW* 142.
38. Ellmann, *Identity*, p. 154.
39. McCartan knew Clarke and brought Pearse to see him in 1910; see Edwards, *Pearse*, p. 154. See also Kevin B. Nowlan, 'Tom Clarke, MacDermott, and the I. R. B.', in F. X. Martin (ed.), *Leaders and Men of the Easter Rising: Dublin 1916* (Ithaca, NY: Cornell University Press, 1967) pp. 111–12.
40. For a photograph of the table of contents and a full discussion of its implications for editing Yeats's work, see Phillip L. Marcus, 'Yeats's "Last Poems": a Reconsideration', in Warwick Gould (ed.), *Yeats Annual* No. 5 (London: Macmillan, 1987) pp. 3–14. The photograph appears opposite p. 170.
41. Jeffares's *Yeats's Poems* and Richard J. Finneran's *The Poems Revised* (New York: Macmillan Publishing Co., 1989) both err in this regard.

The only edition to deal acceptably with the problem is M. L. Rosenthal (ed.), *Selected Poems and Three Plays of William Butler Yeats*, 3rd ed. (New York: Collier Books, 1986).

42. See Jon Stallworthy, *Vision and Revision in Yeats's "Last Poems"* (Oxford: Clarendon Press, 1969) pp. 123, 148; hereafter cited as *VR*.

43. *GFM* 69. Yeats probably first encountered this text, and three other poems ascribed to Amergin, in the fifth volume of the *Transactions of the Ossianic Society* (pp. 228–37), which also contained the text that was his primary source for *The King's Threshold*.

44. *UP2* 119–20; *WG* 80–2; *YBIR* 252n, 261–2; Preface to *The Ten Principal Upanishads*, trans. Shree Purohit Swāmi and W. B. Yeats (1937; reprinted London: Faber and Faber, 1970) p. 11: 'The one fragment of pagan Irish philosophy come down, "the Song of Amergin", seems Asiatic'.

45. Dáithí O´ hÓgáin, *Fionn mac Cumhaill: Images of the Gaelic Hero* (Dublin: Gill and Macmillan, 1988) p. 67.

46. W. Y. Evans Wentz, *The Fairy-Faith in Celtic Countries* (London: Oxford University Press, 1911) pp. 439–40; *YL* 2241, 2242.

47. Yeats originally wrote 'imanent', presumably for 'immanent', but when the typist substituted 'imminent' he changed his typescript to accommodate the new word; see Edward Callan, *Yeats on Yeats: The Last Introductions and the "Dublin" Edition* (Portlaoise: Dolmen Press, 1981) p. 59. Citations of 'A General Introduction' refer to the easily accessible *E&I* text, but have been checked against Callan's transcriptions of Yeats's typescripts.

48. Cf. *SB* 227: 'The Rosicrucian magic means the assertion of the greatness of man in its extreme form . . . He may even claim with the Druids that mankind created the world'; and *GFM* xviii–xix.

49. In the first line quoted, 'these' is my transcription: *VR* reads 'there'.

50. Unpublished letter to Dorothy Wellesley, 7 September 1938.

51. See also *E&I* 225, *Au* 364–5.

52. Unpublished letter to Dorothy Wellesley, 7 September 1938.

53. A. D. Godley (ed.), *The Poetical Works of Thomas Moore* (London and New York: Oxford University Press, 1910) pp. 187–8.

54. Daniel Corkery, *The Stormy Hills* (1929; reprinted Cork: Mercier Press, n.d.) p. 42.

55. Friedrich Nietzsche, *The Birth of Tragedy: or Hellenism and Pessimism*, trans. Wm. A Haussmann (Edinburgh and London: T. N. Foulis, 1909) p. 20.

56. Walter Pater, *Greek Studies: A Series of Essays*, 2nd edn (1901; reprinted London: Macmillan, 1922) p. 243; *Renaissance* 163–4. See also Shelley, 'The Age of Pericles', *Essays and Letters*, p. 140.

57. David R. Fideler (ed.), *The Pythagorean Sourcebook and Library: An Anthology of Ancient Writings Which Relate to Pythagoras and Pythagorean Philosophy*, trans. Kenneth Sylvan Guthrie (Grand Rapids, Mich.: Phanes Press, 1987) pp. 58, 123, 128, 142, 145.

58. Walter Pater, *Miscellaneous Studies: A Series of Essays*, 2nd edn (1904; reprinted London: Macmillan, 1924) pp. 142–71; the story was first published in 1893.

59. Jean Seznec, *The Survival of the Pagan Gods: The Mythological Tradition and Its Place in Renaissance Humanism and Art*, trans. Barbara F. Sessions (1953; reprinted Princeton: Princeton University Press, 1972) pp. 143–6; Edgar Wind, *Pagan Mysteries in the Renaissance*, rev. and enlarged edn (New York: W. W. Norton, 1968) pp. 252–3.

60. *The Birth of Tragedy*, p. 22.

61. Alfred Nutt, *The Celtic Doctrine of Re-birth*, Vol. II of *The Voyage of Bran* (London: David Nutt, 1897) pp. 107–23; see also *UP2* 119–21; *YBIR* 251–2; Piggott, *The Druids*, 113–14; Whitaker 243.

62. John V. Kelleher, 'The Táin and the Annals', *Ériu*, XXII (1971) 107–27. For Yeats's awareness of this tradition, see *GFM* x.

63. Thus Declan Kiberd, *Oxford Illustrated History of Ireland*, p. 275 calls him 'one of the foremost poets of decolonization'. See also Edward W. Said, 'Yeats and Decolonization', in Seamus Deane (ed.), *Nationalism, Colonialism, and Literature* (Minneapolis: University of Minnesota Press, 1990) pp. 69–95. In another context Kiberd has written far more negatively of Yeats's influence; his description of 'Yeats's own progress, which began with a youth intent on reshaping an entire nation and ended with a besieged and weary old man merely defending an archaic sensibility', does not stand up to scrutiny in the light of the evidence amassed in the present study, which in fact shows him to have been entitled to Kiberd's title of 'true hero', 'one who imagines future virtues, which would be admirable precisely because others could not conceive of them'; see 'The War against the Past', in Eyler and Garratt, *The Uses of the Past*, pp. 24–54, especially 27, 29.

64. See also *Au* 265–6, where Yeats recalls Mary Battle describing '"the men one sees riding their horses in twos and threes on the slopes of the mountains with their swords swinging. There is no such race living now."'

65. Quoted by Hazard Adams, *Blake and Yeats*, p. 302.

66. See also *IGE* 239, *Mem* 150.

67. To my knowledge, the only previous critic to have noticed this pattern is Daniel Hoffman, *Barbarous Knowledge: Myth in the Poetry of Yeats, Graves, and Muir* (New York: Oxford University Press, 1967) p. 200; he does not elaborate the point or connect it with the question of Yeats's aesthetics.

68. *WB* 79. See C. G. Jung, *Psychology of the Unconscious*, trans. Beatrice M. Hinkle (1916; reprinted New York: Dodd, Mead, 1965) p. 283. See also James Olney, *The Rhizome and the Flower: The Perennial Philosophy – Yeats and Jung* (Berkeley, Los Angeles and London: University of California Press, 1980) p. 6; and Schuchard, 'An Attendant Lord', p. 119.

69. *WG* 70; Elinor Gadon, *The Once and Future Goddess: A Symbol for Our Time* (San Francisco: Harper and Row, 1989) pp. 29, 94. See also Condren, *The Serpent and the Goddess*, pp. 23–78 *et passim*. The definitive archaeological studies of the Goddess are Marija Gimbutas, *The Goddesses and Gods of Old Europe 6500–3500 BC: Myths and Cult Images*, new edn (Berkeley and Los Angeles: University of California Press, 1982) and the same author's *The Language of the Goddess* (San Francisco: Harper and Row, 1989). Yeats had read in Toynbee about the Minoan Mother Goddess religion and its influence upon Greece; see *AV B* 268n.

70. Cf. Mac Cana, *Celtic Mythology*, p. 92: 'We have seen that the Irish, and indeed the Celtic, goddess is primarily concerned with the prosperity of the land. . . . All the seemingly contradictory characters of the deity – maternal, seasonal, warlike, young or aged, beautiful or monstrous – may be referred to this fundamental nexus, and it is significant that, in general, each individual goddess reveals several or all of these characters, and even though one of them may predominate, the others are rarely absent. Thus Anu, who is explicitly described as a goddess of plenty, is sometimes identified with the Morríghan, the war-goddess *par excellence*, and the Morríghan, like Anu, was commemorated in a placename ("The Paps of the Morríghan") that testified to her maternal function.'

71. *Táin*, ed. O'Rahilly, pp. 2–3, 'friendly thighs' is from the rendering by Thomas Kinsella, *The Táin* (1969; reprinted London and New York: Oxford University Press, 1970) p. 55. See Charles Bowen, 'Great-Bladdered Medb: Mythology and Invention in the *Táin Bó Cuailnge*', *Éire-Ireland*, X (1975) 14–34; also Condren, *The Serpent and the Goddess*, especially pp. 30–6.

72. Yeats's final typescript actually read 'subliminal', but his manuscript (*DCU* 53) and later typescripts and printed texts read 'sublunary'; 'subliminal' may have been the result of an error in the process of transmission from manuscript to typescript. On Cuchulain as superannuated hero, cf. also Rees 340: 'The festive occasion, the fateful bride and the elaborate predetermined circumstances of the deaths [of such figures] recall the ceremonial "killing of the king", when his powers failed or when he had ruled for a prescribed term.' His connection with the moon is suggested also by his relationship with Fand in *The Only Jealousy of Emer*.

73. *Irish Fairy and Folk Tales* (1888; reprinted New York: The Modern Library, n.d.) p. 156; noted by Vendler 38.

74. See also *AV A* 241–2; and Vendler 69, 150–1. My own argument here was first presented, in a different form, in 'Myth and Meaning in Yeats's *The Death of Cuchulain*', *IUR*, II (1972) 133–48.

75. Vendler 139ff, especially 145; she does not see such a pattern in *The Death of Cuchulain*.

76. There is a link here with the drafts of 'Under Ben Bulben', one of which reads 'my flesh is heavy it weighs upon my / heart but I shall soon cast it off / be ~~as light as~~ if god wills I shall / be as light as a bird' (*VR* 152).

77. William Faulkner, *Go Down, Moses* (1942; reprinted New York: Vintage Books, 1973) p. 193.

78. Cf. *Au* 86; see also 'Introduction to Essays', in Callan, *Yeats on Yeats*, p. 80: 'I say . . . it is our first business to paint, or describe, desirable people, places, states of mind.' Yeats here followed Wilde ('Decay', p. 306) in using the Pre-Raphaelites as an example of how the great artist creates 'a new public, a new form of life'. This entire essay, as Callan notes (76), deals with the subject of artistic power.

79. Further connections between the two plays, and between them and 'Politics', the final poem in *LPTP*, are explored in Marcus, 'Yeats's "Last Poems"', pp. 7–9.

80. Sandra F. Siegel (ed.), *Purgatory: Manuscript Materials Including the Author's Final Text* (Ithaca, NY and London: Cornell University Press, 1986) p. 197; hereafter cited as *P*.
81. *OB* 9. The lines 'Some have known a likely lad / That had a sound fly fisher's wrist / Turn to a drunken journalist' (*VP* 625–6) suggest a disappointment of the hopes expressed in 'The Fisherman' and Part III of 'The Tower'.
82. See Torchiana 361–3; he also suggests (344) that Yeats looks back here to Georgian Ireland as a norm against which to criticise his own time.

5 CONCLUSION

1. Quoted by Samuel Hynes, *The Auden Generation: Literature and Politics in England in the 1930s* (New York: Viking Press, 1977) p. 350.
2. Seamus Heaney, *The Place of Writing* (Atlanta, Ga.: Scholars Press, 1989) pp. 37–8; hereafter cited as *PW*.
3. Michael Hartnett, *A Farewell to English and Other Poems* (Dublin: Gallery Books, 1975) p. 33.
4. Heaney echoes Yeats's phrase in *PW* 50; see also p. 37 for 'the indomitable Irishry'.
5. Seamus Heaney, *Preoccupations: Selected Prose 1968–1978* (1980; reprinted New York: Farrar, Straus and Giroux, 1987) pp. 56–60.
6. T.S. Eliot, 'Ulysses, Order, and Myth', *The Dial*, LXXV (1923) 480–83.
7. 'Notes and Opinions', *Samhain*, November 1905, p. 13.
8. Neil Corcoran, *Seamus Heaney* (London and Boston: Faber and Faber, 1986) p. 123; hereafter cited as Corcoran.
9. Wallace Stevens, *The Collected Poems of Wallace Stevens* (1954; reprinted New York: Alfred A. Knopf, 1965) p. 239.
10. Seamus Heaney, *Sweeney Astray: A Version from the Irish* (1983; reprinted New York: Farrar, Straus and Giroux, 1985) p. (vi).
11. Ann Valentine, 'Seamus Heaney: Poet in a Destitute Time', unpublished dissertation, *DAI*, 47.10 (1987) 3761A.
12. Seamus Heaney, *Station Island* (1984; reprinted New York: Farrar, Straus and Giroux, 1986) pp. 92–4.
13. Sean Lucy, 'Presences and Powers', *ILS*, Fall 1989, p. 21. See also Joseph Campbell, *The Power of Myth* (New York: Doubleday, 1988) p. 85.
14. Seamus Heaney, *The Government of the Tongue: Selected Prose 1978–1987* (1988; reprinted New York: Farrar, Straus and Giroux, 1989) pp. 100–1.
15. Seamus Heaney, *The Haw Lantern* (New York: Farrar, Straus and Giroux, 1987) p. 17.
16. Ralph Cohen (ed.), *The Future of Literary Theory* (New York and London: Routledge and Kegan Paul, 1989) pp. 102–3; hereafter cited as Cohen.
17. Elaine Showalter (ed.), *The New Feminist Criticism: Essays on Women, Literature, and Theory* (New York: Pantheon Books, 1985) pp. 287–8. See also Howard Felperin, *Beyond Deconstruction: The Uses and Abuses of Literary Theory* (1985: reprinted Oxford: Clarendon Press, 1987) *passim*; Thomas M. Kavanagh (ed.), *The Limits of Theory* (Stanford, Ca.: Stanford

University Press, 1989) pp. 9–18; and Peter Collier and Helga Geyer-Ryan, *Literary Theory Today* (Ithaca, NY: Cornell University Press, 1990) pp. 1–9.

18. See also George L. Geckle, 'Stephen Dedalus and W. B. Yeats: The Making of the Villanelle', *MFS*, XV (1969) 87–96.

19. James Longenbach, *Stone Cottage: Pound, Yeats, and Modernism* (New York: Oxford University Press, 1988) pp. 10–11, 16–17, 259 *et passim*; hereafter cited as *SC*; A. Walton Litz, 'Pound and Yeats: The Road to Stone Cottage', in George Bornstein (ed.), *Ezra Pound Among the Poets* (Chicago and London: University of Chicago Press, 1985) pp. 128–48; hereafter cited as Litz.

20. See William M. Chace, *The Political Identities of Ezra Pound and T. S. Eliot* (Stanford, Calif.: Stanford University Press, 1973) p. 10.

21. Ezra Pound, 'Art Notes', *The New Age*, 26 September 1918, p. 352.

22. See Ronald Bush, *The Genesis of Ezra Pound's Cantos* (Princeton: Princeton University Press, 1976).

23. Valerie Eliot (ed.), *The Letters of T. S. Eliot*, Vol. I, 1898–1922 (San Diego, New York and London: Harcourt Brace Jovanovich, 1988) 455; 'Ulysses, Order, and Myth,' p. 480.

24. T. S. Eliot, *Selected Essays*, 2nd edn (1934; reprinted London: Faber and Faber, 1949) p. 15. A striking example of the process is Flann O'Brien's co-optation of Joyce in *The Dalkey Archive*.

25. On the anti-'transcendental' bias of deconstructive theory, see Collier and Geyer-Ryan, p. 2.

26. *Oxford Illustrated History of Ireland*, p. 278; for a similar point, see Marcus, 'Artificers of the Great Moment', p. 90.

27. *Beltaine*, No. 2, February 1900, p. 21n.

28. See also *L* 831 and *Myth* 365. Positive aspects of hatred in Yeats's work have been discussed by Fahmy Farag, 'Needless Horror or Terrible Beauty: Yeats's Ideas of Hatred, War, and Violence', in *The Opposing Virtues: Two Essays* (Dublin: Cuala Press, 1978) pp. 7–19; and Joseph M. Hassett, *Yeats and the Poetics of Hate* (Dublin: Gill and Macmillan, New York: St. Martin's Press, 1986); see also Marjorie Perloff, 'Between Hatred and Desire: Sexuality and Subterfuge in "A Prayer for my Daughter"', in Warwick Gould (ed.), *Yeats Annual* No. 7 (London: Macmillan, 1990) pp. 29–50.

29. In response to Conor Cruise O'Brien's suggestion that Yeats sent the poem to de Valera's *Irish Press* as an effort towards rapprochement with the leader, Krimm has pointed out (231) that Yeats had originally sought publication in the *Irish Times*, so that such a rapprochement, if sought at all, was not part of his original plan.

30. Seamus Heaney, *Field Work* (New York: Farrar, Straus and Giroux, 1979) p. 58.

31. 'Notes and Opinions', *Samhain*, November 1905, p. 13: 'Coventry Patmore has said "the end of art is peace"'.

32. For a number of suggested qualifications, see Corcoran 150–1.

Index